DATE DUE			

Argentina & the Jews

Judaic Studies Series
Leon J. Weinberger, General Editor

Argentina & the Jews
A History of Jewish Immigration

Haim Avni

TRANSLATED FROM THE HEBREW BY GILA BRAND
Published in Cooperation with the American Jewish Archives

THE UNIVERSITY OF ALABAMA PRESS
TUSCALOOSA AND LONDON

Library of Congress Cataloging-in-Publication Data

Avni, Haim.
[Mi-biṭul ha-Inḵvizitsyah ye-ʿad "Ḥoḳ ha-shevut". English]
Argentina and the Jews : a history of Jewish immigration / Haim
Avni ; translated from the Hebrew by Gila Brand.
p.   cm.—(Judaic studies series)
Translation of: Mi-biṭul ha-Inḵvizitsyah ye-ʿad "Ḥoḳ ha-shevut".
"Published in cooperation with the American Jewish Archives."
Includes bibliographical references and index.
ISBN 0-8173-0554-8
1. Jews—Argentina—History. 2. Argentina—Emigration and
immigration. 3. Argentina—Ethnic relations. I. Title.
II. Series: Judaic studies series (Unnumbered)
F3021.J5A946 1991   90-47314
982'.004924—dc20

British Library Cataloguing-in-Publication Data available

To Esther
Guideon, Yoav, Adi, and Nili

Contents

Preface   ix

1. The Beginning, 1810–1876   I

2. The Formative Years, 1876–1896   21

3. The Avalanche, 1896–1914   45

4. The Last Chance, 1914–1932   93

5. The Closing Gates, 1933–1945   128

6. The Survivors, 1945–1950   175

7. Conclusion   196

Epilogue   204

Notes   211

References   242

Index   257

Preface

Mass migration has been, without question, one of the dominant features of the nineteenth and twentieth centuries. During these years, millions of people decided to leave their homes and cross the ocean in search of new channels for their talents and energies, new lives for themselves and their families, and, often as not, refuge from economic and political discrimination. In return, the countries that took them in gained a valuable source of manpower. A prime example of the symbiosis between the needs of the newcomers and the host society is presented by the United States, where immigrants helped to forge a powerful new nation. The only parallel in Latin America is Argentina, where a conscious effort was made to imitate the United States. Brazil, Chile, and Uruguay made similar though short-lived attempts to attract immigrants in later years, but the countries in the Andes and the Amazon Basin, as well as those in Central America, remained totally unaffected by the global tide of immigration and its influence on culture and life-style. In respect of culture and life-style, immigration was of supreme importance for the Argentine Republic.

Migration was a highly significant historical phenomenon for many peoples—for the Italians, the Spaniards, the Irish, and others. For none, however, did it play as pivotal a role as for the Jewish people. For the Jews, immigration was closely bound up with other fundamental historical processes, both directly and indirectly. Some of the problems that characterized the Jewish political experience in Europe during the nineteenth century, such as lack of emancipation and the spread of anti-Semitism, could be solved by emigrating to emancipated countries. In the same way, economic hardship, which often stemmed from discrimination but was also a product of the backwardness of the Eastern European and Near Eastern countries where the Jews lived, could be remedied by moving to more-developed nations. Although the newcomers started out poor, in these countries there were at least prospects for change and advancement.

Spiritually, the adjustment was difficult. While the trend away from religion was already evident in Eastern Europe, the Jews were living in tightly knit communities with a common mother tongue, customs, and social values that created for them, at least psychologically, a virtually Jewish-majority society; the same situation prevailed in communities throughout the Turkish Empire. Immigration brought masses of individual Jews into a non-Jewish cultural environment and involved both a different experience of living as a minority and the erosion of Jewish culture. From a historical perspective, however, it is clear that all those who left their homes in Europe spared both themselves and their descendants the horrors of the Holocaust.

The decision to emigrate, which plays such a central role in contemporary Jewish history, was largely a personal one. Until the mass immigration to the State of Israel in the second half of the twentieth century, there was virtually no Jewish body that organized members of the community for the purpose of resettlement. The one exception was the colonization scheme of Baron Maurice de Hirsch, which we shall look at closely. Basically, the efforts of the Jewish emigration organizations were geared toward helping those who had already decided to move. The assistance they provided was invaluable to the immigrant during the move and especially afterward, in his new home, and a special area of concern in this book will be the extent to which such organizations were instrumental in enlarging the scope of Jewish immigration to Argentina. Nevertheless, the starring role in the immigration drama is reserved for the immigrants themselves.

Another important player was the host society, which allowed immigration to proceed in the first place. Jewish immigration to Argentina was unique in that Jewish and Spanish cultures had been out of contact for hundreds of years. While the Jews reaching the United States were not unfamiliar with the Dutch and English cultural traditions they found there, Jewish immigration to Argentina constituted a renewed physical contact with a culture that had sharply and cruelly severed all relations with the Jewish people. Since the days of the Inquisition, Jews had been prohibited from immigrating to Spanish territories in the New World, and the Limpieza de Sangre ('purity of blood') laws extended this ban to the New Christians and their offspring. Until Argentina's independence in the early nineteenth century, Inquisition ceremonies were familiar spectacles in its cities. Inhabitants were urged to inform on anyone suspected of "Judaizing," or performing Jewish customs such as changing the tablecloths and linen in honor of the Sabbath, fasting on Yom Kippur, and eating bitter herbs on Passover. A phantomlike "Jewish presence" was thus conjured up, demonstrating the utter illegitimacy of a real Jewish existence in Argentina.

After Argentina's independence, the legal status of the Jews changed, paving the way for the eventual establishment of the largest Jewish community in the Hispanic world. However, while outdated laws could be reformed by enlightened legislators, enforcing the reforms depended upon their acceptance by the society at large. The legitimacy of Jewish existence was the crux of the matter. Legal status can be examined simply enough, but to determine legitimacy we must probe not only the attitudes toward Jews prevalent in the host society, but also the society's social ideal and the extent to which the Jews fit into this framework. In this book, we use Argentina's attitude toward immigration in general, and Jewish immigration in particular, as a truthful barometer of its willingness to accept the Jews in its midst. By delving into the fluctuations of Argentine immigration policy, we hope to unravel some of the knots in this complex issue.

Argentina and the Jews covers a period of 140 years, from the beginning of Argentine independence (1810) to the establishment and consolidation of the Jewish state in Israel (1950). It was the changing need for immigrants that opened and closed Argentina's doors to newcomers during the formative years of the Republic. At the same time, it became increasingly urgent for the Jews to leave the Old World as Jew-hatred moved toward its tragic climax in the 1930s and 1940s. We shall examine the correlation between these two historical needs: the needs of Argentina as a developing nation eager for working hands; and the needs of the Jews as a persecuted people seeking a home. Our study ends with the establishment of the State of Israel, which opened an independent channel for Jewish immigration. A brief survey of the last forty years, during which many Argentine

Jews resettled in the Jewish state and other countries, is provided in the epilog.

This edition of *Argentina and the Jews* is an abridged and updated version of a more detailed study that has appeared in both Hebrew and Spanish. Although scholars and researchers specializing in the history of Latin America and its Jews have access to these other editions, we have introduced new material into this English-language version that was not available previously.

On a final note, the reader will find numerous references to the Jewish Colonization Association (JCA) throughout this book. Argentina was the JCA's sole focus of activity during the days of its founder, Baron de Hirsch, and continued to be its chief interest for many years to come. The work of the JCA represents a unique phenomenon in the history of Jewish migrations: Here we have a Jewish organization that shaped the creation of a Diaspora community and played an important role in its growth and consolidation. We are grateful to the JCA for allowing us free access to its archives, both in London and in Buenos Aires, and for its financial assistance in bringing this work to print. Its publication now, as the JCA celebrates its centennial, brings us much satisfaction. Needless to say, we have not allowed this to affect content in any way.

Chapter 5 is based in part on the research project "Latin America and the Jewish People during the Holocaust Era" undertaken by the Latin American Division of the Institute of Contemporary Jewry, The Hebrew University of Jerusalem, with the kind support of the Basic Research Foundation, the Israel Academy of Sciences and Humanities. The material gathered by Leonardo Senkman, Elvira Rissech, and a group of interviewers who worked on the project in Argentina was of great importance in writing this chapter, as was the permission granted by the Delegación de Asociaciones Israelitas Argentinas (DAIA) to use its archives.

When this book appeared in Hebrew, Jacob R. Marcus immediately recommended that it be translated for the benefit of the English reader. Abraham Peck, the director of the American Jewish Archives, not only encouraged me to do so but stepped in as a moving force and loyal helper, providing invaluable and much appreciated assistance. Sincere thanks are also due to Gila Brand for her talented rendering of this work into polished English.

Argentina & the Jews

I

The Beginning,
1810–1876

Argentina's rebellion against the suzerainty of Spain began in May 1810, and independence was finally achieved in July 1816. The nine years that followed were a time of internal strife and political instability. In February 1825, the new nation signed a treaty of friendship, trade, and navigation with Great Britain, but four years later Argentina drifted into a prolonged era of dictatorship under General Juan Manuel de Rosas, who remained in power for the next twenty-three years. Although Rosas fought vehemently against the unitarians and their demand for centralized government, his term was crucial for the true unification of the Republic. Argentina entered its second constitutional era only after Rosas's defeat in 1852. The devastating civil war that continued until 1860 was both the price paid for a consolidated federal Republic and the fiery furnace in which it was forged.

The seven decades after the first uprising of the criollos (or Creoles) of Buenos Aires thus saw the formation of a new nation. Intensive efforts were now necessary to boost the sparse population—some 40,432 people in the capital in 1810, and barely half a million throughout the immense country.[1]

For the Jewish people, concentrated almost exclusively in Europe, North Africa, and the Near East, these same decades evidenced a unique demographic explosion, from an estimated 2.5 million souls in 1800 to some 7.7 million in 1880. Faced with discrimination, persecution, and growing economic hardship in Eastern and central Europe, the Jews nonetheless continued to hope for a change in their legal status. When they were disappointed time and again, emigration began to emerge as the only solution.

Did the constitutional changes in Argentina create a practical outlet for Jewish immigration? Was any visible Jewish presence created during this period, and if so, was it merely tolerated or was it solidly based on legal equality and social acceptance?

Constitutional Evolution

No official change in the attitude toward Jews and other non-Catholics was brought about by the revolution that began in Argentina on May 25, 1810. The rebellion was sparked by the news, reaching Buenos Aires on May 13, that the French army had captured the city of Seville and overthrown the Spanish government set up as a stopgap when King Ferdinand VII was deposed by Napoleon and exiled to France. In this governmental vacuum, the Cabildo Abierto, a forum of Buenos Aires's distinguished citizens, convened to decide the future of the colonies in the Río de la Plata. Their revolutionary decision was the establishment of a provisional government to "maintain these possessions in our most constant fidelity and adherence to our very beloved king and lord Don Ferdinand VII and his legitimate successors in the Spanish Crown." In its first manifesto, the government also undertook "in every way possible to preserve our holy faith."[2]

At a time when revolutions in Europe sought to overthrow the ancien régime, reduce the power of the church, and institute emancipation and freedom for all regardless of religion, the revolution in Argentina was colored by loyalty to the old order. As such, it heralded no change for the Jews. Similarly, no attempt was made by the provisional government to defy the authority of the Inquisition. When the commissioner of the Holy Tribunal in Buenos Aires requested on July 14, 1810, that one of its prisoners be transferred to the tribunal in Lima, Peru, the provisional government provided an escort just as the Spanish viceroy had done in the past.[3]

The revolution was followed by years of tumult and political change.

The first government lasted barely a year before another took its place; successive administrations were also short-lived as various political elements vied for power. The overall trend, however, was the growing independence of the United Provinces of the Río de la Plata.

The Inquisition was officially abolished in Argentina on March 24, 1813, one of several steps taken by the General Constituent Assembly to create a break with Spain. A decree separating the Argentine and Spanish churches was followed by decrees barring Spaniards without Argentine citizenship from civil and ecclesiastic service. Thus, the abolition of the Inquisition was not necessarily an endorsement of religious freedom; it could equally be regarded as a declaration of national sovereignty.[4]

One of the proposals put before the assembly was the opening of the mines in the provinces, which officially included both Bolivia and southern Peru, "to any persons desiring to come from any place on the globe." To allow for the participation of non-Catholics, it was stated that "no foreigner who initiates mining activity or owns an industry, neither he, nor his family, servants, or dependents, will be disturbed for religious reasons on condition that they respect the public order, and they will be able to worship God in their homes privately, according to their customs."[5] After lengthy discussions, the proposal was approved. This was the first time that the right of non-Catholics to observe their own faith, even in private, had been openly broached in Argentina. It was also as far as the assembly, known for its revolutionary and radical decisions, was able to go during this period. However liberal compared with old regime, the new regime in Argentina could not overstep the social limit, which was still very far from nondiscrimination and full equality for all religions.

The situation in Europe soon changed: Napoleon was defeated and the king of Spain, Ferdinand VII, regained the Crown in Madrid. When the king attempted to restore his authority over his colonies in the Americas, the United Provinces of the South (as the country was now known) organized a congress in Tucumán and, on July 9, 1816, declared its independence from "the king, his successors and the metropol." In so doing, it brought the move toward independence to a successful end. However, the position of non-Catholics did not improve. The discrimination against them was not a product of Spanish rule; it was the will of the Argentine people, as was clearly demonstrated when outside interests led Argentina to forge close ties with Great Britain through the Treaty of Friendship, Trade and Navigation.

The treaty, signed in February 1825, was worded in such a way as to place Argentina on a seemingly equal footing with the mightiest power of that time. Yet, from the Argentine point of view, it contained a most controversial clause: According to Article XII, British subjects living in the United Provinces were to "be neither harassed nor persecuted nor troubled for religious reasons. They will enjoy perfect freedom of conscience there and may celebrate Divine Worship either at home or in special churches and chapels that they will be authorized to build and maintain in suitable places approved by the government of the said United Provinces." These rights were to be conferred reciprocally on Argentine residents in Great Britain. The delegates of all the provinces except Buenos Aires were shocked by this clause and tried, unsuccessfully, to have it omitted. Owing to the political importance of the treaty they signed it anyway, but the actual implementation of freedom of worship was left to the discretion of the local governments.[6] The provinces of Córdoba and Santa Fe immediately declared that non-Catholic worship violated their laws and could not be permitted within their boundaries. Other provinces followed suit. When the liberal governor of the province of San Juan tried to incorporate a clause guaranteeing religious tolerance in the local constitution, he was forced out of office and the document was publicly burned in the town square.[7]

The treaty had a direct impact on the status of Protestants only in Buenos Aires, where a provincial law permitting them to practice their religion was passed on October 12, 1825. Twenty-eight years later, this law was to influence the Constituent Assembly called to Santa Fe by General José Urquiza, the caudillo who had defeated dictator Rosas. It was here, on May 1, 1853, that the assembly promulgated the Argentine Constitution—the same Constitution, with only minor amendments, in effect today. Article XIV, dealing with civil liberties, was the main source of controversy: Should freedom of religion and religious practice be granted to all inhabitants or only to Roman Catholics? One of the major arguments of the liberal assembly members was the precedent created by the treaty with Great Britain. Another was the importance of attracting immigrants, whatever their faith. Earlier, the assemblymen had discussed Article II, which defined the relation between church and state. The conservative delegates called for a declaration of Catholicism as the one true faith to which all the nation's inhabitants owed their respect and whose practice the federal government undertook to protect. In this instance, the liberal view prevailed; Article II states only that the federal Catholic government "sustains" *(sostiene)* the Roman Apostolic Catholic faith. Up to today, this term remains a source of controversy: Liberals interpret it in economic terms, while conservatives see it first and foremost as a spiritual obligation. The liberal assemblymen thus won religious liberty for non-Catholics, but not without a long and bitter fight.

Non-Catholics' right to be appointed to all administrative and political positions was also guaranteed by the Constitution in spite of conservative opposition. However, when the assembly was called upon to determine the qualifications for presidency and vice-presidency, liberals and conservatives united. In a unanimous vote, it was decided that these positions would remain the exclusive domain of "those who belong to the Catholic Apostolic Roman Communion."[8] Non-Catholics could not aspire to become president of the Republic. Nonetheless, they were promised total religious freedom, equality before the law, and the opportunity to be appointed or elected to other public offices. The decisive factor here, constantly repeated by the legislators, was the need for massive immigration.

The Need for Immigration

When Argentina declared its independence, half a million people were living in the provinces of the Río de la Plata. There were also Indian groups scattered over the vast lands in northern and, especially, southern Argentina, over whom the young Republic had no effective control. Headed by their caciques, they continued their autonomous existence, periodically raiding the small Christian settlements in the region.

From the earliest days, the founders of the Republic were conscious of the crying need for more inhabitants. In 1810, the year of the first uprising, the provisional government extended an invitation to the "English, Portuguese, and other foreigners not at war with us" to come to Argentina. Those who devoted themselves to crafts and farming would be granted all civilian rights and the protection of the government. Two years later, in September 1812, the government, led by the blatantly liberal Bernardino Rivadavía, promised "full enjoyment of all the rights extended to man in society" to immigrants of any nationality settling in Argentina. Both this manifesto, which was the first legislative act in the sphere of immigration after the birth of the Republic, and the earlier invitation alluded to the possibility of non-Catholics entering Argentina. At this time, however, the Inquisition was still in force and these invitations conflicted with a basic situation that had not yet changed.[9]

Meanwhile, the presence of foreigners began to be felt in both the province and capital city of Buenos Aires. This trend increased in the first years after independence. According to one source, the number of Englishmen reached several thousand, and this group enjoyed a prestigious position in society.[10] In 1823, Rivadavía, as governor of the province of Buenos Aires, adopted the policy of actively encouraging immigration and settlement. In February 1825, at the very time when the treaty was signed with Great Britain, a group of Scots took advantage of this policy and set sail for Argentina. They settled in Santa Catalina about twenty kilometers south of the capital and built a church there, thus manifesting the relationship between religious freedom and settling the country.[11]

The liberal forces in the province of Buenos Aires, which upheld commercial ties and immigration from Europe, also strove to establish a strong central government headed by their province. The political failures of the liberals when they were in power in 1826–1827 laid the groundwork for the subsequent rise of their federalist rivals, led by Juan Manuel de Rosas. Rosas did not annul the agreement with Great Britain or persecute Protestants, British subjects, or other foreigners already living in Argentina. However, his style of government and disputes with France and England were totally adverse to any thought or plan of augmenting their number. While immigrants continued to come to Argentina—according to one source, there were tens of thousands of them[12]—they no longer enjoyed the support of the government.

The dictatorship of Rosas drove a large group of liberal intellectuals out of Argentina. From exile in Chile, Uruguay, Paraguay, and Bolivia, these people continued to criticize the state of affairs in their homeland and through their writings established a platform for the liberal Republic of Argentina they envisioned in the future. The issues of immigration and demographic change figure prominently in their work. When Rosas was defeated in 1852, many of these exiled liberals filled key positions in the new political order, and their view of Argentina's problems launched a new reality. One of the foremost among them was Domingo Faustino Sarmiento, who was later to become president of the Republic. "The affliction of the Argentine Republic is its open spaces: The wasteland encroaches from all sides and penetrates the core; the solitude, the human emptiness, the absence of all civilized settlement—it is usually these that form the uncontested boundaries between the provinces": This is how Sarmiento described his homeland in 1845.

As a native of San Juan who had never been to the capital before, Sarmiento's familiarity was with the provinces, and it was his memory of them that sparked his feelings and actions during his exile in Chile. The immense pampas of Argentina, its forests, rivers, and mountains, were then populated very sparsely. On the plains, the occasional family ranch was ten, twenty, or even thirty miles from its nearest neighbor. The enormous distances prevented daily contact and ruled out the possibility of public institutions for education, religious practice, or social discipline. In their manners, outlook, and even dress, the inhabitants of the Argentine hinterland differed from the city dwellers. Whereas the urban populace enjoyed the cultural heritage of Europe, both material and spiritual, and thus represented civilization in Sarmiento's eyes, the Argentines in the back country were up to their necks in barbarism. For Sarmiento, "civilization and barbarism," as he subtitled his book, *Facundo,* about Argentina's social and political problems, encapsulated the battle waged by the Republic since its liberation from Spain. As his book was being written, "barbarism," born of the Argentine wasteland, gained the upper hand. Sarmiento's hope, echoed by many of his compatriots, was that the wheels would turn, bringing victory to that product of Western Europe—"civilization."[13]

Truly to eradicate "barbarism," it was not enough to defeat Rosas on the battlefield. A military victory was only one means to introduce fundamental changes in the fabric of Argentina; another way to achieve this was through immigration. This idea was expressed and methodically worked out by another exile, Juan Bautista Alberdi, who was also living in Santiago de Chile. After the fall of Rosas's government, he quickly prepared a small book of his thoughts and proposals that, despite the haste obvious in its prose, was to have tremendous historical impact. When the provincial delegates met in Santa Fe for the Constituent Assembly in November 1852, some of them had copies of this book on hand. Its great influence on the authors of the Constitution has been agreed upon by all historians, whatever their views.

In his introduction, Alberdi set out his credo: "America was discovered, conquered, and populated by the civilized races of Europe through the impulse of the same law that impelled . . . the inhabitants of Greece to civilize the regions of the Italian Peninsula. . . . The divine purpose of this law of expansion is the indefinite improvement of the human race through the crossbreeding of races, the communication of beliefs and opinions, and the adaptation of the populace to the means of subsistence."[14] Alberdi believed that Argentina, which was closed to immigration until its independence and even afterward, was fighting a law of nature under which a backward country was obligated to open its doors to civilization. One way to do so was to encourage the peaceful immigration of European peoples who would benefit Argentina.

Alberdi's program was grounded in the axiomatic assumption that the people then living in Argentina were by their very substance inferior to the people of Europe. Not only the Indians were considered inferior, but also the racially mixed herdsmen of the pampas —the gauchos—and the Hispanoamerican lower classes, who Alberdi felt were not much better. In his view, it was essential thoroughly to change and replace the elements upon which the Argentine nation was founded: "This is the real revolution . . . a revolution of people and things. We must replace our people, who are unfit for liberty, with others who are suited to it, without relinquishing the character of our native race and even less so our possession of the land."[15]

Alberdi felt that such a revolution was necessary for the preservation and advancement of the true Argentina, considering that all its cities, laws, institutions, and systems of government were essentially European in origin. The Christian faith, the Spanish language, the mode of dress, the manners and life-style—none of these were native to South America. Since Argentines, according to Alberdi, were only Europeans born in South America and nourished by European culture, a recent arrival from Europe enjoyed a distinct advantage. As he put it, "Every European who reaches our shores brings us in his mode of behavior more civilization than in many philosophy books, and this is later adopted by our inhabitants. . . . If it is our desire to plant and absorb in America the liberty of the English, the culture of the French, the industriousness of the European and citizen of the United States—let us take chunks of life from the customs of these people, and root them here!"

This was to be the principal goal of the Constitution. "What would you call a country of 200,000 leagues [5 million sq km] and 800,000 inhabitants?" asks Alberdi. "A desert! . . . And what would you call the Constitution of that country? The law of the desert! Yet what kind of

Constitution is most suited to the desert? A Constitution that will work to make it disappear." Thus Alberdi arrived at the motto that would become his trademark: "In America, to govern means to populate!"[16]

To accomplish this, the Constitution would have to accentuate the economic aspects of such a policy—and if economic development was to be promoted, thereby attracting immigrants, it was important to win the newcomers' trust and assure their future. Alberdi believed that immigrants should be promised full civil equality, without forcing them to become citizens or fulfil other civilian duties. In his view, the legal status afforded foreigners in the treaty with Great Britain could serve as a basis for further anchoring their rights in federal law.

In addition to Englishmen, Alberdi recognized the worth of the Germans and Swiss, whom he specifically mentions. However, from his negative attitude to immigration from Spain and complete indifference to a possible influx from Italy or Eastern Europe, we see that Alberdi's definition of "Europe" was very narrow indeed, limited to those areas inhabited mostly by Protestants.[17]

Both the constitutional draft proposed by Alberdi and the US Constitution were used as references by the legislators at Santa Fe when they wrote: "We, the representatives of the people of the Argentine Confederation, gathered at the General Constituent Congress . . . for the purpose of creating the national union . . . and securing the blessing of liberty for ourselves, for those who come after us, and for *all people of the world who wish to live on Argentine soil* [emphasis added], invoking the protection of God, source of all wisdom and justice, we order, decree, and establish this constitution . . ." This preamble attests to the centrality of immigration in the goals set out for Argentina. Clause XXV translates the legislators' impassioned appeal to foreigners into the language of the law: "The federal government shall promote European immigration; it shall not have the power to restrict, reduce, or impose any tax whatsoever on foreigners entering Argentine territory to engage in farming, improve industry, or introduce and teach sciences and crafts." Echoes of this clause, incorporated in the first section of the Constitution dealing with "declarations, rights, and guarantees," can be found in the section that enumerates the powers of the House of Representatives. Encouragement of immigration is specified as a congressional duty and a means of developing and promoting the nation. In nearly the same words, immigration is presented as a concern of the provincial legislatures.

As they wrote these clauses, the authors of the Constitution pursued Alberdi's line of thinking; sometimes they went even a step further. Evidently, this was a subject upon which all members of the Constituent Assembly agreed: The plenary approved the wording of the clauses unanimously, without discussion or appeal.[18] This consensus carried over into the subject of the rights of Argentina's foreign residents. All the assemblymen accepted the principle, explicit in the Constitution, of full equality for immigrants, foreigners, and citizens alike. This meant equality before the law, the right to a fair trial, and protection of personal property. All inhabitants, including foreigners and immigrants, were at liberty to come and go as they desired, sail the rivers, engage in commerce, and seek employment. They were granted freedom of speech and freedom of the press, freedom of assembly and organization for beneficial purposes, freedom to study and to teach others. Immigrants could become citizens after living in Argentina for only two years, although citizenship was not mandatory. Even after naturalization, they were exempt from military service for ten years. The concessions and privileges so liberally granted to newcomers raised no outcry among the statesmen; in most cases, the vote was unanimous in their favor.[19]

However, when the status of non-Catholic immigrants came up for debate, the consensus vanished. Notwithstanding this, by the time the deliberations were over and the Constitution was signed, non-Catholics in Argentina were also assured of their personal status, property rights, and freedom to engage in business. As a religious group, they were to be treated as *almost* equal.

Although the Constitution was born in times of strife and civil war, it was adopted and signed by all the provinces belonging to the Argentine Confederation. After its military defeat in 1859, the province of Buenos Aires also accepted the Constitution with minor modifications. Not one of the proposed changes was related to immigration, either directly or indirectly. Thus, Buenos Aires, like the other provinces, recognized the encouragement and promotion of immigration as a central goal of the Republic.

One of the first attempts to implement this goal was made by the province of Corrientes. In 1853, the governor signed an agreement with a French physician who promised to bring over forty thousand immigrants from the south of France within six years. These immigrants were to be settled along Corrientes's northern border. Another entrepreneur, Aarón

Castellanos, presented the provincial government of Santa Fe with a plan for settling a thousand European families on government lands in the northern part of the province, a region preyed upon by marauding Indians. From these and other schemes envisioned for Entre Ríos and Corrientes, we see that the immigrants were expected to farm land on the frontier, in effect expanding the territorial boundaries of these provinces. The arrival of the immigrants was to be orderly and planned. However, the fact that one of the schemes involved Protestant immigrants from parts of Switzerland indicates that Catholicism was not a determining factor.[20]

The province of Buenos Aires was also active in the sphere of immigration. In September 1854, a law was passed to prevent newcomers' being exploited by those who had organized and financed their trip, and, in April 1856, several leading bankers and merchants founded a philanthropic society to aid poor immigrants. A hostel was built wherein 150 immigrants could find food and shelter during their first four days in Buenos Aires. Among the contributors were members of Argentina's oligarchy. The implication is that immigrants were expected to reach Buenos Aires on their own, without the intervention of agents and immigration contractors. After their arrival, they had to fend for themselves or turn to a public charity; the government was not set up to take an active part in the immigration process.[21]

While the provincial authorities in Buenos Aires and the Confederation concurred on the necessity of immigration, their outlook was fundamentally different. The Confederation viewed immigration as a means of altering economic and social reality: The newcomers would work to develop agriculture and increase the proportion of cultivated land. The province of Buenos Aires was satisfied with the status quo in which cattle raising was a major source of national income; it was this economic sector that assured Buenos Aires its continued hegemony over the other provinces.

By the time Buenos Aires joined the Confederation, the immigration effort had already suffered several setbacks, leading to a greater need for federal intervention and growing controversy over the type of action required. The first president of the united Republic, General Bartolomé Mitre (1862–1868), who had been a government leader in the province of Buenos Aires, was a firm believer in "spontaneous" immigration. He supported concessions that would attract immigrants to Argentina without the government's involving itself in special arrangements to bring them over. The second president, Sarmiento (1868–1874) believed in planned, sponsored immigration. However, the long, bloody war with Paraguay (1865–1870) and the strong opposition to Sarmiento in Congress prevented the passage of a comprehensive law that would allow for greater national involvement in immigration. Only during the term of the third president, Nicolás Avellaneda (1874–1880), was such legislation finally completed.

In presenting the new Immigration and Colonization Law, President Avellaneda and his minister of interior argued that "the entire Republic is convinced . . . that [its] prosperity and future . . . depend on a solution to the problem of European immigration; hence the great concern over this problem among the people of the nation and the authorities." Without excluding spontaneous immigration, the law was aimed at seeking out immigrants from Northern Europe and those countries in the south where there were better prospects of finding candidates and achieving the desired results.

To carry out this task, two chief mechanisms were established: the Immigration Department and the Office for Land and Colonies. The Immigration Department was to develop a network of agents in European countries to disseminate information and organize immigrants. It would also set up local committees to ensure that newcomers were referred to all parts of the Republic and would "strive, with all the resources at its disposal, to elevate the moral standards of incoming immigrants by granting as much protection as possible to the honest and hardworking and proposing means to halt the flow of the corrupt and useless" (Article 3/2). In the course of its duties, the department would dispatch officials to the ships to help the immigrants disembark and find employment (preferably in the provinces), and to solve any legal problems with the authorities. A detailed immigration roster would also be kept.[22]

The immigrant and his family were exempt from customs duties on their personal belongings and any work implements brought with them. They were entitled to a free five-day stay at the immigrants hostel and would be assisted in finding a job by the employment bureau. When they had decided where to settle, free transportation would be provided to any part of the Republic. These benefits were granted to all immigrants. Certain groups, such as farmers or mechanics hailing from European ports, and whose moral and professional standards were high enough, were entitled to extra benefits. Immigrants in this category would receive a refund on their tickets to make up the difference between traveling to Argentina and going to the United States. As the minister of interior explained to the House of Representatives and Senate, this would enable Argentina to attract immigrants from Northern Europe, especially Anglo-Saxons who were rushing to the United States in hordes. Additional benefits were offered to farmers who were selected to settle in colonies established by the government: a loan to cover all their transportation expenses from port of departure to final destination, as well as free accommodation at the immigrants hostel until their arrangements were complete. Moreover, the first hundred settlers in every colony would receive a hundred hectares of land as a gift.²³

The 137 clauses of the proposed law were grouped in sections dealing with various facets of immigration and settlement: supervision of ships and captains to prevent exploitation and guarantee basic hygiene on board; the sale of government land to private settlers; procedures for establishing federal colonies; responsibilities of the provincial government, and so on. Provision was made for the establishment of two funds—one to finance immigration and the other for colonization. In short, the law was to act as a guideline for every inch of the immigrant's journey, from doorstep in Europe to farmstead on the Argentine frontier. It was through this legislation that President Avellaneda and his government found expression for their fondest hope and dream: immigration as a means of settling the wasteland.

The House of Representatives approved the proposal without reservation, and newspapers supportive of the government praised it and heralded its passage as a historic event that would change the destiny of the Republic. When it reached the Senate, however, opposition began to surface. For a combination of political and personal reasons, two leading statesmen succeeded in postponing the deliberations for an entire year. When the debate finally came up, they provoked long, tiresome discussions of nearly every clause, proposing no fewer than seventy-three reforms. It is notable that opponents of the law did not question the importance of immigration or the need for legislation on the subject. On the contrary, the senator from Santa Fe who led the opposition, Nicasio Oroño, stated repeatedly that he appreciated the need for wholesome, hardworking immigrants to develop the country's hinterlands. Aside from the fact that the minister of interior was a political rival of his from Santa Fe, Oroño's chief argument was that the Republic was taking on more than it could handle from a financial point of view.

The basic agreement between critics and supporters of the law was obvious when the discussion turned to the definition of the desirable immigrant. When one senator inquired about how the department would elevate moral standards among the immigrants, the ensuing debate showed that neither he nor the other legislators had any intention of proposing religious or ethnic restrictions on immigration; they were simply questioning the vagueness of the wording. Critics and supporters also agreed on the preference for Northern Europeans: "Does anyone doubt that it would be convenient to acclimate in our own land this manly, intelligent race that has made the prosperity of the United States? This may be one of the greatest achievements we can aspire to!" declared Oroño during the arguments over compensating immigrants who chose Argentina over the United States. None of his colleagues in the Senate rose to contest this view, which was apparently fully in line with their thinking. In fact, it was financial criticism that led to dropping the clause, not lack of support for the idea behind it.[24]

In the long run, the opponents in the Senate failed to block the law, but supporters of spontaneous immigration, who were constantly putting forward its advantages, particularly its low cost in comparison with sponsored immigration, succeeded in reducing the impact of certain clauses. On October 19, 1876, after the proposed reforms had been discussed in Congress and some of them adopted, the Immigration and Colonization Law was passed. For the sixty years and more that this law remained effective, it worked to reshape the face of the Argentine Republic.

The Jewish Perspective

Very few Jews made their home in Argentina during its first fifty years of independence. Even fewer left any written proof of their existence. When we hear of them at all, it is through casual references and fragments of data in old documents. In his memoirs, an English merchant shipwrecked in La Plata in 1813 states that he was rescued by a Jew named "Mister Jacob." Was this man a resident of Argentina and thus the first Argentine Jew in recorded history? The will of a German Jew drawn up in 1876 attests to the fact that he and his brother were living in Buenos Aires in 1834; no more is known about either of them. According to the records of the prestigious Foreign Residents' Club, Henry Naphtali Hart, an English Jew later active in the Jewish community, was a registered member in 1850. Alexander Bernheim of Alsace was a soldier who fought against Rosas in 1852 and a cofounder of the French-language daily newspaper in Buenos Aires in 1860. Ludwig Brie arrived in Argentina as a youngster during the war against Rosas, grew up to be a rich merchant, and was one of the leading activists in the Jewish community in the 1890s.[25] Each of these individuals maintained close ties with non-Jews and belonged to non-Jewish social organizations such as the Freemasons long before they were active in the nascent Jewish community. Occasionally, their economic pursuits brought them into the courts. Old judicial records, combined with social and communal documents, have thus been able to shed some light upon these few personalities.

Other Jews, neither wealthy nor fortunate enough to have been immortalized in this way, remain obscure. Their existence is documented by a letter to the editor of *Allgemeine Zeitung des Judentums* in July 1846. The writer, a Jew from Buenos Aires, estimated that several hundred Jews were living on the Spanish American continent at this time. "They do not reveal their faith and maintain little contact [with each other] even when they are known to be Jews and do not deny it," he wrote, and he goes on to deplore the loss of their Jewishness. From the context and tenor of this letter, we may assume he was referring principally to the city he knew best—Buenos Aires.[26]

Apparently, then, there were many more Jews in Argentina during the first half of the nineteenth century than our sources reveal. However, as non-Catholics, their legal status prior to the promulgation of the Constitution in 1853 was extremely precarious. The political leadership, cultural elite, and common people of Argentina were slow to drop the country's prerevolutionary tradition of Jew-hatred that had taken root among them without their ever having encountered a live Jew. Before the revolution in May 1810, hostility to Jews was openly and systematically encouraged. Frightening ceremonies were held by the perpetrators of the Inquisition in which the populace swore to seek out and denounce heretics. We know of such a ceremony taking place as late as 1804, when the Jews of Western Europe, parts of central Europe, and the United States already enjoyed full emancipation.[27] How much did this change later in the century, when the Constitution and immigration law were formulated?

Sarmiento, Alberdi, the Constituent Assembly, and the legislators who approved the immigration law did not refer to Jewish immigration explicitly, yet some of what they said and wrote had a direct bearing on the status of the Jews who reached Argentine shores. What strikes us first about Alberdi is that his ideas did not emanate from a general, liberal humanism founded upon the universal principles of equality and rights. On the contrary, the rationale for Alberdi's immigration proposals was entirely materialistic, and his perception of humanity was clearly antithetical to the principles of equality that had led to the emancipation of the Jews elsewhere. Alberdi's chief reasons for encouraging immigration—and for giving preference to immigrants of one nationality over another—were anchored in the belief that people were unequal by nature. It was this that caused him to despair of the natives, gauchos, and lower-class Latins and to seek out immigrants from Anglo-Saxon, Germanic, and other Northern European countries as a means of "civilizing" Argentina. When Alberdi wrote his book, racist anti-Semitism had not yet come into the world. There was, however, an exclusivist religious element in his thinking. He believed that the new Constitution of the Republic "must maintain and protect the faith of our fathers as a primary requisite for our social and political order; however, it must protect it through liberty, through tolerance, and through all the means unique to a democratic and liberal regime, and not in the manner of the ancient colonial law, through prohibitions and bans on *other Christian cults*" (emphasis added). In the early years of nationhood, the legislators were forced to continue in the path of their predecessors. Alberdi understood their actions as tactical concessions necessary for the success of the revolution. However, he reasoned that henceforth "it will be necessary to sanctify Catholicism as the state religion, yet without prohibiting the public practice of other *Christian rituals* [emphasis added]. Religious freedom is as vital to the nation as the Catholic religion itself. . . . Religious freedom is a means of populating this country, and the Catholic faith is a means of educating this population."[28] Thus, the significance of religious freedom was limited to religious tolerance, and, as he explicitly states, with respect to Christian observance only. Alberdi's idea of change was restricted to altering Argentina's status as a Catholic country only to the point at which it would be known as a Christian country. This made it highly unlikely that the Jews would be classified as desirable immigrants.

On certain points, the authors of the 1853 Constitution differed from their teacher and guide. Did they perhaps recognize that Jews might be among the immigrants? The records show four references to Jews during the constitutional deliberations, each made by a legislator opposed to liberty for non-Catholics. On these occasions, the speakers described certain situations that they felt illustrated the shocking implications of religious freedom. One speaker imagined the anguish of Argentine parents confronted with the conversion of their son to Judaism or Islam. Others wondered what would happen if a Jew were elected president and had to sustain Catholicism, represent the nation in dealings with the church, participate in festive services at the cathedral, and perform other, similar duties. The speculative nature of these remarks and the fact that the generalized phrasing of the immigration policy clauses passed uncontested indicate that not even the clerics envisioned Jewish immigration to Argentina as a likely possibility. Whether they would have approved such immigration or proposed explicit clauses to prohibit it thus remains unknown.[29]

The liberal members of the Constituent Assembly remained silent on this issue. Perhaps they did not find the statements of their opponents particularly noteworthy, or perhaps the records themselves are incomplete; from the data available, we do not know how the liberals responded, if they did so at all. There were no moves to alter the immigration clauses so as to bar or limit the entry of non-Christians, and none of the remarks about religious liberty and equal rights seem to imply that only Christians were meant. However, let us not forget that Alberdi, too, couched statements about religion in vague terms, revealing nothing to the reader about the boundaries of his thought. Were the founders of the Constitution in Santa Fe similar in this respect?

Whether or not it crossed their minds that a Jewish presence might arise in Argentina, from the standpoint of the Jews the outcome of this legislation was the same: The stage had been set for the immigration and equal treatment of Jews in Argentina. While there were already a number of Jews in Buenos Aires before the writing of the Constitution, others now made their way to the shores of La Plata, singly and in small groups. Very few names have come down to us from the estimated three to five hundred Jews living in Argentina in 1870, and we know of even fewer who were active in establishing a visible Jewish presence. However, it was the efforts of these individuals that put the acceptance of Jews, implicit in the Constitution, to the test.[30]

The first such case was the attempt of a French Jewish couple, Solomon and Elizabeth Levy, to marry in accordance with religious and civil laws that would be recognized in France if they were to return. The fundamental question put to the Supreme Court was whether previous rulings on non-Catholic marriages also applied to Jews. The couple's first appeal was turned down on the grounds that they did not. However, the swift intervention of a lawyer named Miguel Navarro Viola, later to become a senator, led to a decision in their favor. Their wedding, documented by the lawyer in a highly inaccurate account of Jewish ritual, constituted a breakthrough in the legal status of Jews in Argentina.[31]

Less than two years later, a minyan (a prayer quorum of ten men) assembled for High Holiday services, thereby sowing the seed for Jewish community life. According to one source, the impetus was an incident in which two Jews from different countries spent the whole day of Yom Kippur sitting on separate benches in a park in Buenos Aires. When they became acquainted, they discovered that each of them, in their loneliness, had chosen the same manner of spending the holy day: reading the prayer book and meditating. This led them to seek out other Jews in town and establish a regular minyan. Whether this is legend or historical fact, the first minyan convened in 1862, developing within a few years into a permanent institution known as the Congregation of Buenos Aires, and, later, Congregación Israelita de la República Argentina.[32] Initially, the Jewish community was extremely small. In 1872, according to one source, there were only thirty Jews; a decade later there were fifty-five. Nonetheless, its leaders endeavored by all possible means to bring the tiny community under the jurisdiction of the same laws pertaining to marriages, births, and deaths that governed the other religious groups. In this way, they consolidated the legal basis for the existence of Jews in Argentina, both as individuals and as a group.[33]

Avellaneda's government and the legislative committee responsible for the Immigration and Colonization Law did not stand in the way of institutionalized equality for Jews. Neither in the proposed law nor in the debates surrounding it was there any suggestion that only Christians were potential immigrants and that members of certain faiths or nationalities would be rejected. Nonetheless, the law did contain provisions that in the hands of prejudiced officials could be detrimental to Jewish immigrants. Among the particulars immigration agents in Europe and Argentina were requested to provide was the candidate's religion (Clauses 4/14 and 3/14). The entire network was designed to encourage the immigration of "honest, hardworking people" while filtering out the "corrupt and useless." Thus, Jews could eventually be discriminated against in keeping with the personal views of immigration officers on the grounds of their lack of "usefulness." The obligation to provide clear proof of their moral worth, good conduct, and professional skills to the satisfaction of these officers was a further potential impediment to Jews without the law's openly discriminating against them.

After many years these clauses did indeed become a pretext for discrimination against the Jews. At the time, however, this was not the legislators' intention. When the law was being formulated, the members of Congress were not unaware of the presence of Jews in Buenos Aires. Jewish businessmen, at least the most successful, were in contact with a wide sector of the population. Furthermore, advocate Navarro Viola had published his account of the Jewish wedding of the Levys eight years before, when religious freedom was a pressing public issue; the leaders of the Republic were surely familiar with the case. Had there been any objection to the inclusion of Jews in the law, the congressmen might have proposed restricting all immigration, or at least preferential, government-supported immigration, to Christians. In fact, no such proposal was ever raised.

This should come as no surprise. After the signing of the national Constitution in 1853, the issues of religion, religious coercion, and religious prejudice became a constant source of public debate. In the 1850s and 1860s, when the Freemasons gained considerable influence among the intellectual, political, and social elite in Argentina, and this secret fraternity was joined by many liberal leaders and young people, the well-publicized opposition of the Catholic church for over a hundred years turned even more vociferous. There were also several incidents in which clergymen tried to prevent the marriage and burial of Freemasons. Liberals in Santa Fe responded by attempting to wrest control of the cemeteries from the church and legalize civil marriage. At the urging of Oroño, the provincial governor, laws were passed to achieve this. The church loyalists were infuriated. Under the battle cry "Long live Jesus, death to Oroño!" an armed uprising soon followed in which the governor was deposed. The year was 1867, and among the leaders of the insurrection was Simón de Oriondo, who was later to become minister of interior in the Avellaneda government and one of the authors of the immigration law.[34]

Between 1867 and 1876, liberal views became increasingly widespread, and the number of Freemason lodges multiplied. Sensitivity over the issue of church and state continued to grow. In February 1875, the year the proposed immigration law was put before Congress, Buenos Aires was the scene of violent anticlerical outbursts that culminated in the burning of the Catholic El Salvador Seminary. Under these circumstances, no one, it seems, was inclined to introduce religious discrimination into the law at hand.[35]

This alignment of forces on the question of church and state produced the Immigration and Colonization Law that enabled Jews to make their home in Argentina and establish a solid Jewish presence there.

The Stage Is Set

The Constitution and the Immigration and Colonization Law, founded on the general consensus regarding the vitalness of immigration for Argentina's survival and prosperity, proved able to withstand political fluctuations over many decades to come. If there was any disagreement between political factions at that time, it was over the manner in which immigration should be encouraged and absorbed—not over the immigration of non-Catholics or Jews. With the removal of the colonial legal barriers, a small though visible Jewish community was thus able to emerge.

Yet, the opinions on the *desirability* of non-Catholic immigration that were voiced during the Constituent Assembly of 1853 should not be overlooked. The anticlericalist atmosphere in Argentina in the 1870s and later did not hide the fact that even Alberdi, "the Father of the Constitution," favored a more explicitly Catholic national code. That such attitudes existed, even if the Jews were not cited in particular, considerably diminished the legitimacy of Jewish settlement in Argentina. Nevertheless, as the country opened its doors to immigration for the first time, its readiness to receive Jewish immigrants exceeded by far the interest of Jews in settling there. The history of Argentine immigration was then advancing at a much quicker pace than was the history of Jewish emigration.

2

The Formative Years,
1876–1896

The events in the four years after the passage of Immigration and Colonization Law were crucial for the development of the Argentine Republic. In a series of military campaigns waged against the Indians in 1878–1879 (the "Conquest of the Desert"), the Republic increased the territory effectively under its rule by close to 375,000 square kilometers. Clashes continued over the years in northern Argentina and in Patagonia to the south, resulting in the expansion of governmental authority over even more territory. Julio Argentino Roca, the young general behind this highly successful military operation, rose swiftly in the ranks of power. His candidacy in the presidential elections of 1880 sparked an uprising in the province of Buenos Aires, the failure of which led to the federalization of the capital city. This was a dream come true for all the supporters of centralized federal government and heralded a new era in the history of Argentina. On October 12, 1880, General Roca's inauguration day, Argentina was a unified republic led by a young, vivacious leader. Huge expanses of virgin territory were at the federal government's disposal. This was the moment to put into practice the settlement policies formulated during the days of Avellaneda.

Less than half a year later, Jewish history was also at a turning point. Following the assassination of Czar Alexander II in March 1881, the authorities set out to utilize the already widespread anti-Semitism in Russian society to deflect the bitterness and animosity created by the exploitation and persecution of the populace. The rioting that broke out on April 15 in Yelizavetgrad, a city in the province of Kherson, quickly spread to other provinces and proceeded along the same lines: massacres and looting under the auspices and with the encouragement of the government. The anti-Semitic policies that had restricted Jewish residence and economic activity and kept the community from establishing itself financially, now blossomed into physical violence designed to root out the Jews altogether. Large sectors of the Jewish population in Russia lived in terror, and thousands of them, mainly those along the southwestern border, fled for their lives. The pogroms were soon followed by new laws and decrees that, combined with the deterioration of the economy and the birth pangs of industrialization and modernization, turned mass Jewish emigration from Eastern Europe into an increasingly widespread phenomenon.

At that same moment, the Argentine Republic embarked upon an aggressive policy to stimulate immigration and populate its vast territories. The needs of the Jews and of Argentina thus coincided. Were these two separate historical developments destined to meet? How and to what extent did the Jews discover Argentina? Were they accepted wholeheartedly?

The Invitation

News of the pogroms traveled quickly across Europe. When Carlos Calvo, the Argentine immigration officer in Paris, heard about them, he immediately contacted "important persons" in Saint Petersburg to arrange for the transfer of some of the Jewish immigrants to Argentina. His initiative was welcomed by the Argentine government. On August 6, 1881, an Argentine citizen, José María Bustos, became the government's immigration agent *ad honorem*, whose task was to attract Russian Jews to the Republic of Argentina. Bustos was to receive orders from the immigration department, and Argentina's consuls in Europe were instructed to aid him in his mission.[1]

Two days after the appointment was announced in the daily press, a French newspaper appearing in Buenos Aires, *L'Union Française*, published a vicious anti-Semitic attack: "What nation would conceive of sending an agent to collect harmful pests, parasites, from somewhere else?" wrote the editor. "The Jew belongs by instinct, inclination . . . and race to that category of creatures." To prove this, he reminded his readers that Spain had needed the Inquisition "to get rid of this affliction brought on by the invasion of the Moors." The small Jewish community in the Argentine capital was outraged. In a rival newspaper, two of its leaders challenged the editor to a duel as an "honorable" means of atoning for the insult. Legal action and publication of a rebuttal were other steps considered. Sarmiento's paper, *El Nacional,* sided with the Jewish community. Four days later, the French-language paper published an article in which the editor apologized, so to speak, and retracted his statements.[2]

Despite the provocation of *L'Union Française,* which could not have gone unnoticed in educated circles where the French language was highly regarded, immigration commissioner Samuel Navarro proceeded to issue practical guidelines for Bustos's mission. Hearing that Alfonso XXII, king of Spain, had agreed to allow Jewish refugees into his country, Navarro suspected that the Jews might prefer Spain over Argentina.[3] Bustos was instructed to consult with Calvo; if it was found that the Jews were prepared to go to Argentina, he was to ascertain all the real estate and other benefits to which they were entitled by law and to establish contact with the chief rabbi of Paris. It was assumed that a suitable recommendation from the Argentine ambassador in France, with Calvo as an intermediary, would pave the way to contacts with the French Jewish leaders of the Alliance Israélite Universelle and the Consistoire Central, and, subsequently, with the Jewish leadership of Germany and Russia. Bustos was given fifty copies of a promotion pamphlet in German that was to aid him in persuading the Jews.[4]

Bustos's instructions were incorporated in a letter published in the daily press in Buenos Aires on August 30, 1881. Despite the anti-Semitic responses it drew, and the political opposition voiced in *La Nación,* a newspaper edited by former president Mitre, the Immigration Department appended this letter to its annual report in 1882; the courting of Jewish immigration was a deliberate policy from which the government of Argentina refused to retreat. Even the opposition, which rejected the idea of mass immigration in principle, especially if Jews were involved, was prepared to compromise if the immigrants came of their own accord. In consequence, the Republic of Argentina, for reasons of its own, opened its doors to Jewish immigration.

How was this official invitation received by the Jewish communities and organizations in Eastern and Western Europe? First, the identities of the "important persons" contacted by Calvo in Saint Petersburg after the pogroms remain a mystery. Furthermore, we know nothing about Bustos's dealings with Jewish elements in Paris or Berlin, if there were any; and the Jewish press contains only the slightest reverberations regarding Argentina's willingness to absorb Jews. In fact, the Jewish papers carry no information whatsoever about Bustos's mission, and sources at our disposal show that the issue of Jewish immigration to Argentina was never brought up at Jewish leadership conferences held in Europe at the time. Bustos's appointment, as it turns out, was very short-lived. A daily paper in Buenos Aires reported that he had resigned on December 20, 1881, and would soon be returning to Argentina.

Did the leaders of the Alliance Israélite Universelle and other Jewish figures in Europe know about the Argentine proposal but reject it? This may be so, but we lack source material to prove it. It should be pointed out, however, that Jewish sources available for the year after Bustos's appointment are disappointingly silent on the fate of Argentina's invitation to the Jews of Russia.[5]

Argentina Discovered

The czarist decrees that had made life difficult for Russian Jewry since the pogroms in 1881–1882 remained in effect and became even more unbearable as the years went by. A network of special regulations, some of them old laws now reinstated and others new, placed an additional burden on the Jews, who were already struggling under Russia's general economic turbulence. The exodus, which had abated somewhat in the mid-1880s, began anew. Between 1881 and 1889, hundreds of thousands of Jews left czarist Russia and its neighbor Romania.[6]

Increased emigration led to a search for new places to settle. In the first half of the 1880s, the Jews had not yet discovered the Republic of Argentina. However, a small number did reach its distant shores. Alexander Salzberg, who immigrated in 1886, purchased vineyards in the province of Mendoza. There he met another Russian Jew, Aarón Pavlovsky, an agronomist, who had arrived three years earlier at the invitation of the Argentine government. The brothers Julio and Max Popper also arrived in 1886. Julio was an engineer and adventurer known for his explorations in Tierra del Fuego and his discovery of gold dust; he served as the unofficial governor of the northern districts of Tierra del Fuego for some time and even issued gold coins and stamps for local use. He was assisted by his brother Max, who was officially appointed to public office. These and other figures, some of them active in the Jewish community and others less so, firmly established a Jewish presence in the higher echelons of Argentine society.[7]

Other Jews, also from Eastern Europe, found their way to Argentina around this time and introduced a negative element into Jewish community life: pimps and white slave traders from the Jewish underworld in Russia and Galicia who were attracted to Argentina because of the numerical disproportion between men and women and the rootless life-style common there. The activities of these immigrants, later to be known as the "unclean" by the local Jews, are mentioned in the journalistic debates on the benefits and risks of Jewish immigration to Argentina that appeared in Eastern and Western Europe during the second half of the 1880s.

This is not to say that there was any lack of honorable, hardworking people among the Eastern European Jews bound for Argentina. Their presence is attested to in a letter from a Jewish resident of Argentina published in the *Jewish Chronicle* in June 1887 following a report that Jewish organizations in Europe were considering Argentina as a target for mass immigration. Vague statements, which are difficult to date, can be found about the hardships endured by the first immigrants from Russia. However, most of the Russian immigrants arriving in Argentina between 1886 and 1888 were probably not Jewish at all. This is backed up by the report in 1889 that a group of Russian Orthodox living in the capital had built itself a church.[8]

The year 1889 marked a turning point in Jewish immigration as a direct consequence of the reforms introduced in the Argentine government's immigration and absorption policy. In November 1886, shortly after Miguel Juárez Celman succeeded his brother-in-law, Julio Roca, as president, the House of Representatives approved far-reaching organizational changes in Argentina's immigration agencies in Europe. The object was to embark upon a more aggressive campaign than had been waged until then. A budget was approved for the establishment of information offices in several European cities, and the service as a whole became part of the Foreign Office. The new offices published information booklets and brochures in a variety of languages and organized mobile displays of Argentine products. In September 1887, the Senate and House of Representatives took a giant step in attracting immigrants: They approved government-funded loans to cover the travel expenses of poor but "favorable" candidates for settlement. This idea had been proposed in the early 1880s, but had never passed the House or Senate. Originally, the money was to be used to bring over the relatives of immigrants already in Argentina. Within a year, it was decided to broaden eligibility and offer loans to all potential immigrants. Theoretically, the loans were to be repaid to the government, and the landowners or settlement corporation were to provide guarantees. However, when Navarro was sent to Europe in April 1888 to organize the campaign, subsidized or free tickets were offered instead.[9]

News of this campaign soon reached the ears of Jews in Eastern Europe. In June 1888, two Hebrew dailies, *Ha-Tsfirah* in Warsaw and *Ha-Melitz* in Saint Petersburg, reported on the opening of an Argentine information office in Warsaw, offering free passage to Argentina and a plot of land to anyone settling there. In November 1888, *Ha-Melitz* reported the establishment of another office in Rotterdam, where one could view fresh produce and other merchandise from Argentina. Thus Argentine propaganda reached the Jewish public directly, resulting in an open debate over the pros and cons of emigration to Argentina. Reports began to come in from various communities about individuals and groups who were actively organizing for the purpose of emigration. Prominent among these was the Jewish community of Brisk, Lithuania. On August 27, 1888, *Ha-Melitz* said: "The desire to emigrate to Argentina has increased among the people of [Brisk]. One hundred sixteen families are preparing to leave, shouldering empty sacks to be filled there with gold and silver, according to the Argentine representative in Warsaw. . . . Last week a special emissary was sent to Warsaw with a list of emigrants that was forwarded to the consul general for his approval and signature."[10]

The results of this venture are unknown. If 116 Jewish families from Lithuania had indeed reached Argentina, the implications would have been considerable. However, no Argentine sources mention such a large group. Some members may have gone to Paris to consult with the leaders of the Alliance Israélite Universelle and request assistance. Between eight and ten families, a total of forty-five persons, do seem to have received such assistance in October 1888, and they constitute the first group of immigrants to be handled by a Jewish organization. This is borne out in the European Jewish press, Argentine Jewish sources, and the records of the Argentine immigration authorities.[11]

Upon hearing of the opportunities open to them in Argentina, other Jewish families and individuals began to ready themselves for the trip, with less fanfare, perhaps, than the Jews of Brisk. A case in point was the largest group of all: the immigrants aboard the *SS Weser.*

The *Weser* Immigrants

The *SS Weser,* a German passenger ship and freighter, arrived at the port of Buenos Aires on August 14, 1889, a cold, wintry day. Close to twelve hundred passengers crowded the decks, worn and weary after their thirty-five–day journey from Bremen, Germany. Eight hundred twenty of them were Russian Jews, many with beards and sidelocks, wearing Eastern European garb.[12] They numbered almost half as many as all the Jews believed to be living in Argentina at the time. Unlike their brethren on shore, they were a close-knit, well-organized Jewish community. The two Torah scrolls and religious texts they had brought with them, and the ritual slaughterers, rabbi, and teachers aboard, provided all that was necessary to keep up their Jewish observance en route. That day in August two Jewish communities were brought face to face: one scattered all over the large cosmopolitan city beyond the harbor with only a tiny minority actively Jewish; the other gathered on the deck of the German ship, exhausted, hopeful, anxious about the future. Unknown to the players, the scene was now set for a radical change in Argentine Jewish history.

The immigrants on the *SS Weser* had commenced their long journey in 1887. As the Jews along the western borders of Russia were threatened with expulsion, dozens of families living near Kamenetz Podolsk, the capital city of Podolia, had banded together to search for a new home. At the time, Argentina as a destination never occurred to them; their intention was to go to Palestine. Like many other communities in western Russia, they sent emissaries to Paris to seek aid from the Jewish leadership there, particularly from Baron Edmond de Rothschild and the Alliance Israélite Universelle. The competition was so great that the emissaries relinquished their hopes of emigrating to Palestine. At this point, however, they came into contact with the immigration agents from Argentina.

Heading the Argentine information office in Paris was Pedro S. Lamas, who coordinated all the offices in Europe and supervised the distribution of subsidized tickets through government agents such as Bustos or commercial agents hired by settlement corporations and Argentine landowners. The Podolian delegates were referred to a commercial agent named J. B. Frank, with whom they signed a contract. Upon their return to Podolia at the end of 1888, a number of families began to prepare for departure. Others were held back by their relatives and their own fears of the remote and alien land.[13]

Thirty families embarked on the journey to Argentina in June 1889; other groups followed. After a series of misadventures, they found themselves in Berlin, where they turned to the Jewish community and Rabbi Azriel Hildesheimer for help. Their plight was widely reported in the Jewish newspapers in Eastern Europe. When Hildesheimer first learned of their destination, he scolded them for choosing such a distant, unknown place to take their kin. Later, however, he did his best to insure their well-being.

Siegmund Simmel, a wealthy Jewish businessman and community activist, also came to the aid of the emigrants passing through Berlin. He went to Paris to investigate the reliability of the agent with whom they had transacted. After negotiations that involved the chief rabbi of France, Zadok Kahan, Michael Erlanger, Rothschild's charities secretary, and central figures in the Alliance Israélite Universelle, a new agreement was reached with Frank according to which twenty-five to one hundred hectares of land in Nueva Plata, owned by Rafael Hernández, would be sold to the immigrants at 120 francs per hectare. Upon arrival in Argentina, the immigrants would receive farming equipment, food, and supplies on credit from Hernández until after the first harvest; travel expenses would be subsidized by the government of Argentina. In exchange, each family would pay Hernández an advance of 400 francs.[14]

The intervention of Simmel and the Jewish organizations in France transformed the fate of the Podolian group into a public cause. It was more than simple charity. Each of the parties involved kept watch on the group's progress. The Alliance Israélite sent letters to its members in Buenos Aires informing them of the arrival of the immigrants and urging them to extend aid. Simmel, upon hearing that an acquaintance, Doctor Wilhelm Löwenthal, would be visiting Argentina on behalf of the Argentine government to study the colonization issue, asked Löwenthal to inquire into how "his" immigrants were faring. Although the idea of emigrating to Argentina did not spring from the Jewish organizations, and, to a large extent, they were even opposed to it, they regarded the group aboard the *SS Weser* as a controlled experiment from which they might be able to draw general conclusions.

This was also the attitude of the immigration agent, Frank, and perhaps that of Lamas, director of operations in Europe. On July 6, Frank wrote to the immigration commissioner in Buenos Aires asking that the "eight hundred Russian farmers" on the *SS Weser* be given special treatment. His reasons: the sole purpose of these farmers was to settle and cultivate the land by hard work; and they were the forerunners of thousands of others who needed only a single word of encouragement to join them. These others, he claimed, numbered close to 100,000. Lamas's son, who was then leaving for Argentina, was also asked to oversee personally the welfare of the *Weser* group. The leaders of the Jewish community in France closely followed the progress of this experiment, for which the agent was paid a 5,300 franc commission. To Frank, this demonstration of public interest and support was practically a guarantee that more such transactions would be coming his way.

At the request of Simmel and Frank, the German shipping firm agreed to provide its Jewish passengers with their own kitchen, and livestock was brought on board to insure a supply of kosher meat. With these preparations complete, the *SS Weser* set sail on July 10, 1889.[15]

The financial investment of the immigrants and their supporters in Paris and Berlin came to 35,000 francs. The Argentine government spent much more on their travel expenses. If the Jews had had to pay their own way, chances are they would never have gone to Argentina, and the turning point in Argentine Jewish history might never have occurred. In fact, Argentina's ambitious campaign to attract immigrants was extremely short-lived; the severe economic crisis the year after the arrival of the *Weser* group caused the immigration budget to drop to 8 percent of the allocation for 1889, and the granting of free tickets was abolished.[16]

It should be emphasized that the new phenomenon of Jewish immigration to Argentina emerged during a brief period of radical liberalism that was not pursued with the Jews in mind. On the contrary, long before the liberal policies were dropped, agents in Paris were ordered to cease issuing subsidized tickets to Jews. The hostile reception given to the Jewish immigrants on the *Weser* at the port in Buenos Aires illustrates this point well: When the immigration officer, Carlos Lix Klett, boarded the *SS Weser* on August 14, he was taken aback by the strange appearance of the large crowd of Jewish passengers. His immediate response was that they were not wanted in Argentina and should be returned to Europe. As reported in the newspapers, he claimed that Argentina had no room for Jews, and there was no reason why it had to take in those whom Russia, Germany, "and the United States" had expelled. The Jews on the *SS Weser* remained on board as their fellow passengers disembarked. The central immigration committee to which the passengers appealed overruled Lix Klett's decision, mainly on the contention that these were not ordinary immigrants but settlers who had paid for their land in advance. On Friday afternoon, August 16, the Jews were finally permitted to go ashore.[17]

Stormy Beginnings

For the working-class immigrants who arrived in Buenos Aires in those days, the Argentine Republic was a far cry from the legendary El Dorado they may have expected. The humble Jewish immigrants from Podolia could see this even from the deck of their ship. The dockworkers were in the midst of a massive strike, supported by the foreign shipping crews and other port workers. Their demonstrations led to bloody clashes with the police and the stationing of troops in the southern working-class neighborhoods. The French ambassador to Argentina, who reported these events to his foreign minister, was no supporter of the labor disputes in Buenos Aires, yet even he admitted that the situation was "a logical consequence of the difficulties faced by the immigrants, who are unable to find housing and food at reasonable prices."[18] This social and economic tension helped to strengthen the Socialists in Argentina, for whom 1889 was a landmark year. At the same time, the growing social polarization, government corruption, and civil disturbances led to the emergence of the Radical party, the major opposition faction in Argentina until World War I. Both the Socialists and the Radicals were to play an important role in the future of Jewish life in Argentina.

It was at this point, as the dark clouds began to gather on the horizon, that the Jews from Podolia arrived. They were taken from the ship to the Hotel de Inmigrantes, a hostel run by the government immigration office. This was a gloomy, rat-infested, wooden building with tin siding, poor sanitation, and inadequate ventilation where newcomers sought to make their needs known in a Babel of tongues. The Jewish immigrants were in an even worse position than most. The delay in leaving the ship had forced them to desecrate their first Sabbath in Argentina, and, unlike the other immigrants, they could not eat the food offered at the hostel. The problem was solved two days later through the intervention of the Jewish community in Buenos Aires, which persuaded the authorities to provide separate dishes and live animals for slaughter. "This was the first time I ever saw kosher meat in Buenos Aires," wrote Davíd Hassan, the vice-president of the Congregación Israelita, who helped to obtain these facilities.[19]

A few days later, the immigrants were shocked to find that landowner Hernández refused to honor his commitment because the price of real estate had risen since he had engaged Frank to act on his behalf eight months earlier. Such practices, some even uglier, were common in Argentina at the time, and immigrants of all nationalities fell prey to them. Some complained to their diplomatic representatives, but this was effective only if the case posed a threat to Argentina's policy of mass immigration. Usually, the injured parties had no recourse aside from the solidarity of their countrymen.[20]

The immigrants from Podolia turned to the Jewish community in Buenos Aires for assistance. The Congregación Israelita obtained a permit enabling the immigrants to stay longer at the hostel and engaged in fundraising on their behalf. On the advice of the congregation, the immigrants rejected an offer from the authorities to settle in the north of the province of Córdoba and entered into an agreement with a lawyer by the name of Pedro Palacios who owned large tracts of land in the north of Santa Fe. On August 30, 1889, which was again a Sabbath eve, the immigrants departed for Palacios Station, the last stop of the northbound train heading for Tucumán. The fact that they were desecrating the Sabbath during Elul, the month of repentance, pained them greatly. However, on reaching their destination, they found that their hardships were only beginning.

The gap between the expectations of the settlers and those of Palacios was great: The settlers looked forward to decent housing and a regular supply of tools and food; for their part, Palacios and his agents found the habits of the settlers strange and unfathomable. They "wasted" large amounts of good meat in the name of kashrut, the Jewish dietary laws of which the Argentines had never heard. Many work days were lost because of the Jewish High Holidays and the Feast of Tabernacles that fell on Thursdays and Fridays that year. Palacios thought these days were spent "studying the Talmud," which he saw as a further waste of time. The settlers, who claimed that Palacios was not meeting his obligations, were similarly accused by him. Meanwhile, hundreds of Jews were living in abandoned railway cars and tin shacks, suffering from cold and hunger. Before long, dozens of children succumbed to illness. Infighting among the immigrants also took its toll, with many families leaving for the surrounding villages, Santa Fe, or the capital. A small number fell into the hands of the white slave traders and their daughters were forced into prostitution. By the spring of 1890, at least three families had returned to Podolia.[21]

The dispute between Palacios and the settlers reached the newspapers in Buenos Aires and provided an opportunity publicly to voice opinions for and against Jewish immigration. The small Jewish community in Buenos Aires made its views heard, too: It cautioned Jewish public opinion in Europe against encouraging "thousands of Russian Jews" to come to Argentina. When the suffering of the settlers at Palacios Station was reported in the Jewish newspapers in Europe, it became clear that the whole issue of immigration to Argentina had reached a critical point.[22]

The Alliance Israélite Universelle, which had assisted eight families in 1888 and the Podolian group the following year, did not do so willingly. "We did all we could to keep them from going," wrote the secretary of the Alliance Israélite to Simón Kramer, the chairman of the Jewish congregation in Buenos Aires, on January 17, 1890. Six days later, a special committee of the alliance met to discuss a proposal for Jewish settlement in Argentina; it was categorically rejected. The Anglo-Jewish Association in London had also been debating, since November 1889, what stand to take. Learning of the attitude of the Congregación Israelita in Buenos Aires, the leaders of the association resolved to oppose immigration to Argentina and to publicize their decision in the Eastern European Jewish press, which had long been a forum for this issue.

Throughout 1890, there were no published reports of any Jewish groups bound for Argentina; archival sources are equally silent in this respect. Nevertheless, 1890 was a decisive year.[23]

A National Dream

In Argentina, the economy—and, with it, political and social life—had reached the moment of truth. After several years of dizzying speculation with borrowed and sometimes fictitious stakes, the game was suddenly over. The currency was devalued, stocks lost all worth, and the banks collapsed. The political outrage that had been simmering for two years was now unleashed with a fury, culminating in an attempt to overthrow the president in a military uprising on July 26, 1890. The uprising failed but its major goal was achieved: President Juárez Celman was forced to resign, and the future was to be very different.

As Argentina wrestled with its problems, Jewish existence in Russia was threatened once again. Between the spring and summer of 1890, the Jewish leadership learned from reliable government sources that a new series of decrees was to be imposed that would make life even more difficult for the Jews. Despite the public outcry in England and elsewhere, the Russians continued with their plans, and on Passover 1891 thousands of Jews were brutally evicted from Moscow. Realizing the seriousness of the situation, Jews all over Russia headed for the exit and, in so doing, opened a new chapter in the history of mass emigration.[24]

During these difficult hours, the revolutionary schemes of Baron Maurice de Hirsch were instrumental in making Argentina a focus of Jewish interest. In 1887, after losing his only son Lucien, the baron had decided to contribute a large part of his fortune to improving the lot of the Jews in Russia, which he hoped to achieve by developing secular and vocational education for them. He had allocated a fund of 50 million francs for this purpose and dispatched his representatives to negotiate with the Russian authorities. By May 1889, the baron had realized that the authorities were not prepared to encourage the integration of Jews in Russian society and would use the money for their own ends. He had broken off the negotiations and decided to try another solution: emigration. That same month, Hirsch approached Jewish leaders in the United States with the idea of founding an immigrant relief organization. It soon became clear to him that they were opposed to his basic goal, that is, mass immigration to the United States. Without severing these contacts—which led to the establishment of the Baron de Hirsch Fund in New York in February 1891—the baron continued his quest.[25]

Löwenthal was then in Argentina at the request of the Argentine Foreign Ministry to study the colonization attempts in various provinces. His report to the foreign minister also touched on the plight of the *Weser* group, whom he had visited at the urging of his friend Simmel. The dozens of Jewish families who were determined to farm the land in the face of all adversity had convinced him that it was worthwhile encouraging such

Baron Maurice and Baroness Clara de Hirsch-Gereuth

initiatives on a commercial basis. Löwenthal had drawn up a plan that he submitted to Rabbi Zadok Kahan for the attention of the Alliance Israélite Universelle and Baron de Hirsch. Six days after the alliance had rejected the plan, the baron had pledged to investigate the possibilities and personally to initiate and oversee the ventures involved. In an article Hirsch published a year and a half later, he cited the outstanding achievements of the *Weser* immigrants as proof of the Jews' capacity for agriculture: "The knowledge of this guides me in my work, and I am now setting out to accomplish it with all my strength."[26]

An expedition to Argentina was organized in 1890, and in May 1891, shortly after the expulsion from Moscow, two emissaries were dispatched to lay the groundwork for large-scale Jewish emigration. One was Arnold White, a journalist and member of the British Parliament who, oddly, was known for his anti-Semitic views and his demands to halt immigration to England. He left for Saint Petersburg to negotiate with the Russian authorities and engage their help for an orderly Jewish exodus. The other was Löwenthal, who sailed to Argentina with the power of attorney to purchase real estate and make arrangements for the rapid absorption of thousands of immigrants.

At first, the baron envisaged a scheme in which the Jews leaving Russia would settle in several different countries and become assimilated, full-fledged members of that particular society. Within a few months, he began to see Argentina as a base for concentrated Jewish settlement, extensive enough to permit the Jews to operate more or less independently. He believed this would "permit the establishment of a sort of autonomous Jewish state where our coreligionists would be protected from anti-Semitic attacks once and for all." Such a project would require the collaboration of all public and private elements in the Jewish community. The baron took the first step, contributing 50 million francs (approximately US $10 million) to the Jewish Colonization Association (JCA) founded on August 24, 1891. Meanwhile, he kept the more grandiose plans to himself, waiting for the early schemes to prove him right.[27]

Hirsch's plans and activities, both those he pursued openly and those he kept secret, contrasted sharply with the thinking of Jewish organizations in Eastern and Western Europe. However, it was not long before all these organizations were cooperating with him, in spite of their opposition. The Alliance Israélite Universelle, led by its secretary Isidore Loeb, was the first to do so. The president of the alliance, S. H. Goldschmidt, and the president of the Anglo-Jewish Association of London, Julian Gold-smid, joined the board of the JCA, and the Deutsches Zentral Komitee für die Russischen Juden, although it disagreed with the baron's politics, consented to go along with him, too. When the negotiations with the Russian authorities were complete and a permit was obtained, the Russian Jewish leadership, headed by Baron Horace Gunzburg, also did its part by establishing a network of local immigration committees under a central committee in Saint Petersburg.

Even the Hibbat Zion movement (the early Zionists), languishing since the summer of 1891 because of the Turkish ban on immigration to Palestine, was largely unopposed to Hirsch's plan of settlement in Argentina. When Colonel E. W. Goldsmid, the head of Hibbat Zion in England, left for Argentina to direct the colonization program, veteran Hibbat Zion leader Rabbi Shmuel Mohilewer parted from him with the following words: "As the letter *A* leads to the letter *Z,* so Argentina will lead to Zion." The attitude of the proletarians among the Jews was not yet expressed collectively, as no Jewish labor parties existed at the time. However, the work of Baron de Hirsch, who by now was almost a legend, was highly revered among the masses, and a portrait of the "new Moses" was a common sight in the humble Jewish homes in the Pale of Settlement in Russia and elsewhere.[28]

From 1891 until his death on April 21, 1896, Hirsch played a central role in organized Jewry. The sums he contributed to the JCA—$10 million on establishment and much more as part of a covenant signed in August 1892 bequeathing all his property—far exceeded all sources of Jewish philanthropy in Europe and the United States combined. He established himself as general and chief director of the association and from its inception lavished upon it much of his time, energy, experience, and connections. Thus, the JCA enjoyed a great advantage over other public, volunteer organizations in which the key figures found much less time for their organizational duties.

The fact that the baron was not bound by a particular nationality was also significant. As a citizen of the world, he was equally at home in Bavaria, Belgium, France, Austria, and England. He was not a patriotic Frenchman, German, or Englishman, as were the leaders of the Alliance Israélite, the Deutsches Zentral Komitee, and the Anglo-Jewish Association, and was therefore freer in his Jewish considerations. Perhaps this is why he saw what others did not: the first signs that the gates were closing in the countries of immigration. The Jews of the United States, England, France, and Germany feared that the arrival of large numbers of impoverished and strange-looking Russian immigrants would endanger their own emancipation. The baron's realization of this clearly influenced his choice of Argentina as a target for Jewish immigration. With unprecedented speed, Argentina was elevated to center stage in Jewish affairs and a firm basis established for Jewish life there.

The Baron's Schemes

From mid-1891, Baron de Hirsch took over the role that had been played by the Argentine government until 1889: encouraging Jewish immigration. Hundreds of immigrants reaching Galicia and Germany were referred by the local committees to Hamburg or Bremen, where they set sail for Argentina at the baron's expense. Theoretically, there was a selection process to insure that the first settlers, the "trailblazers," were suited to the task. In practice, however, the committees were caught between their desire to move the refugees as quickly as possible to other destinations and the changing demands of the refugees themselves, many of whom now preferred to become protégés of the wealthy Hirsch rather than go to the United States. During the months of July and August 1891, hundreds of refugees boarded ships for Argentina at the German ports. Some took their families with them; others set out alone to pave the way for those left behind. Descriptions of the motley crowds aboard the *SS Don Pedro, SS Tijuca, SS Lisbon,* and other ships, which included quite a few recruits for the "unclean," appear in the reports of JCA officials and in the settlers' personal memoirs.

The scene replayed itself in November 1891, with the arrival of 817 Jews aboard the *SS Pampa.* This group, from Constantinople, included many who had attempted to emigrate to Palestine but were barred from doing so by the Turkish authorities. As they had been unable to return to Russia or remain much longer in Constantinople, the baron had agreed to help several hundred of them settle in Argentina. Again, however, only a small proportion of those selected had the ability or intention of becoming true pioneers, either in Argentina or Palestine,[29] and the absorption of these "spontaneous" immigrants proved extremely difficult. The first groups reached Buenos Aires before Löwenthal had bought land. They, and those who followed, remained for a long period in enforced idleness, subsisting on virtual charity administered to them by JCA employees. Even after the purchase of land in the provinces of Buenos Aires and Entre Ríos, no farming plan had been formulated and the handouts of food and money continued. The agricultural conditions in Argentina were suited to grain crops (wheat and corn) and flax or cattle raised for the world market. The local market was very small and far from the Jewish colonies, ruling out the possibility of varied, intensive farming for domestic purposes. Under the circumstances, farms had to be large—between seventy-five and 150 hectares (185–370 acres)—with an amount of equipment and work animals to match. For the most part, seasonal crops were grown, which required payment of the farmers' living expenses at least until the first harvest.

When the JCA commenced its operations in Argentina, it was not yet known how great the expenses would be for each family. Only later were various estimates submitted, with the minimal expenditure for a farm of seventy-five hectares reaching US $1,730–$1,800. According to the baron's plans, each settler was to repay this debt over an extended period. Natural disasters such as hailstorms just before harvest and plagues of locusts, which were common in the regions where the Jewish colonies arose, pushed the initial expenditure and debt owed by the settlers even higher.[30]

Hirsch felt that the heterogeneity of the first pioneering groups was an error that could be rectified by better planning and organization. He decided that a new system was needed that would bring large groups of settlers straight from Russia. Rather than penniless wanderers lacking agricultural experience, the new breed of pioneers would be veteran farmers who had sold their property in an organized manner and invested in the colony. As a group, they would be unified enough to organize all stages of the colonization on their own through their elected representatives. The baron envisaged groups of fifty families comprising a total of five hundred people. The first nine groups (i.e., 450 families) were to leave Russia together after all travel, real estate, and other arrangements had been made by the JCA through its branches in Russia and Argentina. An experiment as large and methodically planned as this was an innovation, and carrying it out was no easy task. The candidates had to be experienced farmers with families large enough to provide sufficient manpower; they had to have some savings of their own and a willingness to forge the way in a new, pioneering endeavor. Obviously, such people were hard to find, and some compromises had to be made in selection. The preparations in Argentina took much longer than planned, so that groups sometimes disbanded and had to be reassembled, and the journey itself was more problematic than anticipated. After three years of work (1892–1894), the JCA had managed to bring only 3,444 settlers to Argentina instead of the forty-five hundred envisaged for one year.[31]

In the summer of 1894, the baron still believed that before long, some 300,000 to 400,000 Jews would settle permanently in the colonies. The next year, however, the enterprise entered a critical phase that brought immigration to a standstill and marked the beginning of many months of bitter conflict between the settlers and the JCA administration in Argentina. The core of the clash was a misunderstanding of Hirsch's intentions. The baron, conceiving of colonization in Argentina as a "businesslike" venture, insisted that the settlers sign formal contracts with the JCA in which they undertook to repay the loans advanced to them within a predetermined, relatively short period, at moderate interest rates. The contract was phrased in such a way as to make the settler dependent on the goodwill of the association and its administrators in case of nonpayment. The settlers, discouraged by hardship, crop failure, and the prospects of an authoritarian, overbearing administration instead of the promised group autonomy, refused to accept these terms. The very insistence on contracts seemed to them a deviation from the philanthropic scheme they believed the baron had intended. A fierce clash took place in or near the JCA offices in Buenos Aires, and the resultant press coverage inevitably influenced figures such as Juan Alsina, the head of immigration services. Whereas he had found warm words for the baron's enterprise in his annual report in 1892, he was critical of the JCA in 1895 and subsequent years. He sided openly with the rebellious settlers and gradually developed a negative attitude to Jewish immigration.[32]

Bitterly disappointed by these events, Hirsch resolved to discontinue his massive settlement scheme. However, he died suddenly, during a hunting trip to Hungary, before he had taken any final action. By then, there were a total of 910 farms and 6,757 settlers in Buenos Aires, Entre Ríos, and Santa Fe. This accounted for only two-thirds of the settlers; the remaining third had left the colonies after working there for shorter or longer periods. Baron de Hirsch's great colonization scheme brought only ten thousand Jews to the shores of Argentina, many of whom returned to Europe or departed for the United States. Furthermore, the ineffectiveness of the selection process advocated by the baron was to influence the JCA's colonization procedures for many years to come.[33]

All in all, the colonies in Argentina did little to ease the plight of Russian Jewry. While Baron de Hirsch and his broad network of officials toiled over the settlement of a few thousand people in Argentina, the United States was taking in several times that number every year; even emigration to England was of greater proportions. It should be remembered, however, that Jews who went to these countries usually had relatives living there already. If they had no close kin, they would turn for help to distant relatives or people from their hometown. The majority did not require publicly funded tickets, and many received no financial aid at all.[34] This was not the case in Argentina, where it was the JCA that carved a niche for Jewish immigrants. Furthermore, in contrast to the United States and England, where industrial development and the urban job market provided endless absorption opportunities, Argentina was a land of farming and thus should rightly be compared only with countries where farming was also central, such as Palestine.

According to one estimate, close to five thousand Jews reached Palestine in 1891, before the Turks banned Jewish immigration. By 1896, several thousand more had entered the country despite the ban. However, the great colonization fever that had motivated so many to come was also the source of many departures, so that in the final balance, immigration to Palestine and Argentina in those years was quite similar in scope. Absorption in Palestine was dependent on agricultural colonization and the amount of aid received from Baron de Rothschild and the Hibbat Zion movement. The central role of the two barons, Hirsch and Rothschild, in Jewish life at that time and the resemblance between their philanthropic and Jewish national activities are further evidence of the similar plane occupied by Palestine and Argentina. Moreover, we know that some of the same figures were instrumental in organizing colonization in both countries and that many of the settlers in Argentina were emotionally tied to Palestine.[35]

In light of these similarities and the ideological dimension that permeated both settlement ventures, the social disparity between them is striking. On the whole, immigration to Palestine was a spontaneous initiative. Assistance from outside elements was only a partial factor and, in any case, was offered to settlers only after the move. Immigration to Argentina, on the other hand, was largely determined by the decisions of colonization officials. As a result, the immigrant population in Palestine was much more varied from a social, economic, and, especially, from a cultural perspective. When selecting the pioneers of the colonization endeavor in Argentina, uniformity was one of the goals. "Don't you think that progressive elements are harmful to the colonies?" asked group organizer David Feinberg, when interviewing Noah Katsovitch, one of the few intellectuals seeking to settle in Argentina. Another activist on the screening committee wanted Katsovitch turned down when it was found that he could write perfect Russian; it was due only to Katsovitch's stubborn insistence that he was accepted. This approach, which was fully in keeping with Baron de Hirsh's conceptions of the Jewish farmer, was to have an important bearing on the configuration of the Jewish colonies in Argentina.[36]

The 910 farms operating under the baron's auspices in 1896 represented only a fraction of the real estate acquired by the JCA during his lifetime as a basis for further immigration. During these years, strong bonds were growing between the established Jewish community in Argentina—the Congregación Israelita—and the JCA. Recalling its helpfulness during the early days of the colonization program, Baron de Hirsch asked the congregation to take responsibility for the few immigrants who reached Buenos Aires on their own. This activity, also financed by JCA, strengthened the congregation, and, as a token of gratitude, the baron was elected honorary president.[37] From the outset, these close ties, generated by the similar backgrounds and social standing of the JCA representatives and members of the congregation, were also colored by the congregation's dependence on the JCA in all that concerned the strengthening and expansion of Argentine Jewry.

A Meeting of Paths

As a greater Jewish presence was evolving in Argentina, the country was in the midst of a serious decline, which the new immigrants were the first to feel. In April 1890, the Spanish ambassador in Buenos Aires informed the Foreign Office in Madrid that immigration had fallen off and that a growing number of immigrants were returning to Spain and Italy. A British embassy report published in May 1890 also alludes to the fact that immigrants arriving without means would not succeed in Argentina. In February 1891, when the study mission dispatched by Baron de Hirsch was touring the country to find land for his large colonization project, the French ambassador reported on the growing unemployment and financial hardship, urging his government to discourage further immigration. At the end of May, as Löwenthal was returning to Argentina to work on the practical aspects of the colonization program, the plight of the immigrants in Argentina led the French ambassador to establish an emergency fund to assist those who were starving and homeless. Thus it transpired that as Löwenthal prepared to absorb Jewish immigrants with the aid of the Congregación Israelita, French members of the congregation were asked to donate funds to help their destitute countrymen. Now also, for the first time since the implementation of the mass immigration policy, the Immigration Department published statistics showing that more people were leaving the Republic than were coming in.[38]

The overall picture that emerges is one of asymmetry between the Jewish and general developments in Argentina. When the general mass immigration process was climbing toward its peak in the early 1880s, Argentina was not yet known to the Jewish public and its leaders in Europe. Even in June 1888, when the first news of Argentina's immigration policy reached them, the editors of the Hebrew newspaper *Ha-Tsfirah* knew almost nothing about the country. "Perhaps our readers in North America can tell us something," a leading article hoped, under the supposition that the Jews in the United States might know more because they were closer geographically than were Europeans.[39] When Argentina was finally discovered by the Jewish immigrants from Eastern Europe, the immigration movement had already crested, and the only new direction was down. This was the point at which Jewish and Argentine history converged. Baron de Hirsch's colonization scheme, which brought the paths of history together and created the infrastructure for a new, major diaspora, came at a time when government policy and the general immigration movement to Argentina had lost their momentum.

Large-scale Jewish immigration began when the Republic of Argentina was beginning to evaluate the social outcome of its immigration laws. The hope that the immigrants from Europe would enrich and bring culture to Argentina without undermining its cultural and national heritage proved to be overly simplistic. Before the eyes of the veteran statesmen who had drawn up the Constitution and supported immigration, there now rose national groups, each seeking to maintain its own language, culture, and ties with its mother country. It was not long before the patricians began to voice their dissatisfaction.

Not only the more exotic ethnic and religious groups, such as the Volga-Germans who immigrated from Russia, sparked the ire of the Argentines. They were also disturbed by the patriotism of some of the Spanish immigrants, who organized a broad social, cultural, and welfare network and openly supported Spain's war against Morocco. In a similar bid to express ties with their homeland, an association of Frenchmen in Argentina asked the French minister of war for up-to-date combat manuals so they could train future conscripts to the French army. Each group celebrated its national holidays—Bastille Day, the conquest of Rome, and so forth—and some involved themselves in the politics of their home country.[40] None of these activities, which were pursued openly, escaped the notice of the Argentines. Mass immigration became an increasingly sensitive issue, and the attitude toward Jewish immigration was no different. Fears that the Jews would create a separate enclave in the Argentine Republic had already been expressed when the Roca government extended its invitation to Russian Jewry. The appearance of Baron de Hirsch's emissaries in Buenos Aires and the news of the large-scale colonization experiment he was planning were received with mixed feelings. While welcoming the infusion of resources this would bring, there were misgivings about a salient Jewish entity arising in Argentina. When the baron sought to purchase huge tracts of land in the northern provinces of Chaco, Formosa, and Misiones, the initial reaction of the government was very positive. After a vicious attack in the press, however, which was anti-Semitic in tone, the proposal was blocked by the House of Representatives.[41]

In 1896, as the formative period drew to a close, Argentina appeared to be a disappointment insofar as Jewish immigration was concerned. The number of Jews leaving the country that year was far greater than the number arriving, and the attitude of the authorities and the Argentine public to Jewish immigration, ambivalent from the start, was now moving clearly toward the negative. However, in contrast to 1889, there was already a broad Jewish presence, fairly well rooted, which had learned to withstand the opposition and was trying to change it. The administrative network in the colonies maintained contacts with the regional and local authorities and succeeded in gaining their help. In the major cities, the infrastructure had been laid for organized community life. In the capital city of Buenos Aires, the Jewish community was becoming more varied: In 1891, the Congregación Israelita Latina was founded by immigrants who had arrived from Morocco singly and in groups during the 1880s, forming the basis for the Sephardic sector of the Jewish community; that same year, the first Jewish school was opened in the capital; and in 1894, the delegates of four Ashkenazic organizations banded together to establish the Hevra Kadisha, the burial society that had been sorely needed for many years and eventually became a cornerstone of Jewish life in Argentina.[42]

By the end of nineteenth century, the Jews of Argentina, both in colony and city, constituted a vibrant community. Although further organization was necessary, strong foundations had been created that would enable them to meet the challenge of growth and development.

3

The Avalanche,
1896–1914

In the eighteen years preceding World War I, fundamental changes took place in Jewish life; economic and social processes that had commenced in the late 1870s played themselves out with even greater intensity. The seeds of political activism sown in the previous generation ripened, and, as they continued to grow and produce offshoots, the Jewish landscape became pitted with rifts and chasms. In one year, 1897, both the World Zionist Organization (WZO) and the Jewish revolutionary-socialist party, the Bund, emerged, each with its radical solution to the problems of the Jews. During this eighteen-year period, the Jewish proletarians established parties, and factions grew up within the WZO itself. Each group had its own vision and version of what it felt was the ideal response to the Jewish question. New philanthropic societies also emerged at this time, ostensibly only to do good works but actually with a political view of their own. Among them were the Hilfsverein der Deutschen Juden, founded in Berlin in 1901, the Hebrew Immigrant Aid Society (HIAS) founded a year later in the United States, and the American Jewish Committee, founded in 1906, also in the United States. This was the beginning of a shift in the focal point of Jewish community life, away from Eastern Europe and toward the New World.

Emigration was one of the outcomes, as well as an influential factor, of these momentous changes. During this interval, close to a million and a quarter Jews left Poland alone, and a million and a half Jews entered the United States—as many Jews as the State of Israel was able to absorb in its first twenty-eight years.[1] In varying intensities, emigration became a major life experience for individuals and entire communities in Russia, Romania, the Balkans, and some Islamic countries. As Jewish life dwindled in the "old countries," new roots were struck elsewhere. According to one estimate, some 250 "major communities" were added to the US Jewish scene, and key sectors joined the small groups of Jews in Canada, South Africa, and Australia.[2]

This brief period also heralded important changes in the economy and social history of the Argentine Republic. As the nineteenth century drew to a close, Argentina recovered from the depression of the early 1890s. Foreign investment, primarily British, extended the railway network from a total of 8,768 miles (14,116 km) in 1895 to 19,319 miles (31,104 km) in 1914. The volume of goods transported by rail more than tripled, and huge expanses of land became available for development. The establishment of cold-storage shipping facilities boosted the packinghouse and breeding industries. As the European demand for wheat, corn, and other cereals increased, agricultural production in Argentina grew by leaps and bounds. Between 1895 and 1914, plant crop exports multiplied more than five times over (534 percent), replacing livestock and its by-products, which more than doubled in value (230 percent), as Argentina's top export. This virtual revolution on the pampas required a continuous supply of working hands. In addition, the population swelled from 4 million in 1896 to almost 7.8 million in 1914, creating a growing local market. This increased both imports and local production, although the latter was mainly of low quality. Between 1895 and 1913, the number of Argentine manufacturers doubled (210 percent), and the country's motor capacity increased elevenfold (1,162 percent). All this intensified the demand for urban workers.[3]

For both the rural and urban sectors of the Argentine economy, the answer was immigration. As fate would have it, the Jews were just then searching for a new home that would offer them freedom and security. Was Argentina open to Jewish immigrants at this point? To what extent did the JCA, as an organization with a foothold in Argentina's main economic sector, use its abilities to increase rural Jewish immigration? Was there any organization to promote and offer assistance to urban Jewish immigrants? Once settled in Argentina, were the Jews regarded as an integral and legitimate part of its now growing and changing society?

Argentina as a Refuge

The economic recovery that was clearly felt during the final years of the nineteenth century reopened the question of whether to subsidize the travel expenses of immigrants bound for Argentina. Such a proposal was made on at least one occasion in 1899 but was rejected and never came up again—evidence of the consensus in Argentina against repeating the mistakes of the past[4]—yet there was also a consensus on the need to keep the doors of the Republic open to European immigrants. The Immigration and Colonization Law of 1876 was operating now in full swing. However, the vagueness of the law with regard to the preferred category of immigrant left much of the decision making in the hands of the Immigration Department. Before entering the country, potential settlers were required to prove that they were able-bodied and of good character. One of the jobs of the ship captains was to ascertain that none of the passengers was physically incapable of work, a beggar, mentally ill, a convicted criminal, or over the age of sixty if he or she was traveling alone. Immigration officials had the final word, and in November 1902, following a nationwide strike that paralyzed the country, the Ley de Residencia (Residence Law) was passed, giving them even more authority: They now had the power to bar entry to anyone who had been tried for a crime or political offense in his home country and anyone who might be a threat to public peace. According to the law, such people could be expelled even after they had been allowed to disembark. Argentine immigration officials thus had powers that in England and the United States were reserved for the courts. There is no evidence, however, that these officials tried to restrict the flow of immigration during 1902–1914.[5]

Unlike immigrants to the United States, who had to prove solvency on arrival, newcomers to Argentina were put up at an immigrants hostel, given medical attention, and transported free of charge to their final destination—all in keeping with the 1876 law. That this policy was maintained throughout the period is attested to by the fact that a new, more comfortable immigrants hostel was completed in 1910, after a long planning and building process. A Jew from Paris described the hostel in 1911, shortly after its dedication: "I was amazed to see the immense dining halls, the spacious, airy bedrooms, the well-equipped libraries where, interestingly, I had the pleasure of finding many Hebrew prayer books."[6]

In the late 1890s, in a carryover from preceding years, Jewish immigrants were received by the immigration commissioner, Juan Alsina, with open suspicion. "The department has not taken its eyes off Russian Jewish immigration and settlement. . . . We are constantly observing it to ascertain whether its peculiarities do not conflict with our institutions and the character and needs of the Republic," he wrote in his annual report in 1898. He admitted in this same report that the scrutiny had yielded no significant results. However, his hostility remained, and in 1901, when the number of Jewish immigrants increased, he clearly discriminated against them. When a group arriving by ship in March demanded the services to which it was entitled by law, the immigration officials refused to comply. This was on the orders of the commissioner, who felt that all aspects of Jewish immigration should be handled by the JCA. The complaint of JCA administrators in Buenos Aires to the minister of agriculture, who also supervised the Colonization Department, achieved its purpose: On May 19, 1901, the major morning newspapers in Buenos Aires reported that Alsina had been reprimanded for violating the Immigration and Colonization Law and discriminating against Jewish immigrants on the basis of race and religion.[7]

Alsina did not repeat his actions; that year and the next, groups of Jews arriving from Romania had access to all the state services offered to other immigrants. It was not long before the immigration commissioner had a total change of heart—at the end of January 1905, he expressed his willingness to secure employment for all future immigrants. Jewish craftsmen would find work particularly easily, he assured the directors of the JCA who came to see him, because employers liked the fact that they were nondrinkers and quiet by nature. Over the years, Alsina made similar statements and reported the continual demand for Jewish laborers and craftsmen in the inner cities of Mendoza, Córdoba, and Tucumán. "The government considers the immigration of our coreligionists favorable to the development of the country," the JCA administrators in Buenos Aires informed the office in Paris.[8]

The extent to which this evaluation continued to be true is demonstrated by a "diplomatic incident" in the second half of 1907. The vice-consul of Argentina in Basel, who was also responsible for reporting on the progress of immigration, drew his superiors' attention to the fact that the number of Jews heading for Argentina had dropped considerably because they were being directed to Canada and other countries. "This can be attributed in no small measure to the JCA administration in Paris, which, as I have seen myself, has lately taken a hostile attitude to immigration to Argentina," the vice-consul reiterated at a later date, when asked to clarify his position. The recipients of the report apparently agreed with the vice-consul that hindering Jewish immigration to Argentina was an undesirable phenomenon. Alsina, who brought this complaint to the attention of the JCA officials in Buenos Aires, seems to have shared this opinion. The officials were anxious to know the identity and sources of the complainant. Armed with this information and JCA's annual report, they returned to Alsina to deny the accusation and assure him that Argentina was quite acceptable to the JCA—even more so than other countries. "Mister Alsina has reassured us that he is positively disposed toward the immigration of our coreligionists," concluded the JCA director in Buenos Aires.[9]

The cordial relationship with Alsina continued until his retirement at the end of 1910, after twenty years of service that were crucial to the fate of Jewish immigration. As a token of appreciation, the Jewish community presented him on December 18, 1910, with a gold medallion inscribed with the words "Justice to a just man!" and an album containing thousands of congratulatory messages in Spanish, Russian, and Hebrew. The cover of the album shows a wandering Jew offering up his offspring to the Republic. Yet, Alsina's actions on behalf of the Jews contrasted with his fundamental beliefs on immigration and the correct proportion of heterogeneous groups, of which the Jews were an example. Alsina voiced these views on occasion and accentuated them in his book *La Inmigración en el Primer Siglo de la Independencia* that appeared around this time and in proposed legislation specifically to limit such immigration.[10]

Meanwhile, the waves of immigrants reaching Argentina swelled the ranks of the urban proletariat and intensified the class struggle. The number of strikes and workers who took part in them rose, and the Anarchists and Socialists gained headway. The annual May 1 demonstrations became a target of clashes with the police. On May 1, 1909, the police fired into a crowd of Anarchist trade unionists, leaving eight dead and forty wounded. The rage of the workers was then directed toward Buenos Aires's chief of police, Colonel Ramón Falcón, who was murdered, along with his assistant, on November 14, 1909. The young Anarchist responsible was Simón Radovizky, a twenty-year-old Jew who had immigrated two years earlier from Yelizavetgrad. The incident created a furor in

Homenaje al Doctor Juan A. Alsina.

דבר טוב חדש לבו של אחינו מר דוד עלקן להביא הגשי
תודה בשם כל בני ישראל היושבים בארץ ארגנטינא להאדון
יוחן אלסינא בעד ישרת לבו ואהבתו לכל אדם בלי הבדל
דת וגזע.

עשרים שנים רצופות עמד הדר אלסינא בראש הפקידות
של בית האיטיגרנטס. ובכל משך שנות עבודתו הפריה הנאמין
בעשרים שנים אלה רצופות. ובכל משך שנות עבודתו הפריה הנאמין

גם רבים מאחינו ידעו ויזכרו את אשר עשה לטובתם
בעתית מצוקה באשר יק דרכה עלם באין לא יהיה והוא
עזר להם למצא עמדה ינחלם בעציתו באב רחמו.

Di Yudische Hofnung (The Jewish Hope) reporting on the Jewish community's
homage to Juan Alsina

Buenos Aires and was deeply felt in the Jewish community. In fact, the authorities pointed an accusing finger toward the Jews as a whole, and particularly the Russian immigrants among them. "The government is firmly disposed toward taking strong measures in order to prevent the entry into the country of dangerous people and to evict those already here," Alsina informed JCA officials on November 25, 1909. Jewish community representatives heard a similar statement from the new chief of police, who added that "Argentina belongs to the Latin race, whose impressions are not easily erased." Under the state of siege that reigned for two months, the police began rounding up nonnaturalized union leaders. Under the Residence Law of 1902, hundreds were thrown on ships and banished from Argentina. New immigrants were scrutinized more carefully, and dozens of them, mainly Russians, were prevented from getting off their boat.[11] The assassination of the police chief and the prominence of Russian immigrants among the Anarchists were of great consequence for the status of Jews in Argentina. However, a deliberate change in immigration policy was not yet evident.

While prior to World War I, Jewish emigrants could find refuge in Argentina, some traditional countries of immigration, such as the United States, were also open to them during these eighteen years. What made them prefer one country over another? What was their conception of Argentina? To answer these questions, we must take ourselves back to the humble homes of the potential immigrants. The decision was made there, often as not, while poring over a letter from overseas by the dim light of an oil lamp. For the most part, the circumstances and considerations that moved each of the hundreds of thousands of immigrants to pack up and leave will remain a closed book. We do know, however, that the mass migration of Jews, which changed the map of Jewish dispersion in modern times, was the result of many thousands of personal dramas that came together to create a tremendous historical and national force. The individual decision to seek refuge in one place or another was surely dependent on the information received from relatives or acquaintances who had gone before. In the Republic of Argentina, immigration had just begun, and there were relatively few who could supply such information. Immigrants to Argentina were therefore more reliant on organized assistance than were those settling in the more traditional countries, and the JCA played a greater role than did any other Jewish institution or organization in rendering such assistance.

The Role of the JCA

When Baron Maurice de Hirsch died in 1896, the JCA had at its disposal the enormous sum of £8,830,116 sterling (US $43,002,664, calculated by $4.87 to the pound), most of it in stocks and bank deposits, and annual profits on this capital reached £335,000 sterling ($1,631,450). Although an inheritance tax of close to £1.25 million was paid to the British Treasury after five years of judicial contest, the money invested in financial institutions in Europe was still bringing in £300,000 ($1,461,000) annually ten years later. Added to this was the vast amount of property acquired in the New World during these years. There was no comparison at all between this and the funds available to other organizations. The Jewish National Fund, for example, the Zionist movement's major tool for land acquisition and development, reported an income of only £45,580 sterling ($221,974) in 1905, after three and a half years of existence and two years under the leadership of Theodor Herzl. Even the wealthy German Jewish organization, Hilfsverein der Deutschen Juden, was poor by comparison. With nearly fourteen thousand supporters and several donors who had established special funds, Hilfsverein's expenditures for 1906 amounted to only £73,807 sterling ($359,440), and this was a peak year in its activity because of the pogroms and rioting in Russia.[12]

The immense fortune of the JCA allowed its administrative council to enjoy total independence—Jewish public opinion, which may have affected other organizations, had very little impact. From the outset, the council decided against publicly reporting assets, profits, and expenditures or informing the public of its resolutions. Although the council members were from all over Western Europe, certain principles were unanimously accepted: The capital fund would not be touched; ventures in which the JCA would not have the final say would be avoided; and any ideology showing the slightest trace of Jewish nationalism would be opposed. At the same time, the JCA saw itself as the central institution for coreligionists. In 1908, when Jacob Schiff of New York proposed the establishment of an umbrella organization that would allow swift, coordinated action in times of crisis, the JCA offered to organize the bureau in Paris. It helped shape the new federation and, over a number of years, persuaded various bodies to join.[13]

The centrality of the JCA was especially evident in the sphere of immigration. Its declared goals, and its wealth, led it to become an active organizer of emigration or absorption in all the countries Jews were leaving or entering. The executive committee in Saint Petersburg, some of whose members had been working with the JCA since the days of Baron de Hirsch, had initially tried to stop emigration and channel most of the funds into developing agricultural settlement and vocational training in Russia. In 1903, however, the committee proposed the organization of a comprehensive network of information offices for emigrants. By the eve of World War I, there were over five hundred local agencies and information bureaus, and the head office in Saint Petersburg was a bustling center that a former employee, Zalman Shazar, who later became president of Israel, called a "Ministry of the Diaspora." The main emigration office established by the Hilfsverein in Berlin was also funded to a large extent by the JCA, as was the Industrial Removal Office in the United States, an organization established in 1901 to encourage immigrants to move to other parts of the country rather than settle on the East Coast.[14]

The year the baron died, the JCA owned 200,619 hectares (495,529 acres) of land in Argentina's three most fertile provinces. Only half of this land was settled, and even then, only sparsely. As a large-scale property owner and a settlement company investing a fortune in colonization and administration, the JCA developed important contacts in both the district and federal governments. These proved helpful on the few occasions when the attitude of the Argentine immigration authorities to the Jews became questionable.

On September 14, 1905, the JCA directors were received by the president of Argentina, Manuel Quintana. He was presented with a handsome copy of the prayer book in Spanish recently published by the JCA for the use of the colonists' children in Argentina. During the meeting, the president inquired about the JCA's settlement activities and assured his guests that "the government sees Jewish immigration to Argentina very favorably."[15]

While the steps taken by the authorities in 1909–1910 to suppress revolutionaries also affected Russian Jewish immigrants, the JCA never lost its status in government circles. Wealthy Jews and the directors of the colonization organization felt these steps were justified, and the latter even took advantage of them to silence Leon Chasanowitch, leader of the Zionist Socialist party, Poalei Zion, in Russia, who was touring the colonies and severely criticizing the JCA administration there. When the state of siege was at its peak, the JCA directors in Buenos Aires informed the authorities, and Chasanowitch was arrested. From the colony of Mauricio, he was returned to the capital and deported along with others suspected of inciting rebellion.[16]

Concerned that the collective accusation against the Jews was gaining headway in government circles, the JCA set out to paint a true picture of the colonization movement and the Jewish community as a whole. In January 1910, shortly after the abolishment of the state of siege, JCA officials met with the minister of interior. "This visit made an excellent impression, both on the minister of the interior and on the Jewish community in Buenos Aires," the officials later reported to the head office in Paris. The small Jewish community, composed almost entirely of nonnaturalized immigrants, would have been unable to exercise such influence on its own.[17]

The JCA, which Baron de Hirsch originally thought to call the Jewish Immigration Association, was highly influential in Argentina, with vast material resources at its command. The question is how much this situation was exploited to encourage and expand Jewish immigration to the fullest.

Emigrants Bound for the Colonies

At the beginning of the period 1896–1914, the shadow of crisis still hung over the Jewish colonization enterprise. Locusts, heavy rainstorms at harvesting time, and other natural disasters in the provinces of Santa Fe and Entre Ríos in 1895–1897 had ruined the farmers in the region and brought misery to all. From his office in the port city of Rosario, the French consul watched the sad sight of immigrants, French and others, who had abandoned their farms and were wandering the streets, desperate for food and work. Many were pleading to leave Argentina, no matter where they were sent.[18]

Jewish settlers in Entre Ríos who decided to remain on their farms poured out their bitterness to Baron de Hirsch's widow, Clara: "With all our hearts we want to be farmers, with all our strength we are willing to fulfil our obligations to our people, but help us so that we can withstand . . . so that we and our families will not perish of hunger and want before achieving our aim." The state of the Jewish colonies worsened because of bitter conflict with the local JCA administration, the sense of loss over the death of the baron, and the dashed hopes for stability and rapid adjustment. In despair, many settlers sought to leave the country and received assistance from the JCA for this purpose. In 1897–1898, the JCA spent large sums on "repatriation," which had already begun in the days of the baron. According to one survey, the number of families in the colonies dropped by over 20 percent, from 983 to 779, between the end of 1896 and the end of 1897.[19]

The JCA made no attempt at this time to revitalize the colonization project. For caution's sake, it was decided that no new settlers would be sent to Argentina before the colonies were on firmer footing. Unfortunately, such a state was achieved very slowly. Even after the lean years were over and the farms in Santa Fe and Entre Ríos were flourishing again, the exodus continued. Large numbers of settlers left to farm privately owned land in the southern part of the province of Buenos Aires, where they were offered easy terms and contracts with no custodianship. In the span of two years, 1900–1901, 250 families departed, and many took their equipment without paying for it. While economic hardship was certainly a factor, Sigismond Sonnenfeld, director general of the JCA, acknowledged that the arrogance of the administrators and their unhindered maltreatment of the settlers was also to blame.[20]

Samuel Hirsch and Davíd Cazés, the project directors in Argentina, believed that all the ills of Jewish colonization stemmed from the fact that the colonists' trip had been organized and paid for by the JCA. When things went wrong, the colonists felt they were entitled both to financial compensation and a free return ticket. The directors tried to prevent further immigration through JCA officials in Europe on the pretext that any expansion of colonization should be prompted by the settlers themselves, and in fact, the ice did begin to thaw on the strength of initiatives from within the colonies.

At first there were individual settlers who, despite the general hardship, were able to save enough money to bring over more family. The JCA promised to provide discount tickets in exchange for a written commitment that no further financial assistance would be requested. Then came the initiative of a group from Grodno, Lithuania, living in the colony of Moisesville. Close ties with relatives in Russia, a drop in the number of residents—which diminished the quality of social and spiritual life—and modest economic prosperity after the introduction of cattle grazing, all provided an incentive to enlarge the colony. They decided that one of the settlers, Noah Katsovitch, should travel to Russia and select a group of fifty families from among the settlers' closest relatives. His trip, the travel expenses of the families, and a certain percentage of the settlement costs would be paid for by the settlers themselves. Moisesville was to bear sole responsibility for the venture, although the JCA was required to supply land, livestock, and a small budget for settlement expenses.

The directors in Buenos Aires were pleased with the proposal but took it wholly literally. When they heard that some of the families selected by Katsovitch could not pay their own way, they ordered the JCA official in Moisesville to halt all building and other preparations for the new arrivals. Nevertheless, responding to a desperate appeal, the members of the JCA council in Paris provided 3,000 rubles to make up the difference, and Katsovitch was able to include families with limited means. Screening the candidates, obtaining passports, and making travel arrangements took many months. After another month of sailing by way of Le Havre, France, the newcomers reached Argentina. The date was July 12, 1900. Three days later they were in Moisesville, and the dormant period in Jewish colonization had come to an end.

The success of the first group quickly led to a second try. Katsovitch sailed for Russia in May 1901 to organize the immigration of another hundred families. This attempt was also successful. The hundreds of families who joined the colonial effort in 1900–1902 compensated for the mass exodus taking place at the same time and prepared the ground, especially in the province of Santa Fe, for the absorption of a much larger wave of immigrants.[21]

News of the renewed colonization in Argentina spread rapidly throughout the Pale of Settlement in Russia. Rumor had it that a Jew need only pay his way to Argentina and he would be immediately admitted to the colonies of the JCA. The central committee of the JCA in Saint Petersburg was deluged by applications for information and advice. David Feinberg, the secretary and guiding spirit of the committee, and his colleagues were in a state of panic. "We are dealing with a population of millions who live in conditions that are beyond description and who are desperate to make a living, no matter where," they continually warned the JCA administration in Paris beginning in April 1900. They felt that this unplanned exodus would have dire consequences and that "we will be witness to a scene like no other in the entire history of emigration." The

Noah Katsovitch, leader of the Moisesville settlers (Central Archives for the History of the Jewish People, Jerusalem)

directors in Buenos Aires were also against a panic-stricken migration from Russia. After an exchange of letters to determine the correct strategy, it was decided that only those who could pay their own fare and maintain themselves until the first harvest would be accepted to the colonization program.[22]

However, even before this decision was reached, the pogroms and systematic persecution of the Jews in the Romanian town of Iassi had led thousands of them to flee the country in 1900. This sudden exodus, partially on foot, surprised the Jewish organizations and brought about large-scale involvement of the JCA in the evacuation of refugees. Groups of refugees were heading for Canada, the United States, and other destinations, and the JCA felt it had no choice but to open the colonies in Argentina to them, too. As they were totally penniless, the old system of preliminary selection in Europe, passage paid by the JCA, and full maintenance in Argentina had to be employed. A JCA representative from Paris was sent to Romania to organize a group of fifty families. After the lists of candidates were sent to Paris for approval and other arrangements were made, forty-one families, a total of three hundred persons, set sail for Argentina. In 1902, this group, augmented by another nine families, established a new village inside the large colony of Moisesville. These fifty farms were the only mark left by this crisis of Romanian Jewry on the colonization map of Argentina.[23]

A year and a half later, in April 1903, a disastrous pogrom was waged against the Jews of Kishinev. Like other Jewish organizations and public opinion in Western Europe at large, the JCA was horrified by the news of the bloodshed, torture, and plundering in the capital of Bessarabia with the connivance of the Russian authorities. An order was received by the JCA administration in Argentina to prepare two hundred new farmsteads as quickly as possible. Many applications had reached the office in Paris from Bessarabia, and one of them claimed to represent two hundred families whose total assets amounted to 300,000 francs. Cazés, who had recently resigned as director in Buenos Aires after ten years of service, was urgently dispatched to Kishinev together with Feinberg and Wolfgang Auerbach, who had organized the group from Romania, to interview candidates and ready them for the trip.

The list of applicants for colonization had been drawn up hastily and proved less than accurate. The personal assets of the candidates came to only one-tenth of the amount declared, and what is more, many of them had applied for assistance in reaching Palestine—not Argentina. Other groups bound for Palestine also turned to the JCA. Some were willing to pay their own fare and settlement expenses, and requested only land. The numbers and earnestness of the applications so impressed the JCA officials that Cazés proposed, somewhat hesitantly, that the JCA comply with the request of at least one of these groups. As on other occasions, immigration to Argentina was in direct conflict with immigration to Palestine.

Suitable candidates were found, some with serious experience in agriculture, but the selection criteria invalidated most of them from the outset. Families with the proper manpower and farming know-how generally lacked the financial means to pay their own way and maintain themselves until the first harvest; those with means often lacked two grown sons who could run the farm together with the head of the family. Cazés felt that the JCA should be more flexible, urging that roundabout ways of financing the trip be sought for those in need, and a special absorption framework be established for young families. The council discussed these proposals and approved them in theory, thereby paving the way, as it were, for large-scale immigration and settlement.[24] However, in April 1904, a year after the pogroms in Kishinev, only fifty-three families from all of Bessarabia and another eighty-three from the province of Kherson were preparing to emigrate. By the end of the year, only eighty families had reached Argentina, and very few of them were from Kishinev. What had happened to the scores of Kishinev's residents bent on emigrating the year before? Was it the selection process and red tape that were to blame, or a sudden loss of interest in Argentina? These were the questions directed by the JCA in Paris to the central committee in Saint Petersburg.

The truth is that the complicated procedure of carefully screening the candidates, applying on their behalf to the Russian bureaucrats for passports and exit permits, and then arranging for group transportation to Argentina via Western Europe could not be handled according to a predetermined timetable. Many of the disillusioned candidates had simply lost patience and dropped out. Hence, despite the JCA's declarations in favor of continued immigration to Argentina, the pogroms left no dramatic imprint on the development of Jewish farming there.[25]

In the course of 1905, as the pogroms in Russia became a ploy to distract the people from the losses of the Russo-Japanese War and the growing social tension, the JCA's selection and emigration mechanism collapsed. Another strategy, partially in use in previous years, was adopted instead:

Immigrants reaching Argentina were required to work as hired hands for a long period and were accepted as colonists only after their abilities, disposition, and adjustment to farm life were assessed by the local administrators. The immigrants would then pay some of the colonization costs from their earnings. This was the rule for indigents; another rule was applied to those who were well-off.

In mid-1904, forty-eight families from Novi Bug in the province of Kherson applied to the JCA for land in Argentina and a modest building loan. Each family possessed at least 3,000 rubles (roughly US $1,500). The JCA complied, and the first group set out for Buenos Aires not as "colonists" but as farmers in their own right. Other groups and individuals followed and were provided with the same conditions if they could prove they had the required capital—at least 2,000 rubles. Sometimes the family work force was not large enough to run a farm, but if there was enough money to hire help, these families were accepted, too. Around this time, a huge tract of land encompassing nearly 100,000 hectares (247,000 acres) was purchased in the southwestern part of the province of Buenos Aires. This was regarded as choice land, as indicated by the price, and the colony established there, named Baron Hirsch, was open to those with means. Aside from a contract signed by the settlers dealing with the value of the land and the small loan they received, the JCA decided not to intervene in the colony's affairs. No administration was set up, and only one minor official was sent to guard JCA interests and offer advice. Minimizing the amount of bureaucracy was seen as a worthy goal also in the colonies of the less affluent. However, even in Baron Hirsch this was not achieved. Poor yields and crops ruined by natural disasters ended the autonomy of the formerly well-to-do settlers, and the administration of the colony grew until it hardly differed from the bureaucratic network in other colonies. The policy of requiring newcomers to work as farmhands did not reduce the need for administrators and, to some extent, may have had the opposite effect. Thus, the efficiency and size of the administration were major factors in limiting the expansion of Jewish colonization.[26]

A factor of even greater importance was the quality of the land. The JCA had continued to purchase property after the baron's death, and by 1913, it owned 579,917 hectares of land (1,432,394 acres). Agricultural advancement in Argentina was then on an upswing, and broad expanses of frontier were being developed. The spiraling price of real estate in the fertile zones led the JCA to look for relatively cheaper land on the frontier and thus keep the settlers' debt to the JCA within reasonable limits. Part of the Baron Hirsch colony expanded into the cold, semiarid territory of La Pampa. In 1909, a colony named for the president of the JCA, Narcisse Leven, was established farther west in the same territory on forty-seven thousand hectares (116,090 acres) that turned out to be even more barren. On a smaller scale, three thousand hectares of land near a river were purchased in the province of Santiago del Estero for the cultivation of irrigated crops. What all the settlers in these new areas had in common was that in years of drought or agricultural blight, they were the first to suffer.[27]

In 1906, the JCA handled only a few dozen families from among those arriving in Argentina. Every year after that, until 1913, the administrative council approved a budget for 150 to two hundred families who had met the supervised training requirements and were accepted as colonists. In addition, the JCA in Buenos Aires provided dozens of plots and a small amount of financial aid each year to the grown children of settlers seeking to strike out on their own. In this way, the number of farmsteads in the colonies grew steadily. By 1913, there were 2,655 farms run by 3,382 families (some farms were managed by more than one family) and the population had reached 18,900.[28]

While new families were being absorbed, however, there were also those who were leaving—at a rate that was sometimes quite alarming. During the first half of 1904, over sixty families packed up and left the colonies in Entre Ríos. At the same time, and in mid-1906, large numbers of families left Moisesville in Santa Fe. The JCA officials tried to comfort their superiors in Paris by calling this a process of natural selection that was ridding the colonization scheme of undesirable elements. It did not escape their notice, however, that many of those leaving were successful farmers and that some had taken their farming implements and moved to the lands of a private company in southern Buenos Aires province. The exodus from the new colonies was of a different nature. The years 1909–1912 were black for the farmers of Argentina. Continuous drought in the south, coupled with poor rainfall and locusts in the north, slowly weakened the foundations of the Jews' farms established only years before on the outskirts of the fertile zones. The situation was made even worse by the norms for farm size and choice of crop introduced by the JCA on the basis of experience in more-fertile areas. The hunger in the colony of Narcisse Leven, brought on by the ravages of nature, was sharpened by the tension and bad feeling between farmers and administrators.

The rise in the number of settlers from 7,125 in 1901 to 18,900 in 1913 represented only a fraction of all the immigrants who worked in the colonies as a first step toward integration in Argentina. Furthermore, this rise did not yet indicate stability in the colonization enterprise.[29]

Immigrant Workers in the Colonies

Despite the limited size of the colonization project, it was a vital instrument for the absorption of Jewish immigrants. In the first years of the twentieth century, a large percentage of those reaching Argentina went straight to the colonies. This was openly encouraged by the immigration commissioner, Juan Alsina. In 1901, the colonies reported 409 agricultural hands, aside from the established colonists. By 1904, this figure had risen to 836. As emigration from Russia increased in 1905 and colonization expanded in Argentina, there was also a rise in the number of nonsettlers living in the colonies. According to the reports of the JCA administration in Buenos Aires, there were 7,748 in 1913, compared with 2,195 in 1905. The increase was significant as scores of these families were accepted yearly as colonists, whereas many others, discouraged by the poor living conditions, had left. Thus, the figures cited by the JCA hint at a much larger number of immigrants for whom the colonies were only a first stop.[30]

Initially, work at the colonies was not easy to find. The number of hired hands required all year round was small, and labor needs were often met by non-Jewish immigrants or gauchos living in the vicinity. However, in 1901, after a settler in Mauricio was murdered by a gaucho, the colonists there decided to hire only Jewish workers. The JCA tried to encourage this, and directors in Buenos Aires planned to offer the settlers in Mauricio and Moisesville loans to build housing for their Jewish laborers; when wealthy Jews began to show an interest in colonization, the Paris office intended to accept only those who agreed to employ Jewish help. The same policy was followed when the JCA was approached for assistance in financing drainage work in the low-lying areas north of Moisesville. As another incentive to employ Jews, the administration in Paris proposed that the wage difference paid to Jewish workers be funded by a special tithe collected from colonists whose crops had been improved by the drainage. Although this plan was never implemented, the JCA showed that it was willing to employ coercion to ensure immigrant absorption. On many occasions, the directors in Buenos Aires were urged to promote Jewish labor both so that the colonization venture could fulfil its role as a school for the development of Jewish agriculture and so that an unemployed, urban Jewish proletariat would not emerge in Argentina.[31]

Aside from fine words and moral encouragement, however, the JCA did little to solve the problems of these immigrants. In the wake of the pogroms in 1905, when the Paris office expected a dramatic increase in the number of applicants for colonization in Argentina, the idea of offering the immigrants private building loans was raised; after encountering opposition from Buenos Aires, it was dropped. The new selection process introduced in 1906 also did little to ease the plight of the growing immigrant population in the colonies. All it offered the newcomers was the hope that if they could hold out long enough, they, too, might become colonists entrusted with valuable land and farming implements.

The administrator of the colony of Lucienville in Entre Ríos painted a gloomy picture of the housing conditions of the two hundred families of immigrants (some twelve hundred souls) who lived there in 1908–1909. Sigismond Sonnenfeld, who was still honorary director of the JCA after resigning as director general, received a copy of this report and realized that the problem was not unique to Lucienville. He proposed that the administration in Buenos Aires join forces with the settlers' cooperatives to build workers' living quarters and auxiliary farms where they could grow vegetables for market in their spare time. The JCA directors in Buenos Aires were not moved, apparently, by the plight of the Lucienville immigrants. They rejected Sonnenfeld's proposal on the pretext that "experience has shown it is not worthwhile for us to build on a large scale." On a visit to Entre Ríos a year later, the JCA director in Buenos Aires, Davíd Veneziani, saw the suffering of the immigrants with his own eyes. The crops had done poorly that year, and a difficult, jobless winter was in sight. In his report to Paris, Veneziani promised to investigate the matter and propose a plan of action. A half a year passed and nothing was done. Then came the news that the council was sending a special emissary to Argentina on a fact-finding mission.[32]

Nandor Sonnenfeld, the son of the former director general, reached the colonies in August 1910, at the height of winter. He was shocked by what he found: "In Lucienville, in Clara, I witnessed the miserable spectacle of large families cramped in tiny rooms, kitchens, or barns, living in huts of mud and straw open to the wind and rain and drawn by their shocking mixture into a situation that is both unhygienic and immoral." In San Antonio, in a clay hut measuring three by three meters, he saw a large family huddled beside an enormous pile of dried cattle dung that they burned for warmth and cooking. "I do not believe that in the poorest villages in Russia, the living conditions were worse than these," he wrote. In all the colonies with the exception of Moisesville, the housing situation was equally distressing. Even worse was the way the early settlers exploited the newcomers: For the right to live in these hovels, they paid rent that amounted to a third and more of their winter wages—which were made minimal in any case by the great clamor for work and the scarcity of jobs during the winter season.

Some of the colonies preferred to hire non-Jews, who were quick and accepted the meager food and wages they were offered without complaint. In the colony of Baron Hirsch, for example, the settlers took on Russian muzhiks to help out in the fields while over a hundred Jewish families who had been employed during the harvest left to seek a livelihood elsewhere. The problem of Jewish labor, which that same year was the cause of bitter strife in Palestine between the hired workers of the Second Aliyah and the farmers of the First Aliyah, had found a parallel in Argentina.

Decent housing and steady employment—these were much needed by thousands of immigrants who reached the Jewish colonies in Argentina on their own. In the opinion of Nandor Sonnenfeld, they could be solved by establishing small, auxiliary farms. David Cazés and the young JCA director in Paris, Louis Oungre, who visited the colonies a year later, agreed with him. A recommendation to build sixty-five units was submitted to the JCA administration, which approved the proposal; but this was, along with a small number of buildings erected in the colony of Clara at the initiative of the JCA in Buenos Aires and the temporary lease of certain vacant buildings owned by it, the extent of JCA's contribution to solving the housing problem in the colonies.[33]

As an alternative to auxiliary farming, Sonnenfeld and Oungre proposed the development of crafts in the villages that were growing up on JCA land in or around the colonies. Another idea was the development of farm-based industry. Linseed, which together with wheat was one of the chief field crops, could be used in the manufacture of oil and fibers; barley was the basis for malt; straw, which was burnt in the fields, could be used to make paper and other products; cattle raising could be the start of a tanning industry; the great demand for sacks at harvest time could be met by producing them locally. However, the proposers, like the heads of the JCA in Paris, felt that all these industries should be established without the direct intervention of the JCA, through the initiative of entrepreneurs or the settlers' cooperatives. This would promote private enterprise while freeing the JCA from a major financial commitment. In January 1913, at a meeting of all the settlers' cooperatives, the directors of the JCA in Argentina urged them to undertake this mission. Miguel Sajarof and Isaac Kaplan, the leaders of the cooperative movement, were enthusiastic about the idea of manufacturing sacks. They made it clear, however, that the required capital—15,000–20,000 pesos—would have to come from the JCA. This was a condition that the directors refused to accept.[34]

Despite the talk about improving the plight of the newcomers that began only a few years before World War I, very little was done in this sphere by the JCA or the colonists. The early settlers were concerned about turning a profit, while the more recently settled were fighting for survival. The newcomers did not interest the colonists unless their own flesh and blood were involved—in which case they were prepared to assist both from afar, by sending money to Russia, and by bringing them over to join them on their farms. The settlers' cooperatives extended aid to the newcomers only when they were on the verge of starving. The comprehensive Jewish perspective on immigration to Argentina was not lost on the JCA leadership. However, all their efforts were devoted to settlement of the land: The Jews who reached the colonies were regarded as agricultural manpower and transforming many hundreds of them into farmers remained the major concern of the JCA and its apparatus in Buenos Aires. The attitude of the administration in some of the colonies was summed up by Abraham Sidi, the administrator of Clara in Entre Ríos, who felt that the departure of many immigrants in 1910 was a positive sign of natural selection: "We believe it serves no purpose to preoccupy ourselves exceedingly with their situation: True farmers know how to be patient, and we are doing enough by settling a certain number of them each year." Apparently, this did not conflict with the position of the JCA council, which approved Sidi's report without comment prior to publication. In the annual statement submitted the following year, the drastic reduction in the immigrant population from 6,826 to 4,477 was actually applauded. This strict, businesslike approach was guided by the implicit belief in the "productivization of the Jews" and the survival of the fittest.[35]

Thus, the tremendous financial strength of the JCA and its capacity to exert direct and indirect pressure on the settlers were not used to promote large-scale absorption of spontaneous Jewish immigration to Argentina. If there was any interest in these immigrants, it was for philanthropic-humanitarian reasons or out of concern that they might become a rebellious urban proletariat liable to spoil the image of the colonization venture in the eyes of Argentine authorities. As it stands, the colonization scheme did attract immigrants to Argentina and enable some of them to settle there permanently. However, if the scheme was to be an impetus for immigration on a larger scale and offer a variety of absorption opportunities, it was necessary for the JCA to take action in this respect. During the decisive eighteen years until 1914, this was not to be.

Urban Absorption Frameworks

The mass exodus from Argentina during 1896 and the two years that followed was widely reported in the Jewish press in Europe and acted as a deterrent to spontaneous immigration. The attitude of the JCA directors in Buenos Aires also discouraged "private" immigration attempts, with the exception of small groups with special qualifications. During the years 1899–1902, for example, the JCA extended aid to a handful of graduates from the Alliance Israélite Universelle's vocational schools in Izmir, Tangier, and Tetuan. Upon their arrival in Argentina, the Moroccans among them found several hundred of their countrymen who had been living in the capital and inner cities for at least ten years. The JCA schools in the colonies were then employing teachers brought over from Morocco because they knew Spanish, and, in a letter to the bulletin of the Alliance Israélite Universelle, immigration to Argentina was presented by one of these teachers as a desirable solution for young Moroccan Jews. In contrast, the newcomers from Izmir had no one to greet them, as emigration from Turkey was still in its infancy. The immigration of both groups was arranged by the JCA because their vocational skills and knowledge of Judeo-Spanish (Ladino) were considered a guarantee for success. However, once they reached Argentine shores, they found no organized body to which they could turn for assistance; the aid provided by the JCA before their departure had been extended indirectly, with the stipulation that the source remain anonymous.[36]

The same cautious, selective approach was maintained when the JCA was asked to aid the mass of refugees from Romania. In view of the failed attempt of several hundred of them to settle in Turkey, the selective and restricting conditions of the US Jewish organizations, and the difficulty of gaining admission to England and Canada, at least some of the Romanian refugees had to be sent to Argentina. However, the JCA in Paris and, even more so, the directors in Buenos Aires were determined to keep the number very small: In August 1900, seven Romanian craftsmen and their families were sent to Argentina by the Alliance Israélite Universelle; in January 1901, the JCA in Buenos Aires was asked to absorb a group of fifty families with trade skills, and half a year later, twenty young people and ten families (a total of ninety persons) set out for Argentina—among them five dockworkers and five builders; arrangements for another group went on for a year. All told, less than one hundred Romanians were sent to Argentina before the project was halted.[37]

While a flurry of correspondence was going on over a handful of refugees, the spontaneous immigration of Jews who, as far as we know, received no aid from Jewish institutions was attaining substantial proportions. In mid-March 1901, JCA directors in Buenos Aires reported the arrival of a large body of immigrants, seventy-five of whom remained at the immigrants hostel after the others had departed for the colonies or settled independently in the city. According to the JCA official responsible for liaison with the immigration authorities, some eight hundred Jews arrived that month. This figure was actually an overestimation, but immigration activity was indeed brisk. This was not only because the Jews of Romania and Russia were being persecuted, but also because of the more positive image Argentina was projecting and the news that colonization efforts had been renewed. In 1902–1903, the number of arrivals dropped but rose again in 1904. In the second half of that year, Jewish arrivals were believed to have reached forty-five hundred persons or more. In January, two ships were expected simultaneously, carrying, together, a passenger load of five hundred. At this rate, the number of Jewish immigrants that year might have reached ten thousand—20 percent more than all the inhabitants of the JCA colonies after fifteen years of settlement efforts.[38]

This rising tide of Jewish immigration, caused by the 1905 pogroms in

Russian immigrants arriving in Buenos Aires in the early 1900s

Russia, coincided with a period of rapid economic growth in Argentina. Absorbing newcomers would be no problem, the JCA directors in Argentina assured their superiors in Paris. When the situation in Russia deteriorated even more, the JCA council allocated a sum of 200,000 francs to help Russian craftsmen settle in Argentina. It was arranged that JCA representatives in Odessa would send off fifteen families a week. However, encouraging immigration was one thing and handling the immigrants was another. The officials in Buenos Aires, fully backed by the council, avoided direct responsibility for the newcomers and, whenever possible, referred them to the Immigration Department or local Jewish bodies. Throughout this period, the JCA offices in Buenos Aires employed a single official to handle contacts with the Immigration Department. When he retired, the Paris administration even considered entrusting this activity to a junior clerk in the JCA office, thereby saving expenses.[39]

The JCA was prepared to support local Jewish organizations if they would undertake responsibility for the new immigrants. The most natural candidate was Ezrah, a welfare society established by the Jews of Buenos Aires in 1900. The JCA had used this society in 1902 to extend aid to Romanian refugees heading for Argentina. In March 1905, the JCA council offered Ezrah a budget of 3,000 pesos, half to be distributed among the immigrants in the form of small loans to be repaid into a permanent revolving fund, and half for charitable purposes, Spanish classes, and the organization of an employment bureau. "In any case, it is essential that you refrain from direct activity and do not allow the immigrants to know the aid comes from us," the director general of the JCA in Paris warned his employees in Buenos Aires. The Ezrah society accepted the offer and later received additional sums for the same purpose. However, it does not seem to have been interested in immigrant relief as a permanent job. Uncertainty about its ability to guarantee repayment of the loans, other welfare interests that culminated two years later in the decision to establish a Jewish hospital, and perhaps also disappointment in the JCA's slow response to the proposal of contributing regularly to its budget—all these kept Ezrah from becoming an organization specializing in immigrant absorption.[40]

At this point, several activities in the Ashkenazic community stepped in to fill the gap. On April 25, 1905, they founded Shomer Israel, the "Association for the Protection of Jewish Immigrants." Within three months, the association had mobilized 225 supporters and financial assets of over

11,000 pesos—more than twice the amount allocated until then by the JCA. Shomer Israel immediately took steps to organize a soup kitchen and an employment bureau; within its first few months it helped many hundreds of immigrants find work. This had not been particularly difficult, it was reported at the association's second meeting on July 30, 1905, owing to the great demand for workers of all kinds. From the beginning of its operations, and again in the second half of 1905, Shomer Israel applied to the JCA for financial assistance. The council immediately transferred 1,000 pesos and, after receiving more information, authorized officials in Buenos Aires to grant another 5,000 pesos to either Ezrah or Shomer Israel, as the situation required. The central committee in Saint Petersburg was given the address of Shomer Israel as an organization to which it could refer requests for information and vocational guidance, and the Ezrah society also referred to it immigrants seeking employment. Thus, the problem of aid and advice to immigrants not bound for the colonies seemed to have been solved. However, this was only a temporary solution. Behind the philanthropic fervor of the founders of Shomer Israel lurked the knowledge that when the flow of immigration ended—or the activists grew tired—the association would cease to exist. This, indeed, was its fate after fewer than two years of activity.[41]

With no authorized public body to handle immigration, the field lay open to consultants and agents on the free market, some of whom engaged in fraud. One such case with a tragic end involved a disreputable character named Rabbi Doctor A. Hoffman. In March 1907, Hoffman informed a large German shipping company in Bremen that a Jewish communal organization had established an information and employment office for emigrants, of which he was the head. He asked the shipping company to refer to him all Jewish passengers booked for Argentina. A year later, it transpired in court that several Jews in Buenos Aires had lost large sums of money by engaging the services of this office to purchase tickets for their relatives. Hoffman's partner was sent to prison, and Hoffman, released until the trial, committed suicide.[42]

Meanwhile, offshoots from the large body of Jews leaving Europe continued to reach the shores of Argentina. The economic recession that had begun at the end of 1906 and continued the following year ruined the businesses of many Jews, including some who were on the verge of establishing themselves financially. However, the damage to the economy was not severe, and the recession ended before it had any serious effect on the flow of immigration. The pace fluctuated from year to year, with fewer immigrants arriving in 1907, and more in 1908 and subsequent years. Incoming numbers depended on events in the Jewish world, the encouragement of relatives and friends already living in Argentina, and, to some extent, the obstacles posed by other countries. Two problems—securing aid for the immigrants and utilizing Argentina's absorptive potential to the fullest—were assuming major proportions at this time.

Among the large groups arriving now were many who were deeply involved in the proletarian movement. The organization of a Jewish proletariat had begun in 1905, and Socialist-Territorialists and, on their heels, Poalei Zion, the Anarchists, the Bundists, and the assimilationist Social Democrats formed small parties, each with its own ideological slant. Attempts to found Jewish trade unions similar to those in Eastern Europe failed from the outset, but the cultural activity of the parties brought people out of isolation and offered them a measure of companionship and mutual support. With their meager resources, these parties could not help the immigrant financially; neither did they have the necessary contacts to organize employment bureaus. Nevertheless, an umbrella organization for all the proletarian parties, the General Jewish Workers' Society (sometimes called the General Jewish Workers' Mutual Aid Society) was established in 1909 at the initiative of Poalei Zion leader Leon Chasanowitch. One of the goals of this organization was to disseminate reliable information in Argentina and other countries about the real state of the Argentine labor market in order to deter future immigrants from coming. Stated in this way, such an undertaking was in line with the thinking of anti-immigrationists in the general Socialist movement. In practice, however, immigrants reaching Buenos Aires could benefit from this information. Unfortunately, the society reached very few of the Jewish workers affiliated with a party, who themselves constituted a minority in the Jewish proletariat. The police action taken against workers in 1910 further hindered activity, and the society later became the battleground for internal partisan strife. Thus, its impact on the absorption of immigrants remained negligible.

Another organization founded for the purpose of offering mutual aid to Jewish workers and easing the hardship of the immigrants was the Union of Jewish Workers (Unión Obrera Israelita). The union emerged long before the General Jewish Workers' Society but changed its character and goals in midstream. Established in 1896, the union maintained a proletarian slant for ten years. One of its activities was finding jobs for new immigrants, for which purpose it received a budget from the JCA in 1906 with the stipulation that the beneficiaries be sent to inland cities. Shortly afterward, however, the union began to devote most of its energies to medical care for the needy, and its name was changed to the Bikur Holim society.[43]

During those same months that an umbrella organization for the "lower-class," proletarian sector, composed mainly of immigrants, was emerging, a similar effort was being made in the established "bourgeois" sector. Here, unification was orchestrated by Rabbi Samuel Halfon, rabbi of the Congregación Israelita, who had been sent to Argentina by the JCA and had held various JCA positions. His intention was to unite the congregation and other organizations established over the years—the Ashkenazic burial society Hevra Kadisha, Ezrah, and the first Jewish school in Buenos Aires (founded in 1891)—in a federation that would handle all communal affairs. When the platform was first put forward, no mention was made of responsibility for immigrants. Later, an employment bureau was included on the list of activities the federation hoped to pursue. However, nothing was ever done because the framework dissolved in mid-1910.[44]

Between these two organizational blocs, one in its formative stages and the other more established, there were no bodies specifically handling immigrant affairs. The Zionist movement in Argentina was split and limited in scope and influence. It was busy with affairs in Palestine, social and cultural activities, fund-raising, and petty organizational quarrels. Juventud, an organization founded in 1908 by Jewish university students, declared that it would also work on behalf of the immigrants. In practice, it soon became an ordinary social-cultural framework that later took up proletarian ideology. The *landsmanschaft* movement in which Jews from the same country or hometown banded together, later to play an important role in Jewish organizational life and immigrant absorption, had not yet emerged. Such was the state of affairs in the Ashkenazic community. Immigrants from Morocco, Turkey, and the Near East were even more alone. The number of Jews from these countries living in the capital was around four thousand, with another seventeen hundred in the provinces. The communal organizations they established in Buenos Aires, the most notable among them being the Congregación Israelita Latina of the Moroccan community, were incapable of meeting the most primary religious and welfare needs of their members, much less those of newcomers. Hence, the Jewish immigrant reaching Argentina was largely left to his own devices.[45]

A Failed Plan

A very grim picture is portrayed in three eyewitness accounts of the situation in Argentina received by the JCA council in 1910–1911. "There is no one to handle the Jewish immigrants here. No one takes an interest in them either financially or morally, not when they disembark in Buenos Aires nor later when they arrive in the towns of the interior," stated Rabbi Halfon after completing a comprehensive survey of the Jewish population sponsored by the JCA.

> Our immigrants are thus abandoned and are forced to undergo difficulties and critical situations that could be saved with a little organization and goodwill. . . . You frequently hear negative talk about the Jews without anyone trying also to point out their [good] qualities! Incidentally, it must be said that a properly organized immigration service could also contribute greatly to diminishing Jewish prostitution in this country. At the moment, the only Jews usually on hand to welcome the immigrants on their arrival are the agents of the white slave traders.

A similar account appears in Nandor Sonnenfeld's report to the council following his trip to Argentina. Another eyewitness, Louis Oungre, described the JCA's lethargy: The only official involved with immigrant absorption was the clerk, who also compiled the statistics sent in by the administrators of the colonies. Only when he was finished with his office duties would he go down to the port to check out the figures on Jewish immigration submitted by the government Immigration Department. This, claimed Oungre, was the extent of JCA activity in the absorption of immigrants. Davíd Veneziani and Walter Moss, the directors in Buenos Aires, rejected the claim that the JCA should be directly responsible for solving the immigrants' problems. Hence, no action was taken, either by the council or the administration in Paris, to alter the situation.[46]

It was now two years since Rabbi Halfon had submitted his recommen-

Rabbi Halfon (*center*, with tophat) and Jewish farmers in Mauricio in the 1900s (Central Archives for the History of the Jewish People, Jerusalem)

dations. Immigration to Argentina continued to swell, and an active campaign for a world organization to handle Jewish immigration was under way in Eastern Europe. From time to time, the central committee in Saint Petersburg registered complaints about the defrauding of immigrants and their relatives who purchased tickets for them in Argentina. Then came the proposal from the JCA administration in Paris that the directors in Argentina establish an "immigrant protection committee." The JCA would be represented, but only in partnership with local organizations such as the Ezrah society and the Congregación Israelita. This committee would handle monetary transfers, the purchase of tickets at a discount from shipping companies, the finding of jobs for the immigrants in the capital and provinces, and so on. The Buenos Aires administration was asked to meet with the heads of local organizations and prepare a detailed program; the Paris office promised to cover the costs.[47]

On December 18, 1912, the representatives of four organizations met at the JCA offices: the congregation, the Ashkenazic burial society, Ezrah, and the women's charity society affiliated with the congregation. The draft committee had prepared a platform for the new organization, which was approved unanimously. It was resolved that the members of the organization would meet immigrants on the ships, register their occupations, refer them to employers, represent them in contacts with the immigration authorities, and organize Spanish-language courses. There was to be follow-up even after they found jobs, and a special effort would be made to keep the women and girls away from the white slave traders. In addition, the organization was to handle all the commercial aspects, such as transferring money to Europe, purchasing boat tickets, and shipping the immigrants' belongings. These activities would not stop in Buenos Aires; committees were to be established in the important provinces, and close contacts were to be maintained with other immigration organizations in the Jewish world. The entire project would be run by a committee composed of two delegates from each organization, JCA representatives, and Rabbi Halfon. The annual budget would reach 18,000 pesos a year (1,500 pesos a month), not including expenses for setting up and equipping the office. All the organizations agreed to take part in financing the budget: Each would contribute 500 pesos a year for a total of 2,000 pesos.[48]

This broad platform and the relatively modest sum required to set the plans in motion seemed to herald the prompt establishment of an immigrant relief organization. Reality proved otherwise. The JCA council discussed the proposal on February 1, 1913, and decided that it should be simplified. All that was necessary was a committee to coordinate the other organizations, without the need for a separate apparatus and offices. The council was prepared to contribute a total of 6,000 pesos. This was a decision it refused to modify, even when the administration in Argentina protested that only an established, independent organization could do the job. The directors in Buenos Aires proposed cutting the budget to 10,000 pesos a year and commencing work immediately, using the allocation of 6,000 pesos, on condition that the remaining sum be forwarded later. The Paris office remained steadfast in its refusal.

When they convened on May 5, 1913, the delegates of the Jewish institutions in Buenos Aires were shocked to hear the decision of the JCA council. None would consider commencing activity with such a budget. A number of delegates approached some wealthy members of the congregation in the hope of mobilizing the remaining sum. Within a week, they realized their efforts were in vain. In a final attempt to rescue the program, which had taken a year of correspondence and talks to formulate, the council in Paris was asked to reconsider. On June 28, 1913, the original proposal was brought to the floor. However, those who demanded a radical cutback in all JCA expenditures and activities had gained an absolute majority by then, and the appeal of the institutions in Buenos Aires was flatly rejected—Argentina was still without a proper immigration organization even in the last year of mass migration.[49]

The extraordinary thriftiness of the JCA administration in Paris, which blocked the establishment of an immigration protection association over the sum of 4,000 pesos a year, probably did little to endear the JCA to the Jews of Buenos Aires. Their attitude to the JCA had already been influenced by the frequent reports of the ironfisted rule in the colonies that had reached the capital city. Furthermore, the Jewish organizations in Buenos Aires had harbored high hopes that the immense fortune of the baron would be used to help them, too. Their feeling was that Jewish immigration should be the JCA's sole responsibility. When the members of the Executive Committee of the congregation, which included JCA directors, discussed the JCA's decision to limit aid to the immigrant protection committee, they resolved that it was the JCA's duty to provide full support. Organizations that did not have JCA directors on their boards were surely much blunter in their criticism.[50]

On the eve of World War I, the Jewish community in Buenos Aires was still young. It was only twenty-five years since the first sizable group of Jews had arrived, and community activists were still working toward the establishment of autonomous institutions: Hevra Kadisha, which was to become a major Jewish organization in Argentina, was seeking funding to fence in the cemetery it had gone into debt to purchase some time before; and the Ezrah society had acquired a large piece of land on which to build a Jewish hospital and was also in debt. Nonetheless, Ezrah also aided needy immigrants, as did organizations such as Bikur Holim and the Congregación Israelita. However, finding an embracing solution to the problem of immigrant absorption, which involved daily interaction with helpless newcomers, was not a top priority, although the job had been foisted upon the other organizations by the JCA's inactivity. This organizational attitude to immigration and related problems was echoed in the war against the white slave trade.

The conspicuousness of Jewish pimps in the streets of Buenos Aires had been a shadow on the reputation and public image of Argentine Jewry from its earliest days. The need to dissociate itself from this group became a matter of survival for the respectable Jewish community and especially the Europeans. Every Jewish organization incorporated a paragraph in its articles of association prohibiting such people from joining. This ostracism, with its organizational and social consequences, was particularly noteworthy when compared with the situation in the old, established communities in Europe. However, no steps were taken to prevent the entry of pimps and prostitutes into the country by the Jews of Argentina themselves. Throughout the period, it was the Gentlemen's Committee of the Jewish Association for the Protection of Girls and Women in London that was active in this sphere. In 1900, the association empowered a Catholic clerk at the Austro-Hungarian consulate in Buenos Aires to act on its behalf in exposing white slave traders, rescuing their victims, and preventing libertines and their agents from entering Argentina. A three-man board of trustees was set up in Argentina to represent the interests of the London association. The fact that all three were English Jews, the most prominent of them being Henry Joseph, a merchant who acted as rabbi of the Congregación Israelita, further demonstrates the nonlocal character of this activity. From its inception, the Association for the Protection of Girls and Women sought the material and moral support of the JCA in Paris, from which it received a regular stipend. Several JCA directors in Buenos

Aires, and especially Rabbi Halfon, were actively involved in its work. However, this did not evolve into a local Jewish public campaign.[51]

Immigration, Absorption, and Departure

Throughout 1896–1914, Jewish immigrants who were not part of the preplanned colonization effort continued to make their way to Argentina of their own accord and to establish themselves without institutionalized public assistance. If these people had heard anything about Argentina that encouraged them to make the move, it was from the letters of relatives or acquaintances. The information available from Jewish institutions was vague and not very enticing. Argentina was often portrayed as an agricultural country without industry, where one would have to overcome enormous social and economic difficulties in order to put down roots. This contrasted sharply with the image of the United States as a "golden land of opportunity." Rumors about the scope of prostitution in Argentina led the Jews to regard it as a "tainted land"—more so than the other new countries of immigration. In the Jewish communities of Morocco and the Turkish Empire, the negative image was less widespread, and the linguistic and cultural similarity worked to encourage immigration. Indeed, a large part of the non-Ashkenazic community in Argentina arrived in the eighteen years prior to World War I, although its total number was not very great.[52]

From the government immigration figures painstakingly gathered every week from 1905 on by the JCA official in Buenos Aires, we learn that the number of Jewish immigrants on the official register was extremely small even during the peak years of Jewish immigration. Based on supplementary estimates of the Immigration Department, 81,915 Jews entered the country officially between 1901 and 1914.[53] This was not a large number, and absorption difficulties further reduced the role the newcomers might have played in strengthening Argentina's Jewish community.

The job opportunities open to the immigrants, aside from working in the colonies, included employment in the public and private development projects under way in Argentina. The immigration authorities and private investors offered jobs building railroads, digging sewers, and working as lumberjacks in the quebracho forests in northern Argentina. There may have been some Jewish immigrants willing to engage in such physical labor, at least temporarily, but this could not provide a major occupational basis for a large proportion of the incoming Jews. Crafts and industry in the capital and principal provinces proved to be a more familiar and desirable option.

"In Rosario we visited a furniture factory belonging to a Russian Jew, an ex-colonist from Entre Ríos," reported Rabbi Halfon in 1909. "Of the more than one hundred workers, two-thirds are Jews who earn from three to seven pesos a day. In this factory, there is work all year round. . . . At first the Jewish workers had a difficult time finding work in non-Jewish factories as they were unable to speak the language; however, today the Jewish workman is appreciated by all for his ability and productiveness, and is hired even if he is a new arrival still unable to express himself in Spanish." The sixty-odd Jews employed at this factory represented a sizable portion of Rosario's Jewish population, which was around three thousand. From another source, we learn that 540 Jews were then working at clothing factories in Buenos Aires. This may not sound like much compared with the number of Jews who landed in Buenos Aires during that year alone. Nevertheless, adding family members and friends working in the furniture industry and other trades, we find quite a large body of Jewish workers, considering the relatively small Jewish population at the time.

As early as 1909, small Jewish neighborhoods were emerging in towns throughout the Republic. The Jews who lived there typically engaged in wide variety of crafts: There were tailors, carpenters, saddlers, blacksmiths, locksmiths, watchmakers, soap manufacturers, housepainters, and so on, providing the population of preindustrial Argentina with a broad array of vital goods and services.[54]

The number of unskilled immigrants and petty merchants who turned to peddling and soliciting was particularly great. The high profit margin that was common among retailers in Argentina created boundless opportunities for salesmen willing to settle for less. Moreover, the practice of cash sales left a void where the needy were concerned. There remained a very broad sector of the population for whom peddlers and credit payment presented the only means of attaining basic commodities. As peddling required only a minimal knowledge of Spanish and a friend or relative to supply the first consignment of goods, it was very popular among the immigrants. Thus, the *cuenteniks* (literally "on-the-account men") as the peddlers were called, played an important role in the process of Jewish absorption. Risks were high, selling to the poor in full knowledge that collecting payment depended largely on their goodwill and honesty—if not on their naïveté—and peddlers relied on high markups. Before long, if not too many customers refused to pay, the immigrant peddler could put away a nice sum for future, more conventional business ventures.[55]

Despite the developmental upswing in Argentina during the greater part of 1896–1914 and the seeming ease with which immigrants could find work, most of the jobs available were temporary. Both agriculture and industry had their off-seasons. One source for the beginning of the period reports that only 18.6 percent of Buenos Aires's labor force worked all year round; the rest were employed nine months or fewer. The situation remained much the same over the next decade, and probably continued until World War I. When producing for the local market, as opposed to long-range industrial production for more-remote markets, adapting to the pace of seasonal change was unavoidable. Peddling was not a particularly stable occupation, either: Sometimes a peddler would find closed doors when he came to collect his money; sometimes he did well and was motivated to open a more established business before he was financially ready. Peddling was popular among the Ashkenazim, but it was virtually the sole occupation of those arriving from North Africa and the Turkish Empire. Jewish peddlers competed for business between themselves and with immigrant peddlers of other nationalities. However, unlike other Jewish workers, they did not organize to improve their employment conditions, and no union arose during this period to protect Jewish commercial interests.

The poor working conditions in industry and the trades further heightened the sense of impermanence. The clothing industry's sweatshops, which absorbed so many immigrants in the United States, were not lacking in Argentina. However, here they played a much smaller role in the economic integration of the Jews. The typical features of the sweatshops—shameful pay and cramped, unhygienic conditions—were also found in Argentina's furniture industry, where wages were often based on the number of units produced (piecework). Business competition and higher expenses prompted employers to pay their workers even less. Indeed, the income of workers in Argentina decreased in real terms: Between 1900 and 1911, the cost of living index in Buenos Aires rose from 100 to 215 points while wages increased by only 50 percent.[56]

In Buenos Aires and in the large provincial cities, the widening gap between earnings and expenses was chiefly due to the high cost of housing. The tremendous population growth in the capital far exceeded the housing supply; rents soared while quality steadily declined. Horrifying slums developed as huge buildings in the heart of the city were divided into tiny, one-room flats without toilets, occupied by large families. Nothing could have been further from the immigrants' dream of making an honest living and achieving some measure of comfort than the *conventillos* (literally "little convents"). "Not long ago, we visited one of these conventillos," wrote Rabbi Halfon in 1910. "What shocked us the most was the filth and promiscuity we found in the rooms of over fifty Jewish families (some 450 persons) living around the same yard. . . . These were all families working honestly for their bread." The severe exploitation of the tenants in these buildings—and all other rental housing—sparked a spontaneous rent strike in 1907. Although the police were brought in, the tenants held out until the fees were lowered somewhat—albeit not enough to bring about genuine improvement in the housing situation. Thus, it often transpired that even when the Jewish craftsman, laborer, or peddler found work, he was forced to live in disgraceful, overcrowded conditions.[57]

Added to the economic and housing difficulties of the urban immigrants was their longing for the old country. Those who had arrived alone, as scouts for their families, required large sums of money to bring over their kin. The sense of impermanence made many give up hope of ever planting roots and increased their hunger for the warm and familiar world they had once known. The decision to leave was made easier as fares to Europe became cheaper. This was especially so in 1908, when competition between shipping companies reduced the cost of a ticket from Buenos Aires to only 30 pesos—equivalent to fewer than ten days of labor by a skilled workman.[58] From the figures collected each week by the JCA official in Buenos Aires, we learn that between 1907 and 1914 there were 10,761 registered Jewish departures from Argentina, compared with 55,606 arrivals. This indicates a reemigration rate of 19.35 percent a year. No other country to which the Jews migrated seems to have experienced an exodus of such proportions. The rate of reemigration from the United States, for example, was only 7.14 percent during the years 1908–1914.[59]

The hardship involved in settling in Argentina and the knowledge that other countries were still open to immigrants undoubtedly encouraged this reemigration. At the same time, no serious measures were taken in the Jewish community to halt the phenomenon through financial aid to immigrants or, at least, proper guidance and referral. The potential inherent in Argentina for Jewish immigration thus remained largely unexploited.

Meanwhile, the Republic was changing, and attitudes to the Jewish immigrant were changing, too.

The Country of Immigration and the Jews

Argentina's third comprehensive population census on June 1, 1914, revealed that the number of inhabitants had nearly doubled since the previous census in 1895: The population now stood at 7,903,662, compared with 3,954,141 nineteen years earlier. The number of foreigners had risen slightly more, from 1,004,527 to 2,357,952, and now represented 29.9 as opposed to 25.4 percent of the overall population. However, the distinction between "Argentines" and "foreigners" in this and all other censuses was determined by place of birth. This ignored the fact that the offspring of the immigrants, brought up and educated by their parents, were not yet Argentines in any respect except birthplace. Actually, the immigrant presence in Argentina was greater than the 30 percent indicated in the census. Moreover, the concentration of immigrants in certain parts of Argentina, particularly the capital, the province of Buenos Aires, and other provinces in the "humid pampa," left an indelible mark on the population's makeup. When the census was taken in 1914, foreigners constituted 49.36 percent of the city of Buenos Aires and 34.17 percent in the province of Buenos Aires. Together with their "Argentine" offspring, they were probably a majority in the capital and much more numerous than the figures indicate in Argentina's chief province. Beyond the data supplied by the census, the impression of the foreign presence in Argentine society was further augmented by no less than 1,588,096 immigrants living in Argentina for shorter or longer periods between 1895 and 1914, who had reemigrated before the census was taken.[60]

This was not exactly what the patricians had envisaged when they drew up Argentina's immigration law. To many of their descendants, only the second part of the motto "To govern means to populate" seemed true. At

Argentine immigration authorities on board an immigrant ship

the expense of populating the country, they felt their grip on governing was being lost. In their eyes, the idea of a cultivated population ridding Argentina of its barbarism had also proved false. The national-cultural origins of the migrants and the extent of their assimilation in the existing culture was a far cry from the vision of a biological merging. The fact that the newcomers settled mainly in Buenos Aires and the provinces along the eastern coast increased the already existent hostility to Buenos Aires and the federal government in the provinces farther inland.

A whole series of disappointments during the period between the two censuses had created a negative stance on immigrants and immigration that was to have a crucial impact on the status of the Jews. The first disappointment lay in the ethnocultural sphere: The number of "preferential" immigrants arriving in Argentina over this nineteen-year period—Germans, Anglo-Saxons, and Francophones—had reached 142,485. However, during this same period, 102,073 of these had left the country. According to the 1914 census, they represented 6.87 percent of Argentina's foreign population and only 2.05 percent of its overall population. On the other hand, over 2.5 million Italians and Spaniards had settled in Argentina during this time, and even after over 1 million of them had returned to their homelands, they constituted 75 percent of the country's foreign population and 22.26 percent of its general population in 1914. The poor socioeconomic background of most of these immigrants led to a higher percentage of illiteracy in the general population and certainly represented no "civilizing" factor. Furthermore, despite their Latin origins, which were thought to be an advantage in linguistic-cultural absorption, they continued to maintain strong ties with their homelands. Although the majority of the immigrants had a Latin Catholic upbringing, a linguistic, ethnic, and organizational pluralism developed in Buenos Aires and the other large cities that conflicted with the monolithic unification sought by the veteran Argentines.[61]

In the face of this Babel of languages and nationalities, a small group of young writers led by Ricardo Rojas emerged during the first decade of the twentieth century to give expression to a new wave of Argentine cultural nationalism. Argentina in its early, preimmigration days was no longer seen as a wasteland and the home of barbarians. In the hands of these writers, the unruly gaucho was refined into the symbol of positive Argentine attributes and values. Harsh judgment was passed on the immigrants, both Latin and "northern," whose culture had defiled this original state.

Their attempt to bequeath their foreignness to their children and to preserve their own culture was regarded as an attack on the hegemony of the Argentines in their own home.[62]

The resentment against immigration and immigrants for ethnocultural reasons was especially strong in the case of the Jews. Those from the Turkish Empire, and the more numerous Ashkenazim, belonged to a varied group of "exotic" nationals with whom the native Argentines had never previously had cultural or economic contact. The total number of these immigrants at the time of the 1914 census was no more than 207,967, making up 8.82 percent of the immigrant population and a mere 2.63 percent of the general population; nonetheless, the demographic weight of all these national groups combined was sufficient to disturb the cultural hegemony envisaged by the patricians but not adequate to win them a legitimate place in the emerging Argentine nation. To curb their influence, Alsina, after twenty years in the immigration service, proposed that Russian (including Jewish, Greek Orthodox, Lutheran, and Catholic), Polish, Austro-Hungarian, and Turkish nationals—"all these people who differ from the basic population of the Republic"—be permitted to mingle in Argentine society "if they merge with the existing population without making themselves felt." If they did not create a conflict of interests, show hostility or aloofness, affect the labor market by bringing down wages, or set themselves above the local inhabitants—then "public opinion might allow itself to become favorable toward them."[63]

However, the Jewish public in Argentina, despite its small size, was not geared for such anonymity. Like other immigrant groups, the Jews in the capital proceeded to establish their own institutions. When Alsina wrote, the major religious and humanitarian institutions had been founded, Jewish newspapers were being published, and many cultural and social organizations were operating. In a national survey carried out a year earlier, Jewish institutions had also been found in several provincial cities. The 3,059 Jews living in Rosario boasted two communal organizations, synagogues, a cemetery, a welfare society, and a Jewish workers union. The Jews were also organizing in Córdoba, Tucumán, La Plata, and elsewhere. As in other immigrant groups, a national identity was developing among the Jews. A 1904 survey of voluntary associations in Buenos Aires surprisingly lists three Zionist organizations, including a Zionist federation of twelve associations with a membership of 1,123.[64]

If the communal and social organization of the Jews was not yet fully evident in the cities, it immediately struck the eye in the agricultural colonies. Every colony had religious facilities such as synagogues and ritual baths, often, because of the great distances between the farms, housed in separate buildings at a central juncture, thus leaving their mark on topographic maps. The children were given a Jewish education, and the broad network of schools built by the JCA in the early days of the colonization program continued to expand after the baron's death. In 1910, there were fifty schools with 155 teachers and a student population of 3,538. Against the backdrop of neglect in the state schools, the size, organization, and plentiful resources of the Jewish network were all the more obvious.[65] The JCA had created this network to educate a young cadre of Argentines of the Mosaic faith who would continue the farming tradition in their new homeland. This educational ideal went hand in hand with their image of the Argentine Republic as a free country founded upon freedom of religion and equality, also for the Jews. It was quite a shock to the JCA when its educational network in the colonies was presented as a negative example of immigrant separatism.

The Jewish schools were first attacked in November 1908 in an important publication of the governmental National Education Council. Soon the daily press joined in, accusing them of teaching the children only Hebrew and the Bible and nothing about Argentina. Despite the appearance of official denials, the spokesman of cultural nationalism, Rojas, perpetuated these accusations in his book, *La Restauración Nacionalista*, which became the textbook of Argentine nationalism as soon as it was published in 1909. Education in the Jewish colonies was presented as a clear example of the negative outcome of Argentina's overly liberal policy in allowing the immigrants to teach their cultural values to their children. "The danger in the Jewish schools is that by bringing in [Jewish] fanaticism, they are also bringing us the seeds of a Semitic problem that *happily did not exist here,* but that will exist the moment that the creole son of the Semitic immigrant prefers to be a Jew instead of an Argentine in complete communion with his people and the land of their birth," wrote Rojas (emphasis in the original). Were the views of Rojas and the National Education Council a product of a particular hostility to the Jews, of anti-Semitism? In fact, Rojas was drawing attention to the danger presented by all foreign schools in Argentina. Rabbi Halfon, in answer to this question, explained that the motives of the National Education Council were chauvinistic rather than anti-Semitic. In any case, the Jewish community played a conspicuous role in the heterogeneous ethnocultural reality that had grown up in the Republic, to which these spokesmen of the "original" Argentina were opposed.[66]

The Jews were a reminder of yet another disappointment in the area of immigration. The hegemony of Catholicism in Argentina had been relinquished for the sake of the large numbers of Protestant immigrants anticipated by the Fathers of the Republic and the legislators of the Immigration and Colonization Law. In 1909, more than fifty years after the signing of the Constitution, there were no more than 30,791 Protestants among the capital's million and a quarter inhabitants. In the rest of the Republic, in an overall population of 6,805,684, Protestants probably numbered less than 100,000.[67] Of course, the liberal legislation heralding the emancipation of the Jews of Argentina was anchored in the liberal and anticlerical views of many members of the Argentine elite. When immigration did not create an ethnic reality of religious pluralism founded on broad ethnic and demographic elements, only the views remained; but views could be recalled, and with them also the stamp of legitimacy anticipated by Argentine Jewry. Indeed, many members of the governing elite developed an aversion to social liberalism in the wake of the social changes wrought by immigration. As the militancy of the secularists declined, those who demanded a Catholic Argentina, for both historical and demographic reasons, gained strength. Others, abandoning the theories of positivism and rationalism, adopted romantic nationalism and a return to Argentine "roots"—which were embedded in Iberian, Catholic Christian culture. Thus, both proclericalists and secularists met on the common ground of budding nationalism.

Without knowing it, the Jewish community developing in Argentina during this period ran counter to these processes. The community was certainly not religious, as the reports from the capital and provinces illustrate. However, even those lax in observance had certain religious needs that required organization. The most obvious examples were a prayer quorum for the Jewish High Holidays and a Jewish cemetery. Even the Jewish atheists and socialists contributed to the "religious" Jewish presence sensed by the Argentine public, for whom the distinction between Jewish believers and nonbelievers was not at all clear. The colonies, because of their geographic concentration and large population of observant Jews in the founding generation, were perceived as well-defined islands of Jewishness in a Christian environment.

This state of affairs was highly displeasing to the militant Catholics, and the more radical among them, who were blatantly anti-Semitic, did not hesitate to express their hostility. Neither did full equality for the Jews mesh with the ideas of Alsina, ostensibly a supporter of Jewish immigration; in his eyes, the thinkers and statesmen who had created the nation had hoped to establish "the perfect, enduring Christian republic." As a devout but liberal Catholic, Alsina was not against religious freedom in Argentina. He felt that there should be *tolerance* toward non-Catholics, and non-Christians, too. Nonetheless, they had no right to regard themselves as full and equal partners of the "main inhabitants." Rojas, the secularist, also had a clear image of Argentina before him, but the observant Jewish public was certainly not a part of it. After listing the "exotic" names and dates of the Jewish holidays he found in the school calender published by the JCA, he "defended" the Jews by saying that the teaching of "extra-Argentine" languages and religion in their schools was not basically different from the linguistic activities and anti-Argentine imperialism in the Italian, English, and German schools. His argument was that the Jewish school "creates the Jewish family whose patriarchal religion will prevent it from merging with the families of the land and assimilating in our basically secular society."[68]

Since, in effect, the Jews constituted the only body of non-Christian immigrants in Argentina, these views and their different nuances had far-reaching implications for the legitimization of Jewish existence in the country. The actual results were visible only at a much later date; meanwhile, the Argentine community suffered disappointment in two other areas, both connected with the economy.

The authors of the immigration law had intended the newcomers to populate the frontiers and expand the country's agricultural infrastructure. One of the explicit goals of the law was to pave the way for a broad class of small-scale farmers. Although the landowner–tenant relationship created by the patricians to suit their own interests had suppressed the emergence of such a class, many old-time Argentines blamed the immigrants.[69] In fact, large numbers of immigrants turned to urban trades when they found themselves unable to purchase farmland. The census taken in 1914 showed that 72 percent of all the businesses in Argentina were owned by foreigners, as were 64.5 percent of all industrial concerns and 60.36 percent of the real estate in the capital. Of course, this foreign "monopoly" over middle-class occupations and related assets was due to the fact that these areas were underdeveloped and accessible to them. However, the emotional significance for the Argentines was that daily life in the large political centers was being run largely by foreigners.[70]

There was no real reason for the discontent of the Argentines to focus itself on the Jewish community. From the outset, Jewish colonization had developed on the outskirts of the cultivated areas, redeeming many thousands of hectares of virgin land. The JCA, unlike the vast majority of settlement companies seeking to make a profit, devoted itself entirely to promoting small-scale farming—just as the patricians had envisaged. In this respect, the JCA was much more consistent than was the Argentine government, which made no effort to prevent centralized landownership or the decline of production in the few colonies it had established in the early days of its immigration policy. Against the general backdrop of extensive, exploitative farming, the Jewish colonies stood out in their efforts to diversify, introduce new crops, and, above all, create an intensive, multibranched enterprise in which breeding and dairy farming could be pursued alongside agriculture. This did not escape the notice of the government. Both the head of the Research and Statistics Department of the Ministry of Agriculture and an agronomist employed by the department depicted the Jewish colonies in Santa Fe as worthy of emulation. Provincial and federal leaders who visited the colonies publicly expressed their admiration;[71] yet it was the infighting and scandals in the colonies, which reached the courts in Buenos Aires, that most caught the public eye. The JCA was presented as an oppressor, and its "foreign character" as a company managed by Jewish bankers overseas received greater coverage than did its philanthropic and productive work.

In the area of foreign dominion over urban real estate and commerce, the small Jewish community again did nothing to warrant any special hostility. In 1909, a local Jewish survey found thirty thousand Jews living in the capital—a number that may well have been exaggerated. According to a municipal census that same year, Buenos Aires had close to 1.25 million inhabitants. The Jews would have thus constituted 2.5 percent of the overall population. According to the census in 1914, "Russian" and "Turkish" residents, both Jewish and non-Jewish, accounted for only 1.75 percent of the property owners in Buenos Aires, and their assets were low in value compared with other immigrant groups such as the English and French.[72] In only two neighborhoods was the percentage of "Russians" and "Turks" much higher than elsewhere in the city: One was the downtown area with its proliferation of Jewish peddlers and merchants selling popularly priced goods, clothing, and secondhand merchandise. It was also here that the Jewish pimps were most visible, which was sufficient cause for blaming the Jews for the ills of urban immigration.

While the patricians were disturbed by foreign monopolization of the middle class, no steps were taken to hinder the competition between Argentine and foreign capitalists. Many of them had interests in foreign-owned companies and capital, and the nationalist sensibilities in the ruling class did not yet extend to financial matters. When labor unrest commenced, however, all the pent-up feelings against the immigrants began to emerge and the police were called in. Buenos Aires was placed under curfew five times during the first decade of the twentieth century. Except for the curfew in February 1905, when the Radical party called for armed rebellion, all were designed to suppress the working class. Police violence became steadily worse, and, as police fired into crowds and dispersed demonstrators, the list of dead and wounded grew.

Jewish workers first joined the May 1 demonstrations only in 1906. With their Yiddish placards and red banners, they were quite an attraction. However, the Jews were not a major factor in the proletarian movement in Argentina at this time. Only three and a half years later, when the Jewish Anarchist Simón Radovizky assassinated the chief of police and his assistant, did Jewish workers become the target of upper-class enmity. This act caused a great and long-lasting uproar. In March and April 1910, the newspapers dealt with Jewish issues every day, with a pervading tone of unfriendliness.

On May 14, 1910, a group of young nationalists decided to take revenge on the proletarians. They vandalized the offices of the Socialist and Anarchist party newspapers and then proceeded to the "Russian" Jewish library and the two Jewish proletarian clubs then operating in Buenos Aires, whose entire contents were dragged outside and set aflame. As the fire blazed, the nationalists flung rocks at private homes and shouted insults against the "Russians."[73]

These incidents did not change Argentina's immigration policy any more than did the displeasure of the patricians in other domains. The need for workers in the villages and urban centers was still an overriding consideration, and throughout this period, Argentina kept its doors open. However, the demands of the economy could not stifle the sense of frustration, which continued to grow during the eighteen years preceding World War I and was to become a key factor in later years. The Jewish immigrants, so few in number, were not the cause of this frustration. Nevertheless, it was their misfortune to embody three of the four factors that generated it: ethnocultural heterogeneity, non-Christian religious pluralism, and proletarian rebelliousness. These features of the Jewish community, together with conspicuousness on the urban scene, worked together to blur the Jewish contribution to agricultural colonization.

At the End of an Era

Argentina's doors were wide open to Jewish immigration during the critical period in the history of modern Jewish migrations; nevertheless, the extent to which Jewish emigrants took advantage of this situation was largely up to the Jews themselves. The colonization project of the JCA provided newcomers with an address to which they could turn on arrival, and most of those who went to the provinces did settle in the Jewish colonies, attracted by the hope of work and possibly a farm at some later date.[74] Yet, the JCA directors in Buenos Aires, supported by their superiors in Paris, did not see it as desirable, or part of their duty, to encourage Jews to immigrate en masse to Argentina. They were interested almost exclusively in systematic colonization by carefully selected farmers and firmly believed that the hardships endured by the colonists were an aid to the selection process. The same passive attitude was taken toward the absorption of urban immigrants—during this entire period, no soundly organized, permanent organization was founded to help them.

As indicated by the high rate of reemigration, many of the Jewish immigrants failed to sink roots in the new country. Those who remained had to reconcile themselves to the fact that their ethnic, cultural, religious, and organizational profile, as well as their economic and social standing, were not up to the expectations of Argentina's patricians and emerging nationalists.

By World War I, however, the Jewish community was an undeniable reality. According to various estimates, it numbered between 100,000 and 115,600 persons, most of them concentrated in the capital. The others were scattered throughout dozens of cities in the provinces and in the farming colonies. At this point, the Jews of Argentina actually outnumbered the

Jews of Palestine, and there were more Jewish farmers in the Argentine Republic than in the Holy Land. Around this time, Jewish communal organizations, welfare societies, political parties, libraries, and cultural institutions began to dot the capital, and the first Jewish newspapers appeared. Many of these papers closed within a short time, but their existence, however brief, indicates that a vibrant Jewish community was unfolding in the Republic of Argentina.[75]

At this moment, Argentine Jews, like all the rest of world Jewry, were fast approaching a new era.

4

The Last Chance,
1914–1932

T wo prolonged and profound crises shook the world during the eighteen years from the beginning of World War I until the onset of the Nazi era. The war and its aftermath, on the one hand, and the Great Depression, on the other, left scarcely nine years for recovery and an attempted return to normalcy. From the vantage point of the history of Jewish migrations, this interval between the two crises stands out as the Jews' last chance.

Argentina entered this period as a conservative, oligarchic republic but with a commitment, anchored in a new electoral law passed in 1912, to introduce a truly democratic, popular government. By the end of the period, the oligarchy had given way to a conservative, undemocratic military regime. Whereas these political changes had little effect on Argentina's social and economic structure, the two world crises generated conditions to which Argentina was forced to respond. The flow of immigration still depended on the rate of agricultural and, to a lesser degree, industrial development. However, the prospects of a cosmopolitan, pluralistic society and the fear of proletarian "extremism" supplied Argentina's nationalists and upper classes with a counterargument against immigration.

Did the demand for working hands overcome the cultural and social opposition to immigration, as in the past? How did the controversy affect the opportunities for Jewish immigration and the status of the Jews in

Argentine society? How extensive was this last chance, and to what degree did individual Jews and the Jewish organizations take advantage of it?

A Community on Neutral Shores

The inferno set off by the assassination of the Austrian crown prince in Sarajevo spread like wildfire over the globe, from the Baltic shores in the north to broad stretches of western Poland and Russia, and on through the Balkans as far as Palestine and the Sinai Desert. This vast expanse was inhabited by close to 9.5 million Jews—nearly two-thirds of the Jewish people. Within a few days of the assassination, the Jews of Austria, Germany, France, and England were called upon to demonstrate their patriotism; tens of thousands joined the armies of the Central Powers or the Allies. As German aggressiveness reached a peak and the United States entered the war, the US Jewish community was drawn into the fray, as were the Jewish communities in the British dominions of Canada, Australia, and South Africa.

The fledgling Jewish community in the Argentine Republic was among the few that remained outside the war effort. Despite its close commercial ties with England and cultural affiliation with France, Argentina maintained a solidly neutral stance throughout the war. This was particularly significant in view of the far-reaching changes then taking place in Argentina. In April 1916, Argentine voters cast their ballot for a new president in the first corruption-free elections in the history of the Republic. Their choice was Hipólito Yrigoyen, the elderly leader of the Radical party. It seemed as if the aristocratic, elitist Argentina of old had vanished, replaced by a democratic, populist Argentina embodying the hopes and dreams of the middle-class, second-generation immigrants heretofore denied a say.

However, the new administration made no changes in foreign policy and did little to improve the economic and social problems created by the hostilities. The serious recession that had set in a few months before the war steadily worsened: Shipping was affected by the shortage of steamships and, later, by the naval blockade imposed by the Germans; exportation suffered, and many products imported from Europe were no longer available as military consumption outstripped civilian production. A difficult period was in store for the Argentine economy. As grain exports decreased, the demand for agricultural laborers dropped sharply, and poor tenant farmers watched their farms collapse. The absence of imports was an incentive to produce more goods locally, but the opportunity could not be fully exploited without proper planning, technological infrastructure, fuel, and raw materials. The faint stirrings of industry in Argentina proved incapable of providing jobs for all those who sought them, and urban unemployment persisted throughout the war.[1]

This was the political and economic reality facing the Jewish community of Argentina. Hard-hit by the recession, many Jews in the capital and provinces turned for aid to philanthropic institutions such as the Ezrah society, which had been inundated by requests even before the war. Large numbers had returned to their home countries or left Argentina to seek their fortunes elsewhere. When hostilities broke out and these escape routes were closed, the situation worsened. The recession and increase of general unemployment were a harsh blow to the Jewish peddlers, who could no longer collect the sums owed them by their poor clients. Jewish workers traveled to remote parts of the country in search of jobs; many of the unemployed ended up on the doorsteps of Jewish welfare organizations.

When the war was in its second year, some sectors of the Jewish community began to show signs of recovery, with a resulting impact on organizational life. In the small communities near the colonies were quite a few affluent merchants whose businesses had not been harmed by the instability of the market. Along with some of the wealthier farmers, they began to contribute generously to philanthropic institutions in the capital. A successful fund-raising campaign for the building of a Jewish hospital in 1915–1916 clearly showed that urban Jewish businessmen, craftsmen, and manufacturers were recovering, too. The more established and enterprising among them began to produce goods that they had previously imported or distributed. For these people, the wartime years were a period of progress and financial gain. While the Ezrah society was distributing sums of 5 to 15 pesos to the needy, it was also able to hold a cornerstone-laying ceremony for a new hospital on October 29, 1916, attended by government officials.[2]

The large-scale fund-raising appeal on behalf of the war victims in Europe, which began in February 1915, led to the formation of the Central Committee for the Relief of the War Victims. That this committee was able to collect 380,000 pesos by the armistice was a tribute to the internal organization of Argentine Jewry and its solid ties with Jews the world over. In February 1916, a general Jewish congress was held in Argentina, hosting 107 delegates from thirty communal, cultural, and other organizations in the capital, and twenty-eight communities in the agricultural colonies and provinces. In a bid to add Argentina's voice to the peacetime demands of the US Jewish community on behalf of world Jewry, this congress, with its delegations, ceremonies, flags, and anthem singing, constituted a public affirmation of the Jewish national entity in Argentina.[3]

Other organizations were forming, too. The plight of the peddlers led to the establishment of a cooperative association, the Jewish Commercial Society (Sociedad Comercial Israelita) that, after the war, became one of the leading Jewish financial institutions in Buenos Aires. Immigrants from Eastern Europe banded together to found the first landsmanschaften, and in November 1915 the leftist proletarian cultural institutions operating in many cities held their first convention. Another important feature of the Argentine Jewish landscape was the daily Jewish press, which first evolved during the war to supply news from the "old home" front and provide advertising space for Jewish businesses and organizations. The *Di Idishe Tseitung,* a Zionist, petit bourgeois newspaper, began to appear on November 15, 1914, followed by the proletarian *Di Presse* on January 1, 1918. These papers played a vital role in Jewish organizational and cultural life in Argentina. Together with other publications, such as *Israel,* a weekly magazine geared to the non-Ashkenazic sector, they created an important link between the individual Jew in Argentina and the greater Jewish community.[4]

The revolutionary events of 1917, which reverberated all over the Jewish world, also strengthened the national consciousness of Argentina's Jews. The fall of the czar in March, the promise of civil and national equality in Russia, and, above all, the Balfour Declaration in November were greeted with joy by the Jewish community of Argentina; rallies, assemblies, and other public celebrations were held around the country. Following the news of a Jewish Legion being formed by Great Britain, young immigrants approached the British embassy in March 1918, eager to volunteer. A group of fifty was readied by August, with additional groups of this size to be called up as needed. Much fanfare surrounded the departure of the new recruits, who boarded their ship amid a rush of emotion. When the war ended about a month later, Argentine Jewry was at a high point in its history.[5]

Despite the exhilaration and pride felt by many Argentine Jews during the second half of the war, it was difficult to ignore the criticism and hostility of the society around them. The future of Jewish immigration was a chief area of concern, as we see from the report of the Congress of Argentine Jewry held in February 1916. A few months later, two leaders of the Jewish youth organization, Juventud Israelita Argentina, responded to a withering condemnation of Jewish immigration that had appeared in one of the country's most respected periodicals of social and political science. At the same time, thousands of Argentine youngsters were studying from textbooks that declared: "The Jew is not and never will be a farmer. . . . Jewish settlers who abandoned the village for the federal capital and other urban centers left agricultural labor to the Creoles and Italians whereas the settlers' offspring have resumed their traditional occupations: commerce and usury. . . . In summary, Russian Jewish immigration is not a desirable element in the Republic; on the contrary, it embodies a tangible moral and economic danger." In an attempt to have these books banned, the heads of the Congregación Israelita appealed to Francisco Beiro, one of the leaders of the Radical party, a personal friend of the president, and, later, in 1928, his vice-president. Beiro assured them that the books would be recalled by the authorities on Argentina's independence day in 1917, as a gesture of goodwill. The Jews realized, however, that removing the offending material from the classroom did not guarantee an end to the bad feeling that had engendered it.[6]

To what extent did attacks such as these reflect Argentine public opinion on continued Jewish immigration? This question became increasingly important as World War I ended, and the enormity of Jewish suffering in Eastern Europe came to light. The fate of Argentina after the war and the desirable attitude toward immigration were major concerns for its citizens. Between 1914 and 1918, many thousands of inhabitants left the country, resulting in a population drain of over 200,000 people. On the basis of a survey in July–August 1918, conducted by the Museo Social Argentino, a prestigious nonacademic institution founded in 1911 to disseminate reliable information about Argentina, all but three of the politicians, philosophers, university lecturers, and public opinion–makers questioned felt that immigration was vital for the advancement and development of Argentina. All the respondents held that farming ability in the immigrants was of utmost importance, as was the integration of the newcomers into Argentine society. Immigrants were considered essential not only as a source of manpower but for their contribution to the fiber of the nation. A few of the respondents voiced clearly racist opinions: By bringing in immigrants of "choice stock," they hoped to produce a superior white race in Argentina. They even specified preferred nationalities, along with the traits they were believed to represent. The Faculty of Economics of the University of Buenos Aires echoed the widespread notion that immigrants from Northern Europe were most desirable, "so that their personal qualities of orderliness, industry, willpower, and discipline will influence our overly Latin habits and way of life." Next in line were the Latin peoples, whom some considered on a par with the northerners. The immigration of blacks and Orientals was strongly opposed by nearly all the respondents. While the majority carefully distinguished between those races considered desirable, less desirable, and undesirable, three respondents supported unrestricted mass immigration. Even those with the most liberal views felt that an essential condition was full integration in Argentine society.[7]

The views expressed in this survey were of potential consequence for the future of Jewish immigration to Argentina. If the general consensus indicated that immigration policy should be changed or more tightly controlled, this was hardly encouraging for a community that owed its very existence to the liberality of the current laws. The fact that only three respondents expressly supported free immigration, while unimportant statistically, demonstrated how little the public stood by the principles, anchored in the federal Constitution, that offered the only hope for Jewish immigration. The belief that immigrants should merge with the local population did not bode well for a group such as the Jews, whose capacity for assimilation was doubted from the start. The same held true with regard to farming ability. The impressive achievements of the Jewish colonists had not erased the image of the Jew as a city dweller firmly rooted in the "parasitic" commercial trades. Furthermore, the Jewish masses leaving Eastern Europe and the Turkish Empire were not from the countries designated preferential by the survey respondents. They would be considered for immigration by only a few of the respondents, and only if there were not enough workers from other countries. Four respondents were opposed even in this case and openly expressed their antipathy to Jewish immigration.[8] Again, this is insignificant statistically but does demonstrate the existence of such feelings among Argentine intellectuals. Nevertheless, the threat to Jewish immigration lay more in the attitude to immigrants as a whole than to Jewish immigrants specifically.

Argentina's Immigration Policy

The end of World War I did not eliminate the suffering of Eastern European Jewry. On the contrary, while the Western countries were celebrating the armistice, the Poles and Ukrainians were battling for power and territory, and attacks on the Jewish populace resumed. West of Russia, in defeated Austria and Germany, and in the former lands of the Turkish Empire, the persecution of the Jews continued. This was in striking contrast to the tremendous political gains of the Jews in 1919. The assurance of civic rights and abolishment of racial discrimination was a major provision in all the peace treaties. Whether or not they so desired, each of the new states in Eastern and central Europe signed a commitment to accept the Jews as equal citizens. Minority rights for all the national and cultural minorities in the fallen empires were guaranteed, and the Jews, too, were awarded the status of a cultural and religious entity. To the apparent satisfaction of the Jewish proletariat, these principles were adopted in Soviet Russia as well. Furthermore, the Zionists, repeatedly assured since the Balfour Declaration that their aspirations would be recognized, won international endorsement in 1920 from the League of Nations when the mandate over Palestine was granted to Great Britain. Thus, within the span of a year all the foundations had been laid for a political solution of the Jewish question. Nevertheless, the Jewish masses were increasingly pressed to seek out new terrains.

War refugees were the first on the list. Tens of thousands of Jews who had fled from the Slavic provinces of Austro-Hungary to Vienna, Budapest, and their German and Czechoslovakian provinces again found themselves homeless when the empire was split up into separate nations. The Jews were ordered to return to their "homeland," but the Polish and Romanian administrations that now ruled these areas refused to let them in. In 1919–1921, Jews fleeing the Soviet regime and the pogroms in the Ukraine reached Poland, Romania, Turkey, and the Baltic states. None were willing to absorb them. Even when the torrent of refugees abated, migration was a major preoccupation among the Jews, who continued to suffer from economic hardship and discrimination.

As the need for a friendly home intensified, the country that had absorbed the largest number of Jews—the United States—began to close its doors. In effect, June 1921 marked the end of an era in the history of Jewish immigration to the United States. Classification by national-racial origins, which had been in force since 1882 only with regard to immigrants from the Far East, was now extended to all immigrants. Newcomers of all nationalities were to be admitted henceforth at an annual rate of 3 percent of their national presence in the country in 1910. This policy bit into immigration from those countries from which the majority of Jewish immigrants hailed, reducing their number drastically. Three years later, the legislation became even stricter: The cutoff date for immigration quotas was pushed back to 1890, a year when the proportion of Eastern Europeans living in the United States was small; only 2 percent of the immigrants from each national group residing in the United States before this critical date was allowed in. In this way, the number of immigrants from Eastern Europe and the Near East, where the Jews were being oppressed, was radically diminished. The quota system, with all its racist implications, became a permanent and, in many eyes, hallowed fixture of US immigration policy. In time, these laws were to have a tremendous impact on other lands of immigration, one of them Argentina.[9]

Shall we imitate the immigration policies of the United States? This was one of the implicit questions of the Museo Social Argentino in its 1918 survey. Labor unrest in the months that followed led to a Red scare in Argentina similar to that in the United States, where the fear of revolutionaries had been cited as a major argument against immigration. On January 7, 1919, a labor dispute at one of the largest metal factories in the capital culminated in a bloody clash with the police and marked the beginning of what has since been called La Semana Trágica (tragic week). Faced with the constant deterioration of their wages, the workers of Buenos Aires had been battling against their employers and striking on and off throughout the year. The violence at the metal factory led to a general strike in Buenos Aires that quickly spread to the provinces and was denounced by employers as a proletarian, "maximalist" uprising. The government reaction was to call in the army, although there were also attempts to mediate between the parties. Meanwhile, patriotic nationalists formed "White guards," and groups of vigilantes volunteered to assist the army and police in quelling the uprising. With the full cooperation of the authorities, they swiftly descended on the "Russian"—that is, Jewish—neighborhoods on the pretext of searching for maximalists, victimizing and torturing old people, women, and children. Hundreds of Jews and "Jewish-looking" passersby were arrested and beaten; others were publicly humiliated and their property vandalized. "The raid on the Russians," as the vigilantes called it, ended two days later with the sensational news that a Bolshevik conspiracy had been uncovered and all members of the Soviet "shadow government" headed by the Jewish Bundist journalist, Pinie Wald, had been incarcerated. The belief that all Russians were revolutionaries, which was already evident in 1910 and openly expressed in the Museo Social survey, thus produced an anti-Jewish outrage sanctioned by the government.[10]

"Are we still wanted here?" the Jews of Argentina asked themselves in shock after the pogrom in Buenos Aires and the threat of more atrocities in the provinces. The reply of several prominent statesmen and intellectuals interviewed by the Jewish literary magazine, *Vida Neustra,* appeared to satisfy them. Moreover, a Jewish delegation that met with President Yrigoyen was assured that the persecution of the Jews was "incompatible with the traditions of the country and the spirit of its laws, and with Argentine culture and character. Public opinion and the government consider Jewish immigration an advantageous and important element, and it is hoped that this immigration will continue and the newcomers will assimilate and become an integral part of the Republic." Thus, despite the pogrom and the rumblings against immigrants that preceded and followed it, Jewish immigration to Argentina was allowed to continue.[11]

From a detailed report of the International Labour Office in 1922, we learn how Argentina compared with seventy-six other countries regarding attitude to immigrants. In Argentina, as in most of these countries, the regulations governing immigration were largely in the hands of the consuls. During World War I, it became their job not only to check out local registration papers and the reliability of documents proving integrity, but also, as of August 1921, to keep careful records and draw up a personal profile for each immigrant. In this respect, Argentina was no different from other absorption countries. The stipulation that potential immigrants have no criminal record or revolutionary affiliations in their home country—and that they prove this by appropriate documentation—was also made by other countries, some of which were even stricter. On the other hand, the labor office reported only one restriction on the basis of race, religion, and nationality in Argentina, and this applied to Gypsies. Compared with the numerous discriminatory practices in countries such as Canada, Australia, and South Africa—and also the United States— this one restriction indicated a quite liberal policy. The fact that no requirements were imposed in the area of literacy or finance, apart from barring entry to "professional" beggars, was further proof of Argentina's relative liberality.[12]

In 1922–1923, however, calls to reduce the flow of immigration and tighten restrictions were sounded even in Argentina. On December 31, 1923, a new regulation went into effect that granted entry to immigrants on the basis of how beneficial they were to the country at the given time. Anyone suffering from a chronic or infectious disease, mental illness, physical disability, or any other handicap that would hinder earning a livelihood was thus ineligible for immigration. Entry was also barred to criminals, revolutionaries, women traveling alone or with their children, and both minors from the age of fifteen and those persons over the age of sixty who were unaccompanied. All others were required to obtain a valid passport from their home countries and papers from the police proving there had been no involvement in criminal activity, begging, or social agitation in the five years preceding their application. The Immigration Department also issued detailed instructions to the consuls, urging them to ascertain the occupations of potential immigrants and, even if all papers were in order, to approve only those whose skills were needed in Argentina. In another published circular, the consuls were ordered to refrain from all immigration propaganda, discourage those planning to settle in the cities, and give preference to farmers.[13]

These policies, which placed numerous obstacles in the path of potential immigrants, were criticized by certain sectors of the public. In view of the drastic changes in US immigration laws at this time, those in favor of mass immigration to Argentina argued that the time was ripe to steer large numbers of Europeans toward the Río de la Plata. This seems to have convinced the minister of agriculture, Tomás A. Le Breton. In April 1924, only months after the enactment of the new regulation, he wrote to Juan P. Ramos, director of the Immigration Department, who was attending a League of Nations meeting in Rome devoted to the subject of immigration:

I allow myself to draw your attention to a matter that has serious and decisive implications for us: immigration is not increasing. . . . This country
must augment its population as rapidly as possible, and plots of land must
be made available for colonization. . . . It is desirable that our representatives and general consuls consider the circumstances when applying the
regulations and exercise leniency toward all those coming to our country,
taking care only to avoid their becoming a burden or doing harm. Strictness
in the matter of passports should be the exception, and leniency, the
rule. . . . We bear prejudice against no one. We are willing to modify, simplify, and clarify; we shall accept any logical solution . . . and, in summary,
our aim must be to populate Argentina with honest and working elements.
This is the greatest task of the present and we count on your collaboration to
achieve it.[14]

When the contents of this epistle became known, hope was planted in
many hearts that the severe regulations would be rescinded. "A new policy"—trumpeted the Jewish newspaper *Mundo Israelita,* which all along
had called for Argentina to throw open its gates. However, the attempt to
turn the tide and restore liberality was flatly rejected by the director of the
Immigration Department. "Our country needs workmen—manual laborers, people who want to take up the plow. . . . Those we do not need
are those who want to remain in the city, the petty intermediaries between
men, the small-time merchants," Ramos told a Jewish journalist upon returning to Argentina after several months in Europe. Prior to his return,
he had made similar statements to an Italian journalist. The conference in
Rome, at which Ramos had been a major speaker, seems to have increased
his steadfastness in this regard, in addition to heightening his prestige.
The demand of Benito Mussolini, who presented the opening address, and
the delegates of other lands of emigration, that they be allowed to super-
vise and protect their expatriates in their new homes, was certainly no
encouragement for a more liberal immigration policy in Argentina. On this
question, which was central on the agenda, Ramos had taken the stand on
behalf of the countries of immigration. The majority vote of the uninvolved
countries seems to have convinced him all the more of the necessity of restricting immigration. The impact of these debates on Minister Le Breton, who
was also in Rome, is unknown; the sources do not indicate whether the minister and his subordinate, Ramos, ever came into direct conflict as a result of
their differences. On the other hand, it is clear that the liberalization reflected
in the minister's letter never became Argentine policy.[15]

To circumvent the many cumbersome regulations, some immigrants tried to enter the country illegally. In November 1924, small groups of immigrants were stopped after they had crossed over from Uruguay. Lacking one of the numerous documents required for an Argentine visa, they had arrived in Montevideo and sought the assistance of smugglers who had transported them across the river to Argentina in small boats. When rumors of this strategy began to circulate in Europe, helped along by enterprising travel agents, Jewish immigration to Uruguay in 1924–1925 suddenly surged out of all proportion both to its previous dimensions and to the economic opportunities the tiny republic could offer. It was not long before the first accident occurred: One night in February 1925, a rickety boat left the small town of Salto, Uruguay, carrying thirteen Jewish immigrants from Russia and Romania, among them women and children. They were bound for Concordia, an Argentine town on the other side of the river, not far from the Jewish colonies in Entre Ríos. When they were halfway across the river, the boat sprung a leak and began to sink. In a panic, the immigrants jumped overboard and tried to swim ashore. In the morning, it was found that only three had survived. This episode, which was featured prominently in the newsletters circulated among emigrants in Europe in order to discourage illegal immigration, also made headlines in Argentina. The general papers called it a criminal act and a warning to potential lawbreakers; the Jewish papers saw in it dramatic proof of the serious consequences of Argentina's immigration policy.[16]

The regulations adopted by Ramos and his deputies, however strict, were not intended to halt immigration entirely. Even they realized that the future prosperity of Argentina was highly dependent on large-scale immigration. In his annual message to the people in 1925, the president called the decline in immigration a regrettable phenomenon that deserved to be fought against. Solid economic interests rested on a constant influx of workers, and, even now, the ideology behind Alberdi's motto "To govern means to populate" retained its influence.

Attitudes to Jewish Immigration

Demanding that potential immigrants to Argentina show valid passports and police statements from their home countries was pure mockery in the case of Jews who had fled for their very lives. On several occasions, the JCA appealed to the Argentine government to accept its character recommendations or those of another Jewish institution in place of the state documents that were impossible to obtain. During the last year of President Yrigoyen's first term, these efforts bore fruit. In an agreement reached on November 10, 1921, with immigration commissioner Remigio Lupo, Samuel Halfon, chief rabbi of the Congregación Israelita, was authorized to handle three aspects of Jewish immigration outside the confines of the existing regulations. First, the colonists and other Jews in Argentina would no longer personally have to make all the complex arrangements involved in bringing over their families. The recommendation and signature of Rabbi Halfon on their applications would free them from the need to appear before the authorities in Buenos Aires. Second, Halfon's voucher would be recognized as a substitute for the official documents of the immigrants' home country when such documents could not be procured. Third—and furthest from accepted practice—was Halfon's appointment as the personal guarantor not only of the Jewish elderly, women, and minors, who were the sole subjects of the *llamadas*—the procedures set for the immigration of relatives—but also of other blood relatives who were legally immigrants in their own right.[17]

Within a few months, on February 24, 1922, these special arrangements became even broader. Many Jews who had fled Russia for nearby countries, among them Romania, had czarist or Soviet passports. Holders of Red passports were ineligible for immigration because the Soviet government was not recognized by Argentina. Those with czarist, or White, passports were eligible if they could prove they had lived outside Russia for five years prior to submitting their application. There were many in this category and for those who had relatives in Argentina the immigration authorities were prepared to accept Halfon's word as a substitute for documents from Romania, Poland, or other countries. In effect, even those without White passports were admitted under this arrangement. When it was found that the Argentine consul in Romania was ignoring the new regulation, the immigration authorities took action to ensure that it would be honored.

While this solved the problem of the Russian refugees who had kin in Argentina, it only highlighted the plight of those who had no one. The rabbi brought this issue before the immigration commissioner, who finally agreed that Halfon could act in the capacity of a relative and submit immigration applications on their behalf. At his request, they would also be given visas. "Now, with all the concessions we have been granted, *the problem of free entry into Argentina on the part of our immigrants has been happily and definitively resolved. . . . The gateway to Argentina is now open to Jewish immigration, fully and without restriction*" (emphasis in the original), Halfon wrote to the JCA directors in Paris and, soon after, stated publicly. Only one thought troubled the rabbi: the heavy personal responsibility he would shoulder if seditious, criminal, or revolutionary elements penetrated Argentina in the wake of these arrangements. "Let us hope the heavens will protect us from being put to such a test, and we will be able fully to justify the extraordinary trust and faith that no other community has enjoyed in such measure and that we have been shown by the authorities of this country," he ended jubilantly.[18]

These concessions to the Jewish community were granted in close proximity to the presidential elections on April 8, 1922, won by Marcelo T. Alvear. Before his election, Alvear had been Argentina's ambassador to France, and his relations with key JCA figures in Paris—as well as with Rabbi Halfon and others in the Argentine Jewish community—were even closer than those of his predecessor, Yrigoyen. Thus, it seemed that the new regulations would remain unaffected by the change of government. By mid-1923, however, Halfon's reports had changed their tone. On June 3, 1923, he wrote that the Immigration Department, now headed by Ramos, had abolished privileges to Jewish immigrants. When Jewish immigration from Romania, which had been flowing freely since May, was halted suddenly on July 14, Halfon blamed the intervention of a rival Jewish organization in Buenos Aires; yet the growing unemployment among Jewish immigrants in the capital, also mentioned in Halfon's reports, was probably a factor of no less importance.[19]

In June 1923, the JCA wrote the minister of agriculture, Le Breton, asking him to reinstate the special arrangements for Jewish immigration. The letter described the JCA's work in colonization and education, and expressed the hope that more immigrants could be brought in to strengthen this project. In April 1924, the JCA appealed to Ramos himself. In a ploy to gain the support of this former member of the National Education Council, the JCA declared a fervent desire to see its beneficiaries assimilate and become part of the Argentine nation. It further requested power of attorney to represent those unable to obtain papers from their home country because of their refugee status and other objective reasons. In return, the JCA promised to screen candidates carefully and to send to Argentina only those who were "politically, morally, and physically sound." Moreover, it would consider only farmers, families suited to agriculture, and trained craftsmen. Persons without a trade and unemployed intellectuals would be excluded. In effect, the JCA accepted the strict selection process that had been assigned to the Argentine consuls and offered to assist the consuls in assessing Jewish candidates. The JCA promised to send those found qualified only to the rural areas and provinces. To demonstrate its sincerity, the JCA even proposed that the visas of these immigrants be stamped "visa to Argentina, exclusive of Buenos Aires." In this way, the immigrants would be "officially informed of the conditions of their admission and residence in Argentina." This, of course, was in line with the JCA's own desire to see the Jewish population distributed throughout the provinces, and an official document would lend validity to the JCA requirement that its beneficiaries seek their fortunes far from the port city.[20]

Juan Ramos met again with representatives of the JCA at the immigration conference in Rome. On his return to Argentina in July 1924, he brought with him an official request for a mutual agreement between the JCA and the government of Argentina. Ramos's decision, in the name of the Immigration Department, was issued several weeks later. The JCA would be permitted to arrange the immigration of Jews whose papers were incomplete on condition that they were either trained in a profession required in Argentina, farmers, or qualified to join the colonies, and were not headed for the capital. The JCA would submit a list of candidates specifying why documents were missing, and the Immigration Department would inform the consuls by telegram of the names of those to whom visas, good only for the provinces, should be issued. However, there were three provisos: The consul could refuse a visa to a JCA applicant found deficient in any way or considered "inconvenient for the country"; the Immigration Department could annul the agreement without prior notice if it were proved that JCA applications contained misleading information about the occupations of beneficiaries; and all travel expenses to destinations inside the country would be borne by the JCA. The first proviso left JCA immigrants open to the subjective judgments of the consuls; the second marred the mutuality of the agreement; and the third deprived the newcomers of the aid guaranteed them by the 1876 immigration law.

In spite of these provisos and their degrading tone, Louis Oungre urged the JCA council to sign the agreement. The situation in October 1924 was such that thousands of Jewish refugees were stranded in the ports of Europe, unable to proceed to the United States where new immigration laws had gone into effect. This agreement seemed to offer a glimmer of hope for at least some of these homeless Jews.[21]

Argentina's policy remained unchanged throughout Ramos's term of office. Only when Amadeo Grandi replaced him in April 1926 did a new atmosphere pervade the Immigration Department. Thanks to the agreement with the JCA, which was still in force, Argentina continued to be accessible to the Jews into the late 1920s. This was all the more noteworthy in light of the growing restraints on immigration in other countries. Even so, the extent to which the Jews took advantage of this accessibility depended largely on the information they received about life in Argentina and opportunities for financial assistance on arrival. Those with relatives in Argentina were in a better position, but, on the whole, the Jewish population was small and poverty-stricken. It was thus up to the Jewish organizations, global and local, to insure that Argentina's ability to take in Jewish immigrants in the decade following World War I was utilized to capacity.

The Organizational Challenge

The Central Committee for the Relief of the War Victims, which had raised funds in Argentina on behalf of the Jews of Europe from the earliest days of the war, continued to operate after the armistice. Its new goal was to aid the pogrom victims and rehabilitate Jewish life in Europe. Anticipating a wave of immigration, the committee set up a special immigrant relief division in 1919. However, immigration to Argentina did not assume significant proportions at that time, and the activity of the division gradually waned.

Following a JCA initiative, Rabbi Halfon organized a small group of Jewish activists under Congregación Israelita leader Max Glucksman, a cinema owner and film mogul in Buenos Aires. In March–April 1921, this group joined the representatives of other organizations to found the Commission for the Protection of Jewish Immigrants. Affiliated with the Central Committee, the commission was to receive a quarter of the funds raised by the committee while managing its own affairs and receiving additional funds from other organizations. The JCA, which voted to support the commission on January 16, 1921, was represented on its board and fully backed its activities. Local branches were organized in the provinces to help the commission in its efforts to draw immigrants away from the capital. Here, it seemed, was a united, publicly supported organizational network that could offer assistance to immigrants reaching Argentina. Indeed, one of the outstanding activities of this organization in 1921 was the absorption of one hundred orphans from the Ukraine. Despite this success, problems soon emerged.

Rabbi Halfon and his associates claimed that the Central Committee had not met its financial obligations yet was attempting to influence the nature of the commission's activities. No other public bodies had extended aid, and the commission's subordinate position kept important figures from joining. Rather than providing constructive assistance to the immigrant, it was forced to distribute handouts to the needy. On the other hand, as we have seen, Rabbi Halfon was successful in his personal contacts with the authorities. In the wake of the broad powers granted him in November 1921, a gap was created between the outside opportunities for action and the capacity for action and organization from within. Halfon and his associates were determined to change this situation once and for all. In May 1922, they decided to withdraw from the Central Committee and establish an independent organization known as Soprotimis (Sociedad de Protección a los Inmigrantes Israelitas).[22]

The breakaway of Soprotimis was not regarded favorably by the Jewish community. "At some point, the rivalry and competition [between the two organizations] assumed the form of a great social battle involving not only activists from the capital city but also the subcommittees in the provinces," wrote one of Argentine Jewry's leading journalists and teachers some time later. The establishment of Soprotimis did not, of course, halt the operations of the Commission for the Protection of Jewish Immigrants, and newcomers to Argentina thus enjoyed the "aid" of two organizations.[23]

The powers granted to Halfon by the previous immigration commissioner, Lupo, gave the new organization a tremendous advantage. Halfon's representatives could board ships in port and process the immigrants even before disembarkment. Their applications for visas and passes for those missing papers were also handled more quickly. The Central

Committee was anxious to secure some of these privileges for the officials of the commission. On April 4, 1923, the committee wrote to the new commissioner, Ramos, citing the popular support it enjoyed in Argentina and its close ties with Jewish immigration associations in the United States and Europe. The committee's request was modest: to be permitted to act on behalf of the Jews in Argentina, chiefly in the provinces, who sought to bring over their relatives. The committee was granted this permit, with certain restrictions, but, according to Rabbi Halfon, not before it had maligned the work of Soprotimis. While the truth is difficult to ascertain, Louis Oungre claimed that this was the main reason for Soprotimis's loss of its special privileges. When Oungre met with the immigration commissioner ten months later, one of the major topics discussed was putting a stop to the "intrigues of the commission in Buenos Aires." In this way, an internal dispute between the Jewish organizations became a bargaining chip in negotiations with the chief executive of Argentine immigration policy.[24]

Meanwhile, Soprotimis plunged ahead in two major spheres—smoothing the immigrants' passage into Argentina and helping them settle down. The organization's achievements during its first year were quite impressive. By one account, between May 1922 and July 1923 a total of 4,663 visas were obtained for relatives and other newcomers. A representative of the organization was allowed to board every ship reaching Buenos Aires port. When necessary, the administration of Soprotimis served as a go-between for the authorities to inform immigrants of their rights—the availability of accommodation at the immigrants hostel and free tickets to the provinces. The immigrants were invited to avail themselves of Soprotimis's services after disembarking. Soprotimis officials handled all cases in which Jewish immigrants were prevented from going ashore and, in many instances, as Halfon testified, the entry of sick or disabled passengers was arranged despite the clear-cut laws against this. Glucksman and his fellows were also helpful in straightening out consular misunderstandings, as, for example, when the consuls in Warsaw and Bucharest illegally collected a fee for issuing immigration permits, and when documents were withheld by the consul in Amsterdam.

All this came to an end in the second half of 1923. The license to board ships was revoked, and Soprotimis officials could approach immigrants only on the docks or after they had left the port. According to a senior Soprotimis official, the number of visas secured through Soprotimis's intervention from August 1923 until March 1924 dropped to 122. Nevertheless, contacts with low- and high-ranking officials in the Immigration Department continued to serve Soprotimis in good stead, even when the official policy changed.[25]

The absorption of newcomers was also eased through the "banking" services offered by the Jewish organizations. The JCA handled monetary transfers to relatives in Europe, and discount tickets were sold to Argentine Jews interested in bringing over their families. Soprotimis charged a fee for transferring money, which was one of its sources of income. It also arranged bulk ticket purchases to keep the price low and ran a loan fund that enabled purchasers to pay half the fare in installments. Shortly after its establishment, Soprotimis put up 10,000 pesos for this purpose and an equivalent sum was added by the JCA. In its first two years, Soprotimis provided several hundred Argentine Jews with such loans.

To help the immigrants settle down, an efficient network of committees was required to gather information on employment opportunities and handle absorption arrangements in the provinces. Under JCA pressure, twenty-two committees were established within two years. The Soprotimis office in Buenos Aires maintained contacts with individual activists in another twenty-four locations throughout the country, generally in the agricultural colonies and their immediate surroundings where, however, the JCA reigned supreme. Rival branches of the Central Committee were already operating in most other places. Thus, despite the goodwill and elaborate program drawn up by Soprotimis soon after its establishment, it never became an effective absorption mechanism on a national scale.

Another measure that might have increased Jewish immigration and absorption in Argentina was the creation of a special employment infrastructure for Jewish immigrants. Of all the plans envisaged, the only enterprise Soprotimis managed to set up, with the aid of the JCA, was a sewing workshop, which was actually a shelter to protect women from white slave traders. Although it started out as a constructive, profitable scheme in the second half of 1923, it ended in failure, employing a total of 118 girls and women over a span of three years.[26]

The loss of Soprotimis's special privileges increased its ill will toward the Central Committee and harmed its prestige as a public immigrant relief organization. When it no longer enjoyed an advantage over the private societies handling visas, ticket purchases, and monetary transfers, Soprotimis's activities lost much of their impetus. The situation improved the third year, thanks to the intervention of Jacob Latzky-Bertholdi, a key activist in the "popular" immigration organization in Europe, Emigdirekt, which opposed the JCA's hegemony in Jewish affairs. From the end of 1923 until mid-1924, Latzky-Bertholdi found himself working closely with the Central Committee in Argentina. Observing the unfortunate consequences of the rivalry between the two organizations, he pushed for rapprochement. With the cooperation of Isaac Starkmeth, JCA director in Buenos Aires, and Soprotimis president Glucksman, an agreement was reached on June 4, 1924, ending two years of discord. "From this day forth, the immigration division of the Central Committee merges with Soprotimis; consequently, the protection of Jewish immigrants in the Argentine Republic remains the exclusive concern of the latter," read the first clause of the document signed that day. Leading figures from the Central Committee now joined Soprotimis, and the local chapters of both organizations were expected to work together: Soprotimis would handle immigration, and the Central Committee, fund-raising for Europe. Resources would be divided between them, channeling 40 percent into immigration and 60 percent into overseas relief.[27]

This internal accord was reached just two months before the JCA completed its negotiations with Ramos, and at a time when all the Jewish organizations in Europe and the United States were desperate for a solution for the thousands of refugees, most of them Russian Jews, held up in Romania, Turkey, and the ports of Northern Europe following the draconian immigration measures introduced by the United States on July 1, 1924. Now that the two organizations were working together, there were high hopes that an answer, even if partial, had been found.

The refugees began to be processed in Europe by a joint committee of the JCA and its rival organization in Eastern and central Europe, Emigdirekt. A general census taken to determine the number of refugees found only 5,511—far fewer than anticipated. It soon became clear that many of them were steadfast in their desire to reach the United States and preferred to wait, even years, until they were admitted. Others, willing to go elsewhere, refused to consider Argentina, particularly in view of the requirement of settling in the provinces. On the Argentine side, immigration officers were so scrupulous that only ninety-five of the 158 refugees who submitted applications in the final months of 1925 were approved. This official duress led other Jewish emigrants who were less particular about their destination to cross into Argentine illegally. By the time the

United Evacuation Committee was dissolved in November 1926, the Jewish community in Argentina was richer by a mere 251 persons. Of the 1,272 refugees waiting for their arrangements to be finalized, only twenty-two were headed for Argentina, far fewer than the number of refugees helped to reach Brazil. Thus we see that at this crucial juncture in the history of organized Jewish immigration, Argentina failed to play the role that many had hoped it would.[28]

While the union of the two immigration organizations produced no radical change in immigrant absorption, Soprotimis's personal connections were helpful in securing visas for the relatives of Jews resident in Argentina. Of the 10,998 applications handled by Soprotimis from May 1922 until the end of 1927, 8,227 involved visas. Eight hundred twenty-eight cases were immigrants detained because they lacked certain papers, and only 129 of these applications—that is, slighter more than 1 percent—were rejected by the authorities. The actual number of Jews who reached Argentina as a result of this intervention is unknown, as some of the applications may have pertained to more than one immigrant; nevertheless, if we consider that 48,716 Jewish immigrants legally entered Argentina during this period, Soprotimis's contribution in reducing the obstacles seems quite substantial.

In contrast, the number of applications for assistance after entering the country was low. From 1922 to 1927, Soprotimis received only 7,816 such requests, representing 16 percent of the immigrants settling in Argentina. Of the 4,233 seeking employment, Soprotimis referred 3,191 to JCA colonies and 818 to Buenos Aires proper. The remainder—a mere 224—were sent to the provinces. Furthermore, the fund for ticket purchases disappeared from the scene, and the budget for constructive loans was drastically cut. The grand vision of a central organization in charge of promoting immigration and settling Jewish immigrants all over the country was therefore far from being achieved even after the rivalries had been settled. The oft-repeated excuse of the committee was the indifference and apathy of the Argentine Jewish community. Indeed, the number of contributors to Soprotimis by the end of 1926 was only 631, compared with 1,280 in its first year. Income from membership dues and donations came to only 2,376 pesos, whereas Argentine Jews had contributed 143,719 pesos to Keren Hayesod, the financial arm of the Zionist movement. Even a middle-sized charity such as the Jewish League Against Tuberculosis enjoyed a membership of thirty-seven hundred and an income in 1926 of 39,503 pesos.[29]

Soprotimis was not alone in the sphere of immigrant absorption, even after merging with its rival. Another organization with similar goals was the Jewish Workers Immigration Committee, founded on December 16, 1921, under the auspices of the Comité Obrero Cosmopólita de Inmigración. In the name of the workers unions, to which many Jews belonged, this committee urged immigrants not to accept aid from such bourgeois figures as Glucksman and to apply only to the workers committee when seeking employment. Cocina Popular was a philanthropic society, founded in 1921, that ran soup kitchens and other welfare services for the immigrants. There were also the landsmanschaften, notably those organized by the Polish, Galician, and Romanian Jews, that provided a cultural niche for people of the same hometown, in addition to advice and guidance. The Association of Polish Jewry also operated as an official address for character references, which were required in order to bring over relatives from Poland and to keep out the white slave traders, most of whom were Polish. We do not know how many immigrants bypassed Soprotimis and had their needs met by these other organizations; the number was probably small. In any case, they lacked the resources that would be needed to play an important role in the economic absorption of newcomers.[30]

Soprotimis's difficulty in gaining the support of the Jewish community in Argentina led it to turn to world organizations for help. As the policies of these organizations changed, Argentina was drawn again into the international Jewish public eye.

Immigration Broadly Conceived

As the work of the United Evacuation Committee drew to an end, the organizations involved discussed possibilities for continued cooperation. Talks throughout the second half of 1926 led to the formation of HICEM (HIAS-JCA-Emigdirekt) in February 1927. Its goals were world-embracing: to investigate new countries as targets for Jewish immigration; to render assistance to emigrants in their home countries and en route; and to help them settle down in their new countries. HICEM was to work with all the local committees and societies with which the founding organizations had been affiliated heretofore. After it began to operate officially in April 1927, HICEM approached Soprotimis to discuss financial matters. Following meetings with a Soprotimis delegation visiting Europe toward the end of the year, it was decided to hold a South American congress on Jewish immigration to revitalize the immigration movement. "At the moment, all our hopes turn toward South America, and especially Argentina and Brazil," declared Edouard Oungre, brother of Louis Oungre and director of HICEM on behalf of the JCA, at the HICEM meeting in Berlin in January 1928. To take full advantage of the opportunities still open to the Jewish immigrant in these two countries, HICEM leaders raced ahead with preparations for an immigration congress in Buenos Aires.[31]

"The Argentina Jewish community, whose role in Jewish life was almost nil until fifteen years ago, is now a focus of worldwide public interest," Soprotimis declared as the HICEM delegates arrived in Argentina. The practical goals of the congress were discussed in all the Jewish newspapers. In addition to the existing programs, these included the expansion of immigrant employment opportunities through vocational training networks, a South American Jewish bank to finance small cooperative or private industries, and more-ambitious enterprises such as a grain sack factory or an oil extraction plant for the linseed grown in the Jewish colonies. With HIAS now seriously hampered in its work by the new immigration laws in the United States, there were high hopes that more funding would reach Argentina.[32]

The congress opened on Sunday, May 27, 1928, in a festive ceremony attended by Louis Oungre, director general of the JCA, Miron Kreinin, president of Emigdirekt, Aron Benjamin, secretary of HIAS, and sixty delegates of the welfare societies and landsmanschaften in Buenos Aires and the provinces. Early in the discussions it was decided to end the isolation of Soprotimis and promote closer ties with the community. One of the resolutions at the close of the congress was the establishment of a forty-man council to run the organization. Twenty-seven members would be elected by Soprotimis, ten by its branches in the provinces, and three by the executive board. It was felt that this would involve broad sectors of the population in Soprotimis activity.

Of the numerous proposals raised at the congress on the subject of employment infrastructure, none was discussed further apart from those involving agricultural settlement, which were referred to the JCA. The budget, on the other hand, was debated more intensely. It was hoped that HICEM would recognize Argentina as a major target for Jewish immigration and bear most of the financial burden. In fact, the budget for the first year was set at 70,320 pesos (US $29,522), two-thirds of this borne by HICEM. Soprotimis planned to organize a major fund-raising campaign in July–August 1928 and increase its dues-paying membership to meet its share of the budget, which came to 25,000 pesos.[33]

Despite the emotional closing ceremonies, the immigration congress in Buenos Aires did not live up to expectations. No fundamental changes took place in Soprotimis's ideology or organizational structure, and, publicity notwithstanding, donations the following year reached only 11,287 pesos, compared with 100,000 pesos raised on behalf of Jewish colonization among the Jews of Soviet Russia. Neither was there a substantial increase in membership. Nevertheless, its daily operation improved. With funding from HICEM and local sources, Soprotimis reestablished a loan fund for ticket purchasers, allocated more money for settlement loans, increased the number of Spanish-language classes being offered, and intensified its search for new sources of immigrant employment in the capital and chief provinces. A year after the congress, 1,626 immigrants applied for services rendered by Soprotimis, compared with 962 to 1926.

Liaison with the authorities also improved. Soprotimis representatives boarded every ship reaching Buenos Aires, and 819 women arriving alone that year were protected from the white slave traders. One thousand nine hundred eighty-eight visas were secured, and Soprotimis was able to overturn dozens of earlier decisions barring entry to immigrants or denying them free transportation to the provinces. While there was no doubt that the immigration congress helped to strengthen Soprotimis, there was no change in the type of services it offered. Apart from financial aid to a handful of apprentices, no steps were taken to develop employment infrastructure. As a result, the JCA and the colonies remained the only hope for job-seekers.[34]

In Argentina, where industry was slack and economic policymakers never tired of promoting agriculture, the well-endowed JCA enjoyed considerable stature. Through its special agreement with Commissioner Ramos, the JCA could bring in as many settlers as it desired. In addition to its holdings of farming and grazing land, the JCA supervised the development of towns in the vicinity of the colonies and figured prominently in the colonies' agricultural cooperatives. With so much power, the JCA was in a position to act, either directly or indirectly, to increase employment opportunities for new immigrants, especially in the area of farm products and services.

By the end of World War I, JCA assets in Argentina were enormous. Its real income from the colonies was more than double its expenditures. In 1920, the JCA planned to lay out 618,033 pesos ($206,000), including settlement loans—which were an investment—while it expected to earn 1,921,382 pesos ($640,000). Even after deducting 934,259 pesos to account for possible delays in loan repayment, it foresaw a profit of 369,090 pesos ($123,000). This was almost as much as the Jews of Argentina had donated to relief efforts in Europe throughout the war. The colonization project continued to earn the JCA hundreds of thousands of pesos every year throughout the 1920s.[35]

The farms in the colonies remained much the same after World War I. Extensive grain crops and cattle raising were the staple, although dairy farming was also introduced and proved successful in certain cases. At the same time, the processing of settlement candidates became more rigorous. JCA pamphlets distributed in Europe stated that the colonization program would accept only families with at least two grown sons with farm skills and experience, in addition to the father. Settlers were required to pay their own fare and prove they could maintain themselves during the early days and contribute toward settlement costs. At first, the settler would be given an auxiliary farm of ten to twenty-five hectares (twenty-five to sixty-seven acres) for a training period of up to three years. After this, he would receive his full share of land. However, "if he did not demonstrate his ability to the satisfaction of the association, he would be removed from the colony," the pamphlet warned.

These rigid conditions frightened away large numbers of potential candidates whose family situation, financial assets, or agricultural experience did not fulfill JCA requirements. Those who applied nonetheless were closely scrutinized and the majority rejected. Of the 635 families interested in settling in Argentina or Brazil who contacted the JCA offices in Warsaw in 1926, the "agronomic service" found only 203 acceptable on all counts. This meticulousness was highly commended in the JCA's annual report. According to a 1928 report, the JCA helped a total of 820 families settle in Argentina over a period of eight years. Of these, 326 were the children of settlers and only 494 were immigrant families. No schemes for absorbing newcomers in industry or services were initiated by the JCA, and the thousands of immigrants who reached the towns around the colonies were left wholly to their own devices.[36]

Expanding the colonies became a major topic on the eve of the immigration congress. "Without agricultural colonization as a chief source of livelihood for the immigrants, the entire program and all the activities of the congress lack substance," declared *Di Idishe Tseitung*. Under public pressure, the issue was added to the congress's agenda despite objections from the JCA. Louis Oungre was not present at the debate, and it was boycotted by the other JCA delegates; but the general feeling that the goodwill of the JCA was a crucial factor was reflected in the resolutions. Citing the importance of farming in immigrant absorption, the congress called upon the JCA to step up its colonization efforts and build more housing in the colonies. Established settlers were asked to aid the immigrants and employ them on their farms, and city dwellers were urged to contribute to the settlement fund established by the Federation of Jewish Cooperatives in the colonies. The importance attached to the role of the JCA was demonstrated by the decision to present these resolutions to Louis Oungre through a special delegation.

Oungre's reply appeared in all the Jewish newspapers. To expand the colonization scheme, he claimed, the proper candidates were needed. It was impossible to find more of them in Argentina than had already been found, and the recruitment of colonists in Europe had not gone smoothly. Oungre blamed the slanderous reports in the Jewish press and the open fight against the JCA in Argentina for this state of affairs. Furthermore, he said, capital for settlement would be available only if the established settlers paid their debts on time. In this way, Oungre cast responsibility for the colonization project on the settlers and the Jewish community as a whole.[37]

After a lengthy visit to the colonies and talks with the settlers and administrators, Oungre came to realize that the JCA's entire program was in danger. Very few newcomers had settled in the colonies in the eight years prior to his visit, and a growing number of settlers were striking out on their own after paying their debts to the JCA. By early 1928, one-third of the JCA protégés in the colonies had freed themselves from their bonds to the association, and another 1,140 were expected to follow by 1935—that is, more than half of all the settlers. Out of concern for the future of the Jewish colonization enterprise, Oungre began to consider ways to promote immigration.

He found no fault with the JCA's settlement methods. In his view, the trial period on an auxiliary farm gave the directors time to assess the immigrant's worth. Furthermore, establishing a new farm cost the JCA only 1,200 pesos ($505) compared with 5,000–6,000 pesos ($2,105–$2,226) because the immigrant made up the difference from his own pocket. Thus it did not occur to Oungre to change the settlement procedures or branches of agriculture pursued at the time. He speculated that the activities of HICEM and the immigration congress in Buenos Aires would bring about a wave of spontaneous immigration from which the JCA could select settlers. In addition, the established settlers could be encouraged to bring over their relatives. In light of the concessions the JCA had obtained from the Soviet authorities with regard to emigration, this method seemed to Oungre particularly promising. Tickets could be purchased through the Soprotimis loan fund that had been reestablished after the congress. As a final resort, the JCA could return to the method it had abandoned in 1906: mobilizing "worthy candidates" in Europe.

These proposals, which appeared in Oungre's report to the JCA council on his return from Argentina, were designed to expand the colonization project by a hundred farms a year and "fill the vacuum left by the growing number of emancipating settlers." They were adopted by the council on October 27, 1928. In 1929, the JCA proceeded with its plans to select candidates, both immigrants and others, for one hundred new farms. This was the extent of the "surge of settlement" envisaged by the director and was certainly far from producing a turning point in the economic viability of Jewish immigration to Argentina.[38]

Immigration in Times of Crisis

On April 1, 1928, Argentina went to the polls to elect a new president and renew part of its Congress. Two factions of the Radical party were engaged in a bitter but democratic confrontation that led to the reelection of the seventy-six-year-old populist leader Hipólito Yrigoyen. No change took place in the country's immigration policies or Soprotimis's special relations with the authorities as the new government took office. However, the global economic crisis in the fall of 1929, triggered by the stock-market crash in the United States, drastically changed economic and political conditions in Argentina and, thereby, the possibilities for immigration.

The prices of agricultural produce on the world market dropped to an unprecedented low, while the prices of industrial goods soared. The country's income from grain and beef did not cover the purchase of imports. The price of wheat, which fell in 1930 from 106.6 to 58 pesos a ton, cut into farmers' profits and left them to starve. Coming after two years of prosperity, the sudden blow was also catastrophic for the urban population. The credit scare, the cutback in building, and the plight of the agricultural sector caused the closure of factories and an increase in unemployment.[39] This further compounded the political tension in Argentina set off by profound disappointment in Yrigoyen's government. Surrounded by his loyal aides and out of touch with reality, the elderly president never felt the revolutionary stirrings among his senior army officers. The coup on September 6, 1930, took him by surprise. For the first time since the signing of the Constitution seventy-seven years earlier, Argentina found itself under direct military rule. The brief period of genuine democracy was over. The closeness of xenophobic nationalist elements to the helm of state and the growing economic crisis swiftly took their toll on Argentina's immigration policies.

On December 16, 1930, the provisional government increased the fee for visas by 1,100 percent: Instead of 3 gold pesos (US $3), immigrants would now pay 33, which was a considerable sum for the impoverished families in question. This measure was clearly designed to add to the hardship and reduce the number of immigrants, and in effect it heralded a new stage in Argentine history—restricted immigration.[40] Yet, Jewish farmers immigrating under the auspices of the JCA were exempt.

Meanwhile, spontaneous Jewish immigration continued. Despite the economic crisis, or perhaps because of it, many more Jews reached Argentina in 1930 than in the preceding year of prosperity—7,805 compared with 5,986. During the first four months of 1931, 1,799 immigrants who had managed to secure their papers before the new measures went into effect rushed to Argentina. At the same time, the plight of many of those who had immigrated earlier worsened.

Within six months of the crisis, the chairman of Soprotimis reported great difficulty in providing aid to the new arrivals. In the second year of the crisis, the situation was even graver. In February 1931 it was rumored that the government was sending unemployed immigrants back to their home countries. Hundreds of people, many of them Jews, rushed to the immigrants hostel. When the rumor proved false, two hundred of the Jewish immigrants refused to vacate the premises, demanding that Soprotimis and other Jewish institutions finance their return to Europe. Soprotimis activists were summoned by the secretary of the Immigration Department and asked to remove the immigrants—lest the future of Jewish immigration be endangered. A solution was finally found by the Jewish institutions, but the scandal undermined the prestige of the Jewish community and damaged its relations with the Immigration Department.[41]

The unemployed were particularly vociferous in the capital. The directors of the Jewish organizations tried to avoid confrontation with the masses of job-seekers who besieged the offices of Soprotimis and other welfare societies. Some disappointed immigrants returned to Europe on their own, spending the last of their money on fares. It was around this time that groups of unemployed Jews began leaving for Birobidzhan in the Soviet Union where an autonomous Jewish region was planned. In February 1932, the *Mundo Israelita* bid farewell to sixty immigrants and expressed the hope that this controversial territory in the Far East would attract hundreds of unemployed laborers.[42]

The departures from Argentina did not deter the Jewish immigration organizations from aiding those still interested in bringing over their families. This work continued in conjunction with the consuls and immigration authorities in Buenos Aires, although a HICEM proposal to increase the number of immigrants met with opposition. After a particularly depressing visit to Entre Ríos, a Soprotimis council member urged that immigration be temporarily halted, and the JCA director in Buenos Aires, Starkmeth, agreed. The Soprotimis office in Rosario soon closed, and activities were cut back in other regions, also. Soprotimis's recommendation that small dairy and vegetable farms be set up by the JCA on the outskirts of the principal cities to provide the immigrants with some source of employment remained unheeded. On the other hand, the society's funding from HICEM was drastically reduced, leaving it dependent on local support that had not been forthcoming in the past.[43]

Under the circumstances, the introduction of new regulations curbing immigration produced little outcry. In November 1932, the consuls were told to issue visas only to those who could prove they had work in Argentina or whose relatives could pay for their upkeep. It was not the military regime that ordered these tighter controls but the government of General

Augustín P. Justo, whose election in January 1931, constitutional in the formal sense, had been boycotted by the Radical party and was not without blemish. Despite the regulations, Soprotimis activists were courteously received by the Immigration Department and reassured that Jewish immigration would not suffer. A Jewish daily in Argentina called the regulations "wholly superfluous" considering that "one way or another, immigration is no longer flowing to Argentina."[44]

In truth, with the economic problems plaguing the country and their disastrous results for the Jewish community, keeping out immigrants was more a domestic need than an externally imposed governmental decree.

Opportunity Exploited?

By the early 1920s, the shock and panic aroused by La Semana Trágica in January 1919 had given way to a sense of peace and tranquility. The concern that Jews would be systematically discriminated against soon dissipated. Despite occasional complaints about the hostility of certain consuls, particularly those in Poland and Romania, no consistent anti-Jewish policies were detectable.

During the eleven-year period between the resumption of immigration in 1920 and the peak of the economic crisis in 1930, 1,610,777 immigrants entered Argentina. This was 1 million fewer than, or only 60 percent of, the 2,650,471 arrivals in 1903–1913, which were record years for spontaneous immigration to Argentina. There was little change, however, in the rate of reemigration. Betwen 1920 and 1930, the number of departures amounted to 42.73 percent of arrivals. This was remarkably similar to the rate in 1892–1902 (42.60 percent) and in the record years 1903–1913 (41.97 percent). The fact that the ratio between arrivals and departures remained stable over periods of such social and economic diversity seems to warrant special attention. From our perspective, it demonstrates that in a general, quantitative sense, immigration was as great after the war as it had been before. In the absence of systematic discrimination against the Jews, the potential for large-scale immigration was thus very real.

During this eleven-year interval, 75,505 Jews officially entered Argentina. The figure for 1903–1913 was astonishingly similar—75,483. However, Jews made up 4.69 percent of the immigrants arriving after the war compared with 2.86 percent before the war, which means that the proportion of Jews in the incoming population had grown substantially. Jewish immigrants were also more inclined to remain in the country. Although there were Jews who left Argentina after the war, either returning to the old country or going to some other destination, the percentage was much smaller than for other immigrants. While figures for this period are lacking, the re-emigration rate was probably no more than in 1907–1914, that is, approximately 19 percent. Thus, less than half as many Jews were leaving Argentina as other nationalities, and Jews accounted for 6.6 percent of the remaining immigrant population.[45]

This ratio of arrivals to departures enriched the Jewish community by sixty-one thousand persons, representing a population increase of over 50 percent. The number of Jews entering Argentina was also significant from a global Jewish standpoint. Of the 674,527 Jewish emigrés who settled in various countries between 1920 and 1930, according to HICEM, 11.2 percent (75,505) found a haven in Argentina. More Jews reached the shores of Buenos Aires than went to Canada and Brazil combined, and the flow was only a third less than that to Palestine. After the United States, which absorbed more immigrants during this decade than all other countries put together, Argentina ranked second. Thus it appears that in the ten years after World War I, the Jews took relatively good advantage of the opportunity afforded them by Argentina's immigration laws and general receptivity to newcomers.[46]

Of course, all these figures relate to implemented immigration; they do not tell us about the potential for emigration among the Jewish masses in Eastern Europe and the Near East. While they are important from a local Jewish standpoint and for the insight they provide about Jewish immigration in general, they do not indicate whether the opportunities offered by Argentina were fully exploited in the postwar period.

As large-scale immigration resumed after the war, unemployment posed a serious problem for the urban working class. Despite the improvement in housing conditions, many workers still inhabited the conventillos where a seething ethnic mass lived in unspeakable filth. For the lower classes and poor immigrants, Buenos Aires, the El Dorado of Argentina, was a living hell where a daily battle was fought against starvation and moral decline.[47]

It did not take long for such news to reach the potential Jewish migrants in Europe. The newsletter published by the central office of the Hilfsverein der Deutschen Juden in Berlin warned its readers that Argen-

The Greenhorn in Confusion. The Jewish Workers Immigration Committee warned newcomers in 1922: "Don't hurry to come. There is a crisis going on here. Employers want to exploit you!"

tina was experiencing a severe economic crisis (in April 1924), the outcome of which was unemployment. There were no jobs in the cities, and in the villages most of the work was seasonal and revolved around the grain harvest. The same message was conveyed in even stronger terms by a federal German institution in the spring of 1927: "Even skilled professionals should take with them 500 pesos to tide them over until they find work; unskilled workers, trade clerks, technicians, and engineers who are not promised work in advance have no prospects except to starve in the streets [and] the living standards of agricultural workers are extremely low." Free professionals were cautioned that the government protection extended to graduates of the local university rendered the diplomas of immigrants virtually useless. Immigration activist Latzky-Bertholdi returned from Argentina in 1925 with the disheartening report that Buenos Aires, unlike the provinces, was closed to the Jews. In his view, "this city should be dropped from the list of immigration targets except for uniting of families."[48]

For the many Jews in Eastern Europe and the Near East contemplating emigration, the image projected by Argentina was an important consideration. Aside from the letters received from family and friends, this image was also shaped by incidents such as the bitter feud between the colonists and the JCA, which, according to JCA director Oungre, deterred some of the best candidates, and by tales of the influence and exploits of the white slave traders who supposedly governed the "route to Buenos Aires." There were practical considerations as well, such as travel costs, which had gone up hundreds of percentage points between 1923 and 1929, and the prospects of improving financial and political standing in the countries of origin. A Jew planning to leave his home country had to weigh all these issues and come to a decision on his own. The world Jewish organizations offered some support, but only after a personal decision had been made. "Under no circumstances must we take upon ourselves the initiative of expatriation," declared Edouard Oungre, the director of HICEM, at the international conference in Berlin in January 1928. "If we push for emigration, if we provoke it, we shall bear a very grave responsibility that we have no right to assume. Emigration cannot be healthy unless it is spontaneous," he continued. None of his colleagues at this forum or at the immigration congress in Buenos Aires disputed him.[49]

The constructive rehabilitation projects of the American Joint Distribution Committee (better known as "the Joint") and JCA in Europe were designed to counter the need and desire for emigration. The vocational training centers, occupational cooperatives, loan funds, and commercial banks established with the support of these organizations helped tens of thousands of Jews fight for survival in their home countries. No such projects were undertaken in Argentina. As we have seen, the Jews did not pursue any economic activity outside the colonization scheme and ran its operations independently of emigration needs. No vocational and agricultural training centers were opened, and none of the proposals for developing farm industries or fresh produce and dairy farms in suburban areas were seriously discussed. JCA contributions to Soprotimis, although slated for constructive aid, sufficed only for simple charity. As a result, the economic absorption of Jewish immigrants in Argentina depended upon general trends in the Argentine economy or the spontaneous initiative of individual Jews.[50]

The years between World War I and the economic crisis were crucial for the growth and sense of belonging of Argentine Jewry. The older Jewish institutions in the capital—the Congregación Israelita, the Ashkenazic burial society, and Ezrah—increased their property holdings and building activity. New welfare organizations and landsmanschaften were established. Jewish newspapers appeared in Yiddish and Spanish, numerous books were published on subjects of Jewish interest, and Jewish theatrical groups, both local and foreign, performed to full halls. Among the important cultural clubs founded at this time was the Sociedad Hebraica Argentina, a society of young Jewish intellectuals. This Jewish awakening was not limited to Buenos Aires; a similar phenomenon was evident in Rosario, Córdoba, and other cities.

Amid such a surge of cultural growth, the indifference of the Jewish community toward immigration is all the more striking. Among the Ashkenazim, some of this indifference may have been ideological. While the Zionists focused all their energies on the establishment of a Jewish national home in Palestine, the radical proletarians were promoting Jewish autonomy in Birobidzhan. The newly emerging Sephardic community, composed of Ladino-speaking Turkish Jews and Arabic-speaking Syrian Jews, was even less involved in this sphere. A population census carried out in 1960 shows that nearly half of Argentina's Turkish and Syrian Jews immigrated between 1920 and 1929. The same holds true for over a quarter of the Jews from Italy, the Balkans, and North Africa. If we add immigrants from Aleppo, Damascus, Izmir, Rhodes, and other places, who were no longer alive or resident in Argentina at the time of the census, we see that emigration from these cities was crucial in the consolidation of the Sephardic community. However, immigrants from these regions did not join Soprotimis, and no more than a hundred applied to it for assistance. The Jewish community protocols do not even mention these immigrants, who numbered in the thousands. Here we seem to have a clear case of private and familial absorption, with a large body of immigrants finding a niche in Argentine society unaided by organized Jewish welfare.[51]

Throughout the 1920s, Argentina offered greater opportunities for Jewish immigration than the Jews cared to exploit. At the time, there was no evidence of an explicit discriminatory policy against the Jews. Some intellectuals may have expressed negative feelings toward certain groups of immigrants with whom the Jews could be identified, but none of the immigration commissioners translated these into laws that would keep the Jews out. Outwardly, the well-known nationalist Ramos may have voiced some prejudice, yet he reached an agreement with JCA director Oungre that also implied special recognition of Jewish immigration and its admissibility. Ramos's predecessors exhibited even greater tolerance toward the Jews, as did Le Breton, President Alvear's minister of agriculture, who initially represented the older school of Argentine liberalism and wanted to keep the Republic open to all immigrants, regardless of origin. The legitimacy of Jewish immigration and the presence of Jews in Argentina depended upon such attitudes. As the economic crisis deepened, however, government thinking veered in the other direction and tighter controls were placed on immigration.

The new immigration laws promulgated on November 26, 1932, and implemented on January 1, 1933, coincided with the rise of Germany's new prime minister, Adolf Hitler, who came to power on January 30. As the Nazi era began, Argentina, beset by economic and social problems, proceeded to shut its doors.

5

The Closing Gates,
1933–1945

During the Nazi era, the gap between the emigration needs of the Jews and Argentina's need and desire for immigrants became deep and wide. The economic problems and growing wave of Catholic-Hispanic nationalism in Argentina created a clear opposition to immigration, whereas the Jews were more desperate for a home than ever before. Because Argentina was far from Europe and had vital economic interests in both Great Britain and Germany, it could choose to remain neutral in the evolving European conflict. For the Jews, against whom war was declared from the moment the Nazis rose to power, there was no choice. Emigration from Europe, as we see in retrospect, truly meant survival for them, and the nations who opened their doors became their rescuers.

How great was the demand for Jewish immigration to the Argentine Republic during the Holocaust era? Did Argentina have the potential to take in Jewish refugees or otherwise contribute to the rescue of the Jews? Were the people of Argentina willing to use this potential? Was there any pressure exerted on Argentina to take part in immigration and rescue operations, and how extensive were they in the final tally?

A Time of Panic

A year before the Nazis came to power, many Jewish leaders were openly apprehensive about the serious decline in the security of the German Jewish community. Yet when the cloud burst, everyone seemed taken by surprise. World Jewry was horror-stricken when the Jews of Germany were ferociously attacked at the end of March 1933, and when a boycott was imposed on German Jewish enterprises on April 1. As acts of violence multiplied, it was clear that Germany's 500,000 Jews were in a precarious position indeed.[1]

On March 29, 1933, the directors of Soprotimis convened urgently to discuss a telegram received from HICEM that day: "Seek approval, together with the JCA, for the admission of Jewish refugees from Germany. . . . Provide assurances that they will not become a public burden. Emphasize that they are an outstanding element and a genuine contribution to the economic, intellectual, and moral development of the host country." From the hasty, emphatic tone of the telegram, the directors realized how serious the situation must be. Just two days previously, on receiving word of Germany's first all-embracing, government-sponsored anti-Semitic attack, the Jews of Argentina had held a mass protest in Buenos Aires. Although it had no idea how many refugees would come or whether HICEM would provide funding, Soprotimis now applied without delay for a special dispensation to allow German Jews into Argentina. This request was submitted to the minister of agriculture and the head of the Immigration Department at a time when the streets of Buenos Aires were swarming with starving, unemployed Jews for whom no solution had been found by Argentine employers or the Jewish organizations.[2]

Soprotimis's appeal reached the authorities three months after the new immigration laws approved on November 26, 1932, had gone into effect. Immigration commissioner Guillermo Salazar Altamira and his subordinates were in the midst of preparing an annual report for the Congress in which they expressed their enthusiastic support of the new regulations. Nothing could have been further from their interest than accepting another tide of refugees from Germany; Soprotimis's request was flatly rejected. The immigrants in question had no relatives in Argentina, they had not been hired in advance by Argentine employers, and they were not farmers. Moreover, the term *refugees*, used in the application to emphasize the special nature of the request, was not even recognized in the Argentine immigration laws.[3]

In a meeting with Soprotimis activists, the deputy minister of agriculture implied that potential farmers would not be turned away. Max Glucksman thus proposed the development of a new agricultural zone in the vicinity of Buenos Aires that, unlike the JCA colonies with their extensive grain crops and cattle raising, would concentrate on intensive vegetable and dairy farming. This proposal was supported by all the Soprotimis directors and passed on to the JCA office in Paris, but the JCA claimed that land in the area was too expensive and that it already owned enough real estate in other parts of Argentina. JCA director Louis Oungre suggested instead that fifty German Jewish families settle in the existing colonies, following routine procedures. JCA directors Isaac Starkmeth and Simón Weill, who were also on the board of Soprotimis, opposed the idea because of the ongoing financial crisis plaguing the agricultural sector. Legal, organized immigration to Argentina was thus virtually closed to the Jews of Germany during the months of panic after Hitler's rise to power.[4]

When it was found that the refugees could not be brought to Argentina in a straightforward manner, other means were considered. At the end of June 1933, the JCA directors in Buenos Aires reported the offer of a senior immigration official who was prepared to secure a permit for one hundred families if the JCA nominally declared that they would be settled on JCA land. The "charge" for this service was 10,000 pesos. The JCA directorate in Paris was not prepared for such responsibility and turned the offer down. Even when the number of families was raised to 120 and the fee reduced to 6,000 pesos, the JCA would not reconsider. After further bargaining with the Buenos Aires directors, the official agreed to admit two hundred families for the same fee. It was still necessary to declare the newcomers colonists, as required by law, but it was promised that the authorities would look the other way. On September 16, 1933, the JCA council met to discuss the benefits and risks of this proposal. On the negative side, it involved bribes, which would damage the JCA's standing in Argentina if discovered. Other concerns were that personnel changes in the Immigration Department might keep the plan from being carried out, that the refugees might not find jobs in Argentina, and, finally, that it would be difficult to find two hundred families who would meet such conditions. The council was somewhat hesitant in its decision, but the president of the JCA and the Paris administration were authorized to pursue the plan "within the strict limits of the law."[5]

Meanwhile, the persecution of the Jews in Germany led to the formation of a new immigrant welfare organization in Argentina. A group of German Jewish immigrants, who had found a niche for themselves in Buenos Aires's non-Jewish "German Colony," were now turned out and ostracized by that community. On April 26, 1933, seven members of the community founded the Welfare Society for German-speaking Jews (Hilfsverein Deutschsprechender Juden) under the leadership of Adolfo Hirsch. The new organization swiftly took over the care of needy German Jews who could no longer receive aid from non-Jewish German institutions that had succumbed to Nazi propaganda. It was not long before other immigrants were knocking at its door. After investigating the possibility of working with or joining Soprotimis, the society struck out on its own. By the end of its first year, it boasted 175 dues-paying members and over 32,000 pesos in donations, far more than Soprotimis had mobilized that year. The goals of the new society were similar to those of the older organization—finding the immigrants employment and providing maintenance loans until they could fend for themselves. In the early years, an effort was made to attend personally to the needs of each applicant until he was settled and financially stable.[6]

In the wake of the Nazi attack on the Jews of Germany, and indirectly on the entire Jewish people, the Jews of Argentina founded two committees to fight for the political rights of the Jews and wage an information campaign on their behalf. The Committee Against the Persecution of Jews in Germany, which became the Committee Against Anti-Semitism and Racism in December 1934, was made up of delegates from the major Jewish organizations in Argentina and supported by the JCA. The People's Organization Against Anti-Semitism was founded and run by the Jewish Communists. Argentine Jewry also sponsored an emergency campaign to raise funds for the German Jewish refugees. Most of the money was channeled into Zionist operations for the resettlement of refugees in Palestine.

However much anti-Semitic events in Germany roused the Jewish community in Argentina into action—and the organizations set up to handle refugees demonstrated much goodwill—mass immigration from Germany did not materialize. The Immigration Department's figures show that a total of 1,883 Germans reached Argentina in 1933, the majority of them apparently non-Jews. Only 140 German Jewish refugees registered with the Hilfsverein Deutschsprechender Juden, and 820 with Soprotimis. Of the 2,062 Jewish immigrants reaching Argentina that year, the percentage of Germans was very small.[7]

A Lull in the Storm

In the course of 1933, it became apparent that Argentina was less important as a haven than anticipated. Of the thirty-seven thousand Jews who fled Germany that year, only *one-fifth* set sail for countries across the ocean. Moreover, after recovering from their initial shock, the Jewish leadership in Germany was almost totally opposed to emigration. The hardwon political rights attained by the Jews in the nineteenth century seemed to retain a glimmer of hope, and exodus from Germany, which was right in step with the plans of the Nazis, was perceived as deserting the battlefield.

In late October 1933, all the major international Jewish organizations, including the Jewish Agency in Palestine, declared their opposition to the emigration of the German Jewish community. This influenced the work of the Palestine Office, the Hilfsverein der Deutschen Juden in Berlin, and HICEM: Rather than promoting a swift, massive exodus, they dispensed carefully regulated aid to Jews leaving Germany at their own initiative.

During the second half of 1933, Nazi hostility toward the Jews seemed to lose some of its edge and the targets became more selective. The Jews of Germany somehow learned to live with the enmity around them, although the media spewed forth an unending stream of venom and embittered their existence. Emigration from Germany slowed: In 1934, twenty-three thousand Jews left the country; the following year, only twenty-one thousand. Even after the promulgation of the Nuremberg Laws on September 15, 1935, which abolished the emancipation of the Jews and "sanctified the purity" of the German race, there was no dramatic rise in departures. Twenty-five thousand Jews left in 1936, and in 1937, a year before the Nazis annexed neighboring countries, the number dropped to twenty-three thousand.[8]

As the refugees soon found out, leaving Germany did not always solve their problem. During the years of relative calm, between one-third and one-fourth of the emigrants headed for countries just beyond Germany's borders. The majority were denied permission to settle permanently. In view of the restrictions imposed on employment and length of stay, many resumed their search for a new home, and others waited anxiously to be included in the immigration quotas of established countries of refuge such as the United States. In 1936, when immigration to Palestine suffered a serious setback because of the Arab uprisings and Britain's bias in their favor, there emerged a growing need for new countries willing to accept immigrants. Argentina might have stepped forward; instead, its admission requirements became all the more stringent.

On January 19, 1934, a new ordinance was passed to seal the loopholes in the existing regulations. Until then, passengers in transit, brides joining their husbands, and farmers were among the second- and third-class passengers who were entitled to a reduction in immigration duties. Now they were required to deposit the money until it was firmly established that they met the conditions of the Argentine immigration authorities. While the papers required remained the same—proof of honesty, solvency, and good health—greater importance would be attached to the police certification "of good political and judicial conduct, which should specify that the applicant had no convictions for criminal offenses or disruption of the social order over the last five years." If the emigrant had spent five years in his last place of residence, it was necessary to present papers from that country, also. In rare cases, the consuls could waive the need for such documentation if they personally accepted responsibility and provided detailed grounds for their decision. Nevertheless, the immigration commissioner could veto this decision even after the emigrant had reached Buenos Aires. The new ordinance bore the signatures of the president, the minister of agriculture, and the minister of foreign affairs; and, as we see from the commissioner's report to Congress, it was applied very firmly.[9]

This state of affairs greatly hampered the mission of James G. McDonald, the League of Nations high commissioner for refugees (Jewish and other) coming from Germany. McDonald visited Argentina in May 1935 in an effort to find a permanent home in Latin America for the thirty thousand refugees sheltered by Germany's neighbors. Soon after his arrival, he realized there was no point in pressing for changes or deviations in the law. Nationalist spirit was running high, and, as he learned from his associates, the nationalists fiercely opposed immigration. As a result, McDonald's requests were extremely modest: "It is my hope that the Argentinian authorities will, under these circumstances, see fit to permit the admission of approximately fifty (50) families, or not more than two hundred fifty (250) individuals a month during the period of one or two years." These immigrants, he promised, would be furnished with enough money to help them settle productively in the country without becoming a financial burden. They would include no Communists or persons with radical political beliefs. Despite these assurances and the small refugee population in question—only three thousand persons a year and a maximum of six thousand over two years—McDonald went home after three weeks of effort with only vague promises in his pocket.

Actually, McDonald had come away with a positive feeling from his talks with Commissioner Salazar Altamira, who had willingly pointed out instances wherein the regulations could be bent to accommodate refugees. However, these views of Salazar (who is favorably mentioned in the reports of Jewish immigration activists) were unacceptable to Domingo Brebbia, the deputy minister of agriculture, and even less so to the minister, Luís P. Duhau. Minister Duhau, a prosperous cattle-breeder and prominent member of the Argentine oligarchy, was against increasing immigration or easing the restrictions to admit the refugees. According to Brebbia, Argentina was thus demonstrating its "independence" and national sovereignty. "It was not, however, until I explained the possibility of there being a larger number of Catholics among the refugees as the result of the anti-Catholic activities of Nazi leaders, that Dr. Brebbia showed real concern," McDonald reported. The fact that Cardinal Pacelli, the secretary of the Vatican and later Pope Pius XI, as well as the archbishop of Buenos Aires, regarded McDonald's mission in a positive light further softened the minister of agriculture. "Now you are touching me at a weak point," McDonald quoted the minister. "We Argentinians are always sensitive to any appeal on humanitarian grounds."[10]

In spite of these pronouncements, the high commissioner left Buenos Aires with little more than a "gentleman's agreement," as he called it. The main reason was the vociferously anti-Semitic propaganda being disseminated in Argentina, and a chief culprit was the unofficial but highly influential organ of the Catholic church, *Criterio,* edited by Gustavo Franceschi. While McDonald was in Buenos Aires, Franceschi called upon Congress "to reform the immigration laws and sacrifice . . . liberalism on the altar of necessity to keep the Republic from losing its distinctiveness." In his talks with the archbishop, McDonald had been assured of the Jews' right to settle in Argentina. This, however, was not the view expressed in *Criterio,* which clearly enjoyed church backing. "I do not support neo-German racism or Nazi theories in any form," Father Franceschi declared at the close of his article. This did not stop him from denouncing Jewish immigration in blatantly anti-Semitic terms throughout 1935 and in years to come. Three other nationalist publications in Buenos Aires that were influential in senior government circles, despite their limited circulation, were even more prejudiced against the Jews than was Father Franceschi. Confidants of McDonald claimed they were powerful enough to thwart any visible government concessions to the refugees, most of whom were Jews. Indeed, McDonald's efforts to reach an understanding with the Argentine authorities produced no tangible results.[11]

Under the existing laws, Jews could still enter Argentina if they had relatives to vouch for them. The authorities regarded unification of families as the healthiest type of immigration because it encouraged the immigrants to develop roots and kept much of the currency sent every year to kin in Europe from leaving the country. Although it became increasingly difficult to gain admission to Argentina, the llamadas regulations remained intact, allowing a considerable number of Jews from Eastern Europe and the Near East to join their relatives. For the Jews of Germany, this opportunity was all but nonexistent as very few of them had close kin in Argentina during the period of relative tranquillity between 1934 and 1937. One immigration option that continued to be open to them was farm settlement.

In April 1934, a senior JCA official, Georges Aronstein, was sent to Argentina for a year to study all aspects of the colonization effort. In February 1935, Louis Oungre joined him to investigate the possibility of renewing JCA settlement after a hiatus of several years. As they toured the country, they realized how little the association had contributed to the absorption of German Jews: In 1934, the colonies had taken in no more than six families and fourteen bachelors.

To the immigration activists, settling the refugees from Germany in the existing colonies following standard JCA procedures seemed a nearly impossible task. The high living standards and urban life to which the German Jews were accustomed contrasted starkly with the physical labor and relative isolation of life on large and distant farms. The problem could be surmounted only if the entire orientation of the colonization project were changed. Once again, the idea of suburban produce and dairy farms was raised. Oungre asked the JCA to weigh the proposal, although a farm of this type would require a minimum outlay of 10,000–15,000 pesos, compared with 1,500 pesos per homestead allotted by the JCA under the existing system. Another proposal was to introduce more-intensive cultivation on existing colonies and provide them with larger budgets. Aronstein recommended that a minimum of one hundred new homesteads be added each year, that the budget be doubled, and that the settlers be encouraged to plant a variety of field crops. In Aronstein's opinion, these changes were necessary not only for the sake of the German refugees but to insure the future of the colonization project.[12]

Oungre's recommendations were on a more modest scale: the establishment of a colony on JCA land in the north of Entre Ríos. It would start out with twenty families, but with a larger budget than usual. In early May 1935, this proposal was approved by the JCA council, and a scout was sent to Germany to sign up families. The requirements were agricultural experience and sufficient working hands to keep the farm going. So few families with the proper qualifications and a desire to move to Argentina under these conditions were found that the search was extended even to Austria and Czechoslovakia. It took five months—and the appearance of the Nuremberg Laws—to complete the arrangements. Spurred on by the frightening events in Germany, the council also approved a plan to bring fifty young Jews to Argentina. They would be settled in the colonies in groups of five and directly supervised by the colonial administrator. This was apparently as far as the JCA was prepared to deviate from its routine immigration procedures.[13]

At the beginning of January 1936, the first group of forty-six settlers arrived from Germany and was taken to the newly founded colony of Avigdor. By the end of 1937, the number of German families in the colonies had reached ninety-nine. That year, the JCA secured four hundred visas to allow the entry of 1,267 persons. As required by the Immigration Department, it pledged that all the newcomers would be settled in the colonies. The payment for their visas was deposited with the Argentine consul in the country of departure, and the authorities were officially informed after they had been settled on their farms. If a colonist decided to leave, the JCA administration in Buenos Aires informed the authorities in order to withdraw from further responsibility for his actions or place of residence. Breaking his commitment to be a farmer for life did not make the colonist a criminal; however, he was not much better off than the numerous immigrants who entered Argentina illegally.[14]

In 1936, another attempt to bring over Jewish youth from Germany was made by the Hilfsverein Deutschsprechender Juden and Hirsch. Taking advantage of the immigration laws favoring farmers, fifty-five hectares of fertile land were purchased on the island of Choele Choel in the riverbed of the Río Negro in southern Argentina, and an agricultural training farm was set up to educate the young people in growing deciduous fruit trees, afforestation, and dairy farming. It was planned that after they became farmers in their own right, they would be joined by their families. However, the training farm on the island was able to absorb just over a hundred youngsters before the war broke out.[15]

Those ineligible to enter Argentina under a family unification or farming scheme could also try their luck with one of the various illegal methods. In 1934–1936, for example, when Paraguay was prepared to issue visas to Jewish immigrants, travelers took advantage of their transit visas to remain in Argentina. They were required to pay the full price for an Argentine visa at the consulate in Europe but were eligible for a refund when they arrived in Asunción. Instead of going on to the Paraguayan capital, many Jewish immigrants disembarked in Buenos Aires and disappeared into the crowds. Others spent a few days in Paraguay and crossed the border into Argentina after receiving their refund. A tactic common among those who lacked relatives or a full set of papers was to apply for a tourist visa. Despite the restrictions on immigration, the Republic still welcomed tourism. Immigrants could pretend they were tourists and travel first class, although the price had almost doubled since September 1934 and was often beyond their means. The oldest tactic—crossing the Río Uruguay—was the least common during this period, although some probably tried this, too.

Immigrants who reached Argentina without papers were in a precarious position. As illegal aliens, it was difficult to find work and they were forced to accept charity. This issue was discussed by Soprotimis on July 18, 1935. Despite the risks involved, the society decided to assist these immigrants if they agreed to settle far from the capital, particularly in the north. Over the coming months, considerable effort was invested in establishing absorption and welfare committees in Formosa and other towns along the Río Paraná in order to assist illegal immigrants.[16]

A group of settlers from Germany on arrival in Entre Ríos, 1936

This work proceeded between 1934 and 1937 with little support from the Argentine Jewish community. Apart from the German Jews, who were preoccupied with their own welfare society and relatives, the plight of the refugees was far from the public mind. As the local Jewish leadership focused its attention on the anti-Semitic outbursts and sporadic acts of violence against the Jewish community, the Committee Against Anti-Semitism and Racism gained strength. In July 1935, it became the DAIA (Delegación de Asociaciones Israelitas Argentinas), an umbrella organization for all the important Jewish bodies in Argentina apart from the Communists. On the whole, colonization in Palestine sparked greater interest than did the physical and spiritual welfare of the refugees in Argentina. Work on behalf of the refugees was barely mentioned in the daily Jewish press, and there was no public outcry to open the doors of the Republic to those in need, not even on the part of those involved in the struggle against Nazi and Fascist influence in Argentina. This apathy was possible because immigration to Argentina was perceived to be marginal even among the immigration activists in Europe. The Hilfsverein der Deutschen Juden newsletter published in Berlin in 1934–1937 never promoted Argentina as a target for large-scale immigration. On the contrary, it described a harsh climate, poor wages, unemployment, and loneliness in the predominantly male community. Even at the end of 1937, Argentina was not regarded by the Jewish institutions in Europe as a serious answer to the problems of German Jewry. There was no mention at all of immigration to Argentina or Latin America at the convention of Jewish community leaders held in Vienna on November 15 to coordinate relief activities in the countries bordering the German Reich. At a meeting later that month in Paris to discuss interorganizational cooperation among the Hilfsverein in Berlin, the Reichsvertretung (National Committee of German Jews), HICEM, the Joint, and other bodies, the delegates still spoke of the need to study and investigate the possibilities for immigration to Argentina. Meanwhile, Argentina's immigration laws were growing increasingly ironhanded.[17]

In July 1936, the Spanish Civil War erupted. Soon after, it was rumored that immigration to Argentina would be further restricted to prevent Communists from entering the country. The rumors proved true; October 17, 1936, marked a new chapter in Argentine immigration history. The laws promulgated that day were designed to bar entry to elements "liable to pose a danger to the physical or moral health of our population, or conspire against the stability of the institutions created by the national Constitution." From now on, visas would be issued only to those who could present additional papers from their country of origin, such as a set of fingerprints stamped by the local police. "These regulations are pretty monstrous," a clerk of the British Foreign Office remarked on hearing of the new regulations. Even the protests of the British ambassador in Buenos Aires, who demanded an exemption for British subjects, failed to produce any change in the law. Yet it was obvious that it was not "Nordic" immigrants such as those from the British Isles whom the authorities wished to keep out. This is demonstrated by the three international agreements signed by the Argentine government in the course of 1937.[18]

A Dutch delegation visiting Argentina in April 1937 to discuss commercial ties was persuaded to sign an immigration pact at the urging of Argentina's foreign minister, Carlos Saavedra Lamas. Saavedra Lamas had received the Nobel Peace Prize in 1936 and was well known as a legislator and statesman in international circles. In the pact, Argentina declared its fervent desire to absorb newcomers from the Netherlands and promised to set up a joint committee in Buenos Aires to establish guidelines for all immigration and settlement activity. In July, a similar pact was signed with the government of Switzerland, and, on September 21, with the government of Denmark. In interviews with the press, Saavedra Lamas did not conceal his satisfaction at having reached agreements with the "Nordic countries of Europe whose immigration I consider especially appropriate at a time of universal unrest." These agreements, however, proved ineffective in increasing the immigrant population. Four hundred forty more Danes left the country in the 1930s than stayed on; only 406 Dutchmen settled down permanently; and the number of Swiss immigrants—2,124—was 750 fewer than in the previous decade.[19]

Argentina's interest in settlers from these Protestant countries seemed to indicate receptivity toward non-Catholic immigration. Nevertheless, there was a concealed but very real bias against Jewish immigration. Aside from the regulations approved in October 1936, which became effective on January 1, 1937, new obstacles were put in the path of Jews desiring to bring over their relatives. In March 1937, when the number of Jewish applications increased, Soprotimis found that most of those submitted by residents of the capital and vicinity were rejected except in rare cases where there were humanitarian considerations. This phenomenon was attributed to fear of the Communists, against whom special laws were passed in January, and the tendency to identify Jews with leftists or professions that were considered superfluous in Argentina. However, discrimination against the Jews was not yet a systematic policy.[20]

In the span of four years, from 1934 to 1937, an estimated 13,800–16,600 Jews reached Argentina. Of these 5,663 registered with Soprotimis and 4,362 with the Hilfsverein Deutschsprechender Juden. Eighty percent of those who approached the Hilfsverein were from Germany; this was true for only 26 percent of those applying to Soprotimis. Most of the other applicants were Polish Jews. Thus it is clear that immigration during these years was not limited to refugees from Nazi Germany.[21]

Critical Years

The expansion of the Reich, which began with the annexation of Austria in the spring of 1938, placed another 200,000 Jews at the mercy of the Nazis. The Jews of Austria were swiftly excluded from economic life and driven from their homes in an operation that won Adolf Eichmann his first important citation in Vienna. In the "Old Reich," too, legislation was stepped up to thrust the Jews from all spheres of life. In addition to the vile anti-Jewish propaganda and widespread public humiliation, physical attacks, robberies, and vandalism against Jewish property became everyday occurrences. The horror reached a peak on the night of November 8, 1938, known as Kristallnacht. By this time, the Jewish organizations in Germany and neighboring countries no longer doubted that the only real solution for the Jews of the greater Reich was to leave.

The drama in Germany and Austria was so compelling that the serious problems facing the Jews in other countries, particularly Poland, were almost overshadowed. The global economic crisis of 1929 had begun earlier in Poland, in 1928, and had lasted longer than in the West. Depression was compounded by a systematic policy of discrimination against the Jews, an official expression of the Jew-hatred in that country. As their financial and political status had grown steadily worse, the Jews of Poland had suffered terribly even before the war. Despite the minority treaties still in force, Polish leaders and a large proportion of the Polish people did not reconcile themselves to the permanent presence of the 3 million and more Jews residing in that country. The transfer of the Jewish population became a prominent issue in political platforms, public opinion, and government policy. Talk turned to action in 1937 when a government delegation was dispatched to find a new home for the Jews of Poland. The island of Madagascar, then a French colony, was considered for this purpose. Although the delegation found it unsuitable, the idea of shipping the Jews en masse to this island continued to feed the fantasies of those who would be rid of the Jews, and from 1939 to 1941 served to disguise the murderous plans of the Nazis. Romania also tried to solve its problems by dispossessing and driving out the Jews. In 1938, this became official government policy. The Jews were being forced out of Europe on a scale hitherto unknown in all the years of Jewish persecution.[22]

On February 20, 1938, a change of guard took place at the presidential mansion in Buenos Aires: General Justo stepped down in favor of Roberto Ortiz, who was expected to introduce greater liberality and openness, including in the sphere of immigration. Unlike his predecessor, who had come to power when the country was experiencing one of the worst economic crises in its history, Ortiz was elected in the midst of a developmental surge that was to change both the social and economic face of Argentina. Imports were steadily being replaced by light industry, which had developed into a major branch of the economy. From 1935 until 1941, nearly twenty thousand new factories opened, the number of workers rose from 369,000 to 733,000, energy consumption more than tripled, and product value more than doubled. Likewise, the number of industry-based administrative and clerical positions increased, as did the need for commercial and financial services. This created a demand both for manual laborers and for those with skills and experience usually associated with the middle class. Meanwhile, the European market for agricultural produce revived, and the bumper crops harvested in 1937 filled Argentina's coffers with hard currency.[23]

The improving economic situation, Ortiz's liberal promises during the election campaign, and the growing misery in Europe—all these inspired hope that the curbs on immigration would be dropped. In early March 1938, a panel of experts from eighteen countries met in Geneva under the auspices of the International Labour Office of the League of Nations to discuss technical and financial cooperation in the sphere of emigration and resettlement. A few weeks later, President Franklin Roosevelt extended an invitation to thirty countries to meet in the French town of Évian for a conference on the German and Austrian refugee problem. The Jewish newspapers in Argentina welcomed both developments, especially the US initiative, and expressed the hope that the countries of Latin America, led by Argentina, would open their doors to massive immigration. Rumors in May that the immigration laws were being radically revised were greeted by Soprotimis activists with unabashed optimism. Lying on the desk of the minister of agriculture at that moment was a report on the JCA in which the association won high praise for its agrarian planning, cooperative social policies, tireless efforts to "Argentinize" immigrants, and especially its training programs to transform city dwellers into full-fledged farmers. In conclusion, the author wrote: "In my opinion, we can consent to the JCA's request that this colonization organization be permitted to bring over families from Europe, and especially Germany, where they are not farmers."24

The Évian Conference, which opened on July 6, 1938, in an atmosphere of hope and expectation, ended in disappointment. From the podium, Tomás Le Breton, now Argentina's ambassador in Paris, argued that Argentina had absorbed more Jews per capita than had the United States and many more than all the other Latin American countries. He claimed that as an agricultural nation, it could accept no more newcomers in the urban and industrial sectors, and that as a sovereign entity, it retained the right to make its own immigration laws. Le Breton concluded his speech with this pompous declaration: "We are hospitable by nature. This characteristic is expressed in the preamble of our Constitution. . . . We are fully determined to cooperate within the limits of what is possible. Those limits provide an ample field for the noble work of the present conference. . . . We are convinced that our attitude in the past is sufficient to prove the generosity of the view we shall adopt in the future."

At that very hour, Argentina was feverishly completing a new set of immigration laws. By July 12, the Argentine delegation was able to inform the technical subcommittee at the conference of the substance of the new laws: "In view of the country's present economic situation, the Argentine government decides that all nonresident aliens wishing to enter the country must in future have a special landing permit issued by the Central Immigration Department at Buenos Aires. . . . This landing permit will be issued after the case has been considered by a special committee consisting of representatives of the Ministry of Foreign Relations, the Ministry of Agriculture, and the Ministry of the Interior respectively." What the Argentine delegates did not reveal at the conference was the fact that the new laws were passed "because in the present international situation, we can expect an immediate rise in the number of immigrants who wish to travel to the Argentine Republic for 'incidental reasons' *(motivos accidentales)* that do not correspond with the needs of a healthy immigration policy." In other words, they were clearly designed to keep out refugees fleeing for their lives.

As of October 1, 1938, all immigration applications were to be reviewed by an advisory committee that was urged "to give priority to [the] immigration [of those] with the greatest capacity for assimilation in order to meet our social, cultural, and economic needs." The consuls would provide the committee with detailed personal data, such as the reasons for emigrating, and were asked for their opinion in each case. Those submitting applications on behalf of relatives had to prove that they themselves had been residents of Argentina for at least two years, and all expenses incurred during the administrative processing were borne by them. By adding one obstacle after another, the Argentines hoped to deflect as many refugees as possible. The fact that most of the homeless in question were Jews was never articulated.[25]

When the contents of the new decree, signed by the president and the minister of foreign relations on July 28, were publicized two days later, pandemonium broke loose. Hundreds of Argentine Jews demanded entry permits for their relatives. Argentina's consulates in Europe were inundated with immigration requests. All sought to have their applications handled before the first of October. They soon found that they had been outwitted by the Ministry of Foreign Relations and the Immigration Department. On July 12, the ministry had rushed to inform the consuls of the imminent changes and ordered them to "act immediately to enforce strictly all the selection procedures to prevent the flow of immigration to our land from becoming disorderly and preemptive of the plans being finalized by the government." The moment the decree was signed, the Immigration Department halted the issuing of new visas, and on August 25 the offices were closed to the public. The decree thus went into effect not only before the official date, but also retroactively from the moment the president affixed his signature.[26]

"The decisions now taken with respect to the cancellation of entry permits are causing major damage to our colonization work," the JCA directors in Buenos Aires protested to the immigration commissioner. Many of the prospective farming families in Europe had sold their property and paid their fare, and a final date of departure had been set by the German authorities. "Now, on account of the new decisions, not only is it impossible for us to obtain entry permits for these people, but as we learn from the telegram just received, neither will families possessing such documents be given visas." This state of affairs ran contrary even to the new laws, which in Clause 10 specifically provided for the preferential treatment of farmers. Hence the JCA requested that the necessary permits be issued immediately and that a favorable attitude be taken to all future applications on behalf of Jewish farmers.[27]

The plight of the prospective colonists in Germany and Vienna, now prevented from entering Argentina, was referred to the Intergovernmental Committee, which had been set up at the Évian Conference to deal with the refugee problem. The committee called upon the British government to exercise its influence on Argentina and urge it to moderate its policies. Thus, one of the first missions of the committee, which had been founded with such pomp and circumstance and with the full participation of Argentina, was to put pressure on the Argentine government. The request of the JCA was complied with, but not fully: On January 19 it was authorized to proceed with the immigration of seventy-one families. Eight months later, two weeks before the war broke out, the JCA was allowed to bring over another twenty-three families and the relatives of twenty-one colonists already living in Argentina. The stipulations were that no more than 25 percent of each group could be from the same country, and that this ratio would be preserved when settling them on farms. The JCA also undertook to repatriate any settlers who left the colony before two years were up.[28]

"A fine immigration policy!" trumpeted the Catholic weekly *Criterio,* its editor sparing no praise for "such a worthy government measure." He could imagine only two groups who would oppose it: upholders of "anachronistic nineteenth-century liberalism" and the Jews—the former on grounds of "materialistic romanticism" and the latter owing to vested interests. As the editor of *Criterio* gushed over the new policy, some murmurings of protest were heard from the Comité Contra el Racismo y el Antisemitismo en la Argentina, established in July 1937. Among its founders were leading members of the Communist, Socialist, and Radical parties, as well as several conservative statesmen drawn together both in their opposition to nazism and Italian fascism and in their recognition that anti-Semitism was being used by the Nazis to win public and political support in Argentina. When news of the immigration decree reached them, the committee was preparing for its first convention. The refugee problem had not been addressed by the committee during its first year of operation, and formally, it was not on the agenda of the convention. However, when the convention opened on August 6, 1938, the delegate of the Argentine League for Human Rights, Arturo Frondizi, who twenty years later became Argentina's president, denounced the immigration policy as a violation of the Constitution and Argentine tradition. Following a debate on the issue of "racism and international law," the convention adopted the proposal of one of its Jewish delegates: Along with a public censure of racism, it called upon Argentina to open its gates to "the refugees and persecuted of Austria, Germany, Romania, and Poland." This demonstrated the general consensus among the delegates, but, unlike the other resolutions, it was not translated into a plan of action.[29]

A more outspoken condemnation of Argentina's immigration policy appeared in the prestigious newspaper *La Prensa,* which criticized the government for flinging away the opportunity to gain excellent manpower for the development of the Republic. Similar views were expressed in Congress, by the Socialists and certain Radicals. On September 19, 1938, before the new decree went into effect, Socialist congressman Juan Solari demanded an explanation for the arbitrary halt in granting visas; on January 17, 1939, Solari protested the instructions to consuls to ascertain the religion of visa applicants. Earlier, on December 15, 1938, the Socialists had proposed a debate on the treatment of Jews in Nazi Germany and the possibility of opening immigration, at least to Jewish children. This debate never took place for fear of angering the Germans. About a half a year later, two Radical leaders, Bernardino Horne and Leonidas Anastasi, requested a detailed report on Argentine immigration policy from the ministers of agriculture and foreign relations. On August 9, 1939, a year after the introduction of the new regulations, immigration was hotly debated, giving voice to the broad spectrum of ideologies held by Argentina's statesmen. Indirectly, this also shed light on attitudes to the legitimacy of Jewish existence in Argentina. However, none of this moved the government from its position, aptly summed up in the headlines of the anti-Semitic nationalist paper *La Fronda:* "The Semitic invasion must be opposed!"[30]

How did the Jews of Argentina respond to the extreme measures curbing immigration? When presidential decree number 8972 was first publicized on July 28, Argentine Jewry was absorbed in a nationwide campaign to raise a million pesos for the resettlement of Austrian Jews in Palestine. There was no loud protest from the organized Jewish community until the retroactive nature of the decree came to light. Even then, the Jewish newspapers engaged more in refuting the charges that had led to the new measures than in condemning the authorities; there was no call for demonstrations against the government. A lengthy article by A. L. Schusheim, one of Argentina's leading Jewish journalists, on September 6, 1938, was titled "Major Assembly Needed to Discuss Jewish Current Affairs." He mentioned the ineffectiveness of the Évian Conference and the halt in immigration but devoted most of the article to the racist laws in Italy, which he felt might affect Jewish–Italian relations in Argentina.

No major assembly was convened, and no significant public action in the sphere of immigration was reported in the Jewish newspapers. Neither did the protocols of the meetings of Soprotimis reflect any sense of urgency or panic. There are no records of any special meeting or consultation of the board around the time the new laws were being formulated, and they are first mentioned more than two months after their publication, when Soprotimis was already fighting to retain its official status as the intermediary between the refugees and the immigration authorities—a position it had enjoyed for over fifteen years.[31] The Jewish community was demonstrating once again its greater sensitivity to events in Europe than to immigration to Argentina.

The public passivity with which the Jews of Argentina accepted the closure of the immigration gates in September and October 1938 contrasted sharply with their fury in November when news of the Kristallnacht atrocities in Germany reached their ears. At the initiative of the DAIA, all the Jews of Argentina observed a week of mourning that commenced on November 21 with a general business strike. So impressive was the strike that the authorities sent out policemen to draw up a list of the closed businesses with protest signs in their windows. According to the police, this was an indication of the extent of *leftist* influence that the Jews exercised in Argentina. The strike was one of the first and rare occasions on which Argentine Jewry banded together to show its might, and the general newspapers were favorable in their reporting of the event. In many instances, non-Jewish neighbors demonstrated solidarity by closing their businesses, too. No similar attempt was made in 1938 to harness Jewish power on behalf of immigration.[32]

Assistance to the immigrants was pursued in a quieter, more personal vein. This emerges clearly from a systematic study of the files of the Immigration Department on the arrival and departure of passenger ships reaching Argentina from December 1937 until the end of 1941. In several cases, Socialist congressman Solari and others recommended that the applications of certain refugees be considered after their arrival in Buenos Aires. Commissioner Cipriano Taboada Mora was approached by intermediaries on behalf of holders of tourist and transit visas who desired to settle in Argentina. Unsystematic leniency was his policy, and he was helpful in granting permanent entry permits even in some of the extreme cases wherein passengers, held in custody aboard their ship or at the Hotel de Inmigrantes, tried to escape.

The only refugees the authorities strictly refused to admit were those who lacked an Argentine visa of any kind and had been already rejected by Brazil and Uruguay. Usually, it was explained that there was no reason for Argentina to be more lenient than its neighbors, especially when the refugees held visas to these other countries. However, the pact made among Argentina, Brazil, Uruguay, and Paraguay at a meeting of these countries' ministers of treasury in Montevideo in early February 1939 seems to have been influential here. According to this agreement, those lacking papers or "who were undesirable because of their antecedents" would be barred from entering, and information about them would be exchanged among the respective authorities. Jewish refugees of these categories who reached Buenos Aires were simply turned away. This was the case on February 25, when the SS *Conte Grande* arrived, carrying sixty-eight refugees. Although chances were good that they would be admitted to Bolivia or Chile, the Argentine authorities would not allow them even a few days to make arrangements. Relatives watched tearfully as the ship pulled away from the harbor on its way back to Europe. That same day, the SS *General San Martín* arrived with twenty-seven refugees, only two of whom were allowed to stay. The same scenario was repeated many times in the coming months. Reviewing the data in the archives of the Immigration Department, it seems that some two hundred passengers arriving on twenty-three vessels between December 1938 and December 1939 were denied entry to Argentina. From their names, we see that the vast majority were Jews.[33]

Yet even this policy was not totally consistent. Following the discrete intervention of Soprotimis in 1939, the Immigration Department was prepared to reverse its decision in fifty-eight cases. Other intermediaries may have enjoyed similar success. On May 31, seventy-eight refugees from Hamburg arriving on the *SS Monte Oliva* were first detained on board and then brought to the Hotel de Inmigrantes under custody. Thirty-four of them were permitted to stay in Argentina after an intermediary allegedly bribed the immigration commissioner. This same person was said to have organized the release of passengers on other occasions.[34]

The DAIA also took action on behalf of the immigrants. When congressmen Horne and Anastasi called for a parliamentary debate on Argentina's immigration policy, it organized a public meeting in their support. However, the DAIA was too involved with the growing anti-Semitism and alarming magnitude of the Nazi presence in Argentina to promote immigration as a major cause. All the while, the immigration societies proceeded in their routine activities, with no special sense of need for haste. In early February 1939, there was talk of bringing over two hundred children from Germany, who would be maintained through public funding. By the time the authorities were approached and an agreement was worked out regarding a proper framework for the children, the war had erupted; nothing further was done.[35]

The leading immigration society, Soprotimis, continued to lobby for the unification of families, which was still possible under the current laws; it was successful in 324 cases. Other activities such as assisting illegal immigrants also continued. The authorities had established procedures, albeit costly, by which many immigrants could legalize their status. Soprotimis tried to obtain money for this purpose from the emergency fund set up by the Jewish community but came away with very little. Of the 851,600 pesos raised by the end of 1939, 102,000 went to the Hilfsverein Deutschsprechender Juden (which, in keeping with a new law requiring Spanish names, was now called the Asociación Filantrópica) to assist Argentina's Central European Jews. Only paltry sums were devoted to promoting immigration, and even less to legalization. According to the fund-raisers, the illegals were not in danger of expulsion and the money would be better spent to help those who were still homeless. Argentina was perceived as locked and bolted, whereas Palestine offered greater prospects for both legal and illegal immigration, and enjoyed an ideological advantage, too. Soprotimis was granted a total of 45,200 pesos—the same amount contributed to the transfer of an orphanage from Frankfurt to Palestine. Through the generosity of the Jews of Argentina, forty orphan girls and their teachers were sent to the Evelina de Rothschild school in Jerusalem.[36]

The effects of the 1938 immigration decree were strongly felt. Fourteen thousand five hundred six second- and third-class passengers (who comprised the official category of "immigrants") reached Argentina in 1939, compared with 37,762 in 1938. The outbreak of the war on September 1 was only partially to blame. Arrivals in the months leading up to the war had averaged less than half the number arriving monthly the year before (1,437 compared with 3,142). Jewish arrivals in 1939 totaled 1,873, compared with 4,919 in 1938. However, these official figures do not account for all the Jews immigrating to Argentina. Soprotimis had inside knowledge of at least a thousand Jewish tourists who never returned home. Another fifteen hundred Jews crossed the borders from neighboring countries or remained in Argentina after stopping there in transit. If these figures are taken into consideration, the number of Jewish immigrants in 1939 was actually 4,373. The phenomenon of illegal entry is mentioned in the annual report of the Immigration Department, which attributed it almost entirely to the Jews.[37]

As World War II commenced, the Jews of Argentina were caught in a web of contradiction. They demonstrated their support of European Jewry and resettlement in Palestine through protests, periods of public mourning, and especially fund-raising, and continued to contribute to relief organizations for legal and illegal immigrants in Argentina. Yet, they silently resigned themselves to their country's closure to further immigration. The spread of anti-Semitic propaganda and the lack of support for Jewish immigration among the general public and in the House of Representatives probably contributed to the Jewish leaders' passivity on this local issue, although they spoke out, often loudly, on matters of global Jewish concern.[38]

The War Begins

When World War II entered its third day, President Ortiz declared Argentina's neutrality. The minister of foreign relations attended a conference in Panama at the end of September to assure the neutral stance of all the Latin American countries. At this stage, Argentine policy was in perfect harmony with that of its neighbors.

World War II also summoned up one of Argentina's finest economic eras. After the initial confusion, with its shipping, financial, and unemployment problems, enormous strides began in industrial development. The obstacles in overseas shipping encouraged local industry, and markets formerly supplied by the warring nations opened up, if only temporarily, to Argentine manufacturers. By 1943, industry accounted for 20 percent of Argentina's export income, compared with only 7 percent in 1938. The trend toward industrialization, which had begun after the great economic crisis, now moved forward with extraordinary speed.[39] To keep pace with this rapid development, a body of skilled and qualified manpower was a major requirement. At least part of the demand might have been supplied by the Jewish refugees who had fled from industrialized nations in Europe. It was in Argentina's power to save lives and benefit at the same time. Was there any resultant change in its immigration policy?

The one immigration option that remained open in Argentina on the eve of World War II was entry as a farmer. Clause 10 of the presidential decree of July 1938 specified that contracted farmers *(colonos contratados),* which the Immigration Department took to mean experienced farmers with documented skills, were still welcome in Argentina. In 1939, the JCA successfully appealed this interpretation of the decree, which would have brought an end to the Jewish colonization effort. On September 12, the Ministry of Agriculture declared that JCA candidates would be issued visas even without proof that they were "authentic farmers." In exchange, the JCA renewed its commitment to repatriate any settler who left the colonies before two years were up. However, there was no change in the law excluding singles. As a result, the JCA could not go ahead with its plans to organize groups of individuals who would settle in Argentina as "composite families," to be joined later by their real families. Thus, we see that the gates were not totally sealed to Jewish immigrants, as long as a genuine colonization scheme was developed. The war soon put a stop even to this.[40]

On January 2, 1940, the JCA in Paris instructed its directors in Buenos Aires to stop applying for entry permits for new settlers. The order was repeated on January 17, this time by telegram. As the Paris administration explained a month later, the British Treasury had exercised its wartime authority over companies registered in Great Britain to limit JCA investments in Argentina: "Not having received from the British Treasury authorization to proceed with the settlement of more than forty-two

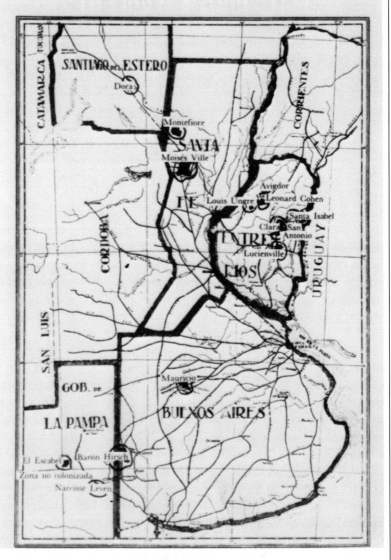

JCA colonies in Argentina

families, we cannot implement our program as it was before. Consequently, it is absolutely impossible to send off the candidates about whom you have written, as well as all the others who are stranded in Europe." Other letters cite the orders of the British Treasury as the reason for holding up further handling of several families who had Argentine visas and were awaiting instructions in Germany. Were these orders negotiable, or could they have been circumvented by using outside funding over which the British Treasury had no control, as alluded to in certain of the letters? As far as we know, no such system for financing colonization was established before France was invaded and the whole situation changed. The abandonment of prospective colonists was caused by a "state of war," while, in fact, the "phony war" was still in process.[41]

The number of settlers in the colonies could still be increased by encouraging the older settlers to bring over their relatives. The JCA in Buenos Aires hoped to pursue this path, but it was imperative that the new settlers remain in the colonies for more than a short time. As the administrators in Buenos Aires wrote in early January 1940: "You will realize our embarrassment: On the one hand we are aware of the moral obligation not to leave unutilized the sole means that our coreligionists might have to emigrate; on the other hand, we realize the risk we take if there is a rise in the number of departures of which we must notify the Immigration Department." The JCA used both incentives and pressure to keep settlers from dropping out, but when this did occur, it stood by its commitment and duly reported each case.[42]

Despite the loyalty of the JCA, the Immigration Department took action that further narrowed the immigrant farmer category. From early 1940, colonists could no longer bring over cousins, and this soon extended to brothers-in-law and siblings. Only the colonists' parents and children were eligible to join them in Argentina. On April 22, 1940, the last of the special concessions was discontinued. The minister of agriculture ordered all earlier decisions revoked and declared that JCA candidates would now be required to be "authentic farmers" and of working age like everyone else. This sudden decision was sparked by the report of the Argentine consuls in Amsterdam and Zurich that certain immigration candidates proposed by the JCA were not genuine farmers and were over the age of sixty. Furthermore, the department had been notified by the JCA of no less than 130 dropouts from the colonies, whom the JCA was now asked to help "repatriate" to Nazi Germany. The JCA wrote a long, defensive letter in an effort to reverse the decision. However, it had no choice but to promise its assistance in repatriating the ex-colonists if and when they were apprehended. Meanwhile, a complete turnabout took place in the status of the JCA in Europe.[43]

Until the defeat of France in June 1940, the directors of the JCA and HICEM supervised the colonization and immigration effort from their seat in Paris. Then, suddenly, they, too, were refugees. In mid-July, Soprotimis received the hasty applications for entry visas to Argentina of several HICEM directors, the deputy director of JCA, and two JCA secretaries. At the beginning of December 1940, the JCA directors in Buenos Aires wrote to the minister of agriculture directly, seeking asylum for the entire administration of the colonization association. In their letter, Simón Weill and Davíd Zvi reviewed the history of JCA activities in Argentina and requested permission to move its central office to Buenos Aires. The list of twenty-five administrators applying for visas included Louis Oungre, the director general. No immediate reply was received; the correspondence dragged on for many months during which some of the applicants found a haven elsewhere. This incident demonstrates how weakened the JCA had become, but it also highlights the extreme harshness of the authorities toward Jewish refugees as a group.[44]

The order signed on July 27, 1940, by Vice-President Ramón Castillo, who had replaced the ailing Ortiz on July 3, seemed like a ray of light in this atmosphere of gloom. The consuls in the warring countries were authorized to arrange temporary visits to Argentina for children under fourteen if "parents, legal guardians, or recognized committees" applied on their behalf. Three days later, Soprotimis and several other organizations formed the Committee for the Admission of Jewish Children from Countries at War. However, there was little this committee could do because most of the procedures made possible by the presidential order required collaboration with the foreign consuls in Buenos Aires. Since support from the Nazi consul was unobtainable, the order could not be used to rescue children from Germany, as proposed by the Reichsvertretung der Juden in Berlin. The only work done by the committee was to apply for entry visas for several dozen German Jewish children in England who had relatives in Argentina, but these children never came to Argentina because of the objection of the Argentine ambassador in London.[45]

No change was introduced in Argentina's draconian policies after the outbreak of World War II. In its annual report for 1940, Soprotimis stated that the authorities' opposition to the llamadas was obstructing and limiting the number of visas granted by the Argentine consuls in Europe, and that, "in the past year, the decree [of July 1938] has been applied with even greater severity than before." The investigation conducted during the greater part of that year against Commissioner Taboada Mora was probably much to blame. From June to November 1940, an inspector was appointed to study irregularities in the Immigration Department; in his final report, he described some of the corrupt procedures through which many refugees bought their way into Argentina. Taboada Mora was moved to another department, and Andrés Maspero Castro, who was probably known to Soprotimis from his work as secretary general of the Immigration Department in 1925, took his place.[46]

Fewer ships were arriving now in Buenos Aires, but the refugees they brought were more desperate than ever. On January 21, 1941, the *SS Montevideo Maru* arrived with fifty-two German Jewish refugees aboard. They had traveled from Berlin to Moscow and continued by train through Siberia until reaching the seaport of Vladivostok, where they set sail for Kube, Japan. When the Japanese authorities refused to accept them, they tried their luck in South America. Neither Brazil nor Uruguay would have them, and when they reached Argentina without visas or papers, it seemed that they would be sent away again, this time back to Nazi-occupied Europe. Fortunately, public opinion was on their side. Forty of the refugees were allowed to disembark and proceed by land to Paraguay, which promised to take them in; the others were rejected. In spite of this seemingly encouraging start, the new year augured poorly for the refugees who reached Argentine shores.[47]

The Argentine immigration authorities remained dry-eyed in the face of the many Jews who came to their offices in the first half of 1941, begging for mercy on behalf of family members who could still leave Germany, France, the Netherlands, and the Iberian Peninsula. In 1940, reports of Nazi spies in Argentina, coupled with the country's willingness to shelter crew members of the *Graf Spee*, a Nazi warship sunk off the coast of Montevideo, infuriated the public and led to a much publicized parliamentary inquiry into the anti-Argentine activities of the Nazis. However, the official attitude to immigration lost none of its coldness. On the contrary, an internal memorandum circulated by the Immigration Department in June 1941 further aggravated the situation. Visas that had already been granted to children, parents, and spouses, but that were sent back to the clerks for whatever reason, were canceled retroactively. Henceforth, applications on behalf of parents would be considered only in the case of widows or widowers who had no offspring outside Argentina. No exception was made for parents taken to concentration camps. Children could join their families in Argentina only if they were minors, and daughters- and sons-in-law could come only if the parent applying on their behalf earned over 200 pesos a month. No applications would be accepted from anyone who had entered Argentina without a visa, even if his status was now legal and he had resided in Argentina for two years. Immigrants who entered the country as skilled workers had to wait three years before submitting requests for their families. When the Argentine consul in Marseilles, then the major port of departure from Western Europe, refused to grant visas to holders of entry permits who lacked a valid passport from their home country, he was fully backed by the authorities in Buenos Aires. These regulations became known to Soprotimis at a time when the world was seething over the news of the German invasion of Russia and the special murder units (Einsatzgruppen) were exterminating Jewish communities across the Baltic states, Belorussia, and the Ukraine. Although emigration from greater Germany and Western Europe was still possible and occasionally assisted by the German authorities, the channels for legal Jewish immigration to Argentina were almost totally blocked.

These regulations, which knowingly ignored the suffering of the Jews, did not arouse any dramatic reaction in the Argentine Jewish community. The records of the DAIA, which represented Argentina's Jews in the political arena, made no mention of any call for community action. At the Soprotimis board meeting on June 24, 1941, two speakers proposed alerting the public and Congress to the new obstacles in the way of immigration. In a majority vote, however, it was decided that rather than condemning the Immigration Department and the minister of agriculture publicly, an attempt should be made to work within the system. Public involvement in this area remained minimal.[48]

Despite its constant prodding of the authorities, Soprotimis achieved little during the first two years of the war. Under the existing laws, its officials obtained entry permits for 271 Jews in 1940, and 351 the following year. Among these were some whose requests had been initially rejected and others who had been ordered to leave the country after disembarking as transit passengers. This number was small when compared with the figures of the Immigration Department, which recorded the arrival of

6,210 second- and third-class passengers in 1940 (1,062 from Germany) and 4,675 in 1941 (767 from Germany). In its report for 1940, the department noted that among the first-class passengers (i.e., tourists) in 1940, there were about two thousand, "mostly German Jews," who never returned home. The 1941 report also stated that 2,006 of all the arrivals that year had declared themselves Jewish. On the basis of these figures and the assumption that illegal immigration continued as before, we may assume that 1,850 to twenty-five hundred Jews entered Argentina in 1940, and approximately twenty-two hundred in 1941.[49]

Compared with their unbending attitude toward visa-seekers, the authorities were mild in their response to border-crossers and tourists or transit passengers who opted to remain in Argentina illegally. Sir David Victor Kelly, the British ambassador in Buenos Aires, attributed this to corruption: "This traffic, which has enriched many with influence in Argentine political circles from the President's immediate entourage to lesser officials in the Ministry of Agriculture, the police and the port authorities, has helped those only whose relatives were ready and able to pay bribes varying from $5,000 to $1,000 [*sic*] in extent." Even if exaggerated, this statement was probably based on classified information and diplomatic hearsay. Such bought favors did not make life easier for the illegals as they tried to sink roots and earn a living in Argentina. Yet, no comprehensive efforts were made to round them up and send them across the border. On the contrary, they were offered an opportunity to legalize their status, which was usually only a financial matter. Soprotimis's argument, then, was not with the authorities but with the organized Jewish community that refused to finance legalization procedures in sufficient measure. A total of 670 immigrants were able to amend their status during the first two years of the war; hundreds more were obliged to wait until World War II was over.[50]

In late October 1941, the SS *Cabo de Hornos* set sail for Europe with 106 passengers who had been refused entry to Argentina. Eighty-six were Jewish, and all held Brazilian or other visas that were declared invalid by the authorities. The non-Jews were later permitted to disembark in Brazil; only after persistent intervention were the Jews allowed to land in the Dutch Antilles. This was a symbolic conclusion to a dismal year in the history of Jewish immigration to Argentina.

On October 31, the Germans prohibited the emigration of Jews from the Third Reich and Western Europe, as they had done after conquering

Poland and Eastern Europe. In the following months, the JCA was forced to notify the Argentine authorities that the visas for which they had worked so hard could not be used for the time being. The deposits put down by the JCA were refunded, but it was requested that the holders of these visas be allowed to renew them when they were able to travel. In most cases, that opportunity never arose.[51]

In the Neutral Republic

With the Japanese attack on Pearl Harbor, the countries of Latin America were drawn into the circle of war. Two days after the attack, Chile's foreign minister called for a meeting of all the foreign ministers in the region to discuss the developments and reach a coordinated position. At their meeting, which opened in Rio de Janeiro on January 15, 1942, the first recommendation was to sever diplomatic relations with Japan, Germany, and Italy. By this time, eleven South American republics had broken off relations with Germany, and several had even declared war.[52]

Meanwhile, on January 20, the major arms of the Nazi administration convened in Am Grossen Wannsee, Berlin, to hear Reinhard Heydrich, Eichmann, and their associates report on the "complete solution of the Jewish question." At the conference, Heydrich surveyed the tactics employed by the Germans in their war on the Jewish people, comparing forced emigration in Western Europe with the "practical experience" of mass murder operations in Eastern Europe; in the course of six months, tens of thousands of Jews had been shot to death. By the meeting's end, it was clear to the bloodthirsty participants that the "Final Solution" led in the direction of Auschwitz and the death camps.

The meeting that opened in Rio de Janeiro ended on a less unanimous note. Two countries, Argentina and Chile, rejected the recommendation to break off ties with the Axis states. Argentina refused to discontinue its extensive relations with Nazi Germany and boasted of its neutrality during World War I. Both economic interests and the broad political influence of Argentina's pro-Nazis were major factors. This essentially anti-US stance was supported in pro-British circles and reflected the mute competition between the two Allied powers. Even when a German submarine sank a clearly marked Argentine merchant vessel three hundred miles off the US coast on April 17, 1942, and a similar incident took place two months later, Argentina did not change its mind. It also remained neutral on other trying occasions, such as when the United States uncovered a broad German spy network operating in Argentina, and it was excluded from the US lend-lease program that supplied arms and military equipment to neighboring countries.[53]

Over the next two years, Argentina maintained full diplomatic, cultural, and economic ties with Nazi Germany. It was the only country in Latin America to do so, apart from a short-lived attempt by Chile, and this heightened its importance in Nazi eyes. Without Argentine neutrality, the Nazis would have been unable to guard their strategic economic interests in the region. Under these circumstances, Argentina and its ambassadors in Europe had a much greater capacity to help the Jews in 1942–1943 than did many other countries. The question is whether this potential was used.

The records of the Argentine Ministry of Foreign Relations indicate that it was not. Upon receiving the family unification permits issued by the immigration authorities in Buenos Aires, certain Argentine consuls were openly hostile. This was particularly true of the consul general in Munich, Ernesto Sarmiento, whose letters on the subject in 1938–1941 were anti-Semitic in tone. He was especially irritated by the fact that some of the applicants themselves had entered Argentina on tourist or transit visas. Although they had legalized their status in the meantime and were entitled to apply, Sarmiento was violently opposed to allowing their families into Argentina. There was no change in his views even after the implications of the Nazis' anti-Jewish policies became fully evident in 1942. With the power to approve or reject immigration applications entirely in the hands of the consuls, who had no instructions to intervene on the Jews' behalf, the processing of applications proceeded slowly, and, by the time the candidates were approved, many of them had been transported along with their fellow Jews to "an unknown destination."[54]

In the midst of this apathy and indifference to the machinations of the Nazis, a scheme to save one thousand Jewish children was noteworthy. In August 1942, the French government at Vichy began to deport Jews from unoccupied France in keeping with its agreement with the Nazis. US relief personnel operating in the south of France appealed to the United States to take in five thousand orphans, and several countries in Latin America were also asked to cooperate. In early October 1942, HICEM's New York office contacted the Jewish organizations in Argentina with the request to arrange entry permits for one thousand youngsters. Delegates of the DAIA, JCA, and Soprotimis, as well as the rabbi of the Congregación Israelita, met with President Castillo on November 2, 1942, and pleaded with him to admit these children into Argentina. They promised to cover all transportation costs and maintain the children until they reached maturity. At that very moment, Great Britain was in an uproar over the news of the systematic extermination of the Jews in the concentration camps, and public figures such as the archbishop of Canterbury had called upon the Allies to act without delay. Argentina's ambassador in London, Miguel Ángel Cárcano, was also approached for assistance. Cárcano reported this to his government on November 3, the day after the president's meeting with the Jewish leaders. With their appeal still fresh in mind, President Castillo and his minister of agriculture, Daniel Amadeo y Videla, signed an order on November 20 instructing the consuls in the regions closest to the concentration camps where children under fourteen were being held to arrange for their passage to Argentina. They were to ascertain the names and state of health of these children and to issue visas only to those who met the Immigration Department's health requirements. The order was limited to one thousand children and was to be implemented by the end of 1943.[55]

The DAIA was pleased and gratified by this response, which was praised by the *Mundo Israelita* and other Jewish newspapers as an expression of the enlightenment of the national Constitution and Argentine society. The anti-Semitic papers, on the other hand, were furious. *El Pampero* and *El Crisol* charged that the president was endangering the future of Argentina. These one thousand little Jews would grow up to enslave the true Argentines, they said, and embellished their articles with "Jewish" caricatures in true anti-Semitic fashion.[56]

Amid this tide of praise and damnation, no one seemed to notice that the children could not even leave France. On November 2, one thousand of the five thousand youngsters awaiting departure for the United States were granted permission to leave. A group of twenty-three caretakers and counselors left the United States five days later, to receive the children in Lisbon. However, the Allied forces invaded North Africa the following night, and the Germans retaliated by taking over the entire south of France on November 11. US relief operations were hastily stopped, and the Germans became the sole decision-makers with regard to emigration. The United States could no longer intervene on the children's behalf except through Swiss intermediaries; not so Argentina, which had direct access to the government in Vichy and the Nazi regime because of its policy of neutrality. Argentina thus enjoyed an exclusive bargaining position and could play upon genuine German interests.

As fortunes turned in France, the Jews of Argentina were preparing for a business strike and mass rally to demonstrate their outrage at the step-by-step annihilation of European Jewry. On December 2, tens of thousands of Jews took to the streets of Buenos Aires to express solidarity with their Jewish brethren. Billboards and homes along the central thoroughfares were plastered with DAIA posters calling upon Argentina to protest the Nazi extermination of the Jews. When the plan to rescue the French children was made public, everyone expected that it would proceed without delay, with the assistance of Jews and gentiles alike. These hopes proved false.[57]

Early that month, Soprotimis activists were warmly received by Commissioner Maspero Castro, who promised to help in rescuing the children. However, precise information, which could not be obtained in Argentina, was needed about their whereabouts. The commissioner was asked to contact the Argentine consul in Marseilles, who could find out particulars from HICEM activists in southern France. Maspero Castro consented but claimed that he could not send a coded cable to Marseilles without the stamp of the Ministry of Foreign Relations, whose cooperation he doubted. To avoid further complications, Soprotimis agreed to send the message by airmail, despite the postal delays caused by the war.

By now, it was perfectly clear that entry permits to Argentina were useless unless the Nazis could be persuaded to let the children leave. The DAIA sought another interview with President Castillo on December 20, but the meeting took place only on March 4, 1943, three and a half months after the order was signed. In its petition, the DAIA stated that "Argentina's ambassadors in various countries had received emotional letters of gratitude from the local Jewish comunities for His Excellency's most Argentine and Christian gesture." However, in order to take advantage of this generosity it would be necessary for Argentina's diplomats in Vichy to secure permission for the children to emigrate. The Jewish leaders came away impressed by the president's courtesy and interest in the rescue mission, but no real steps were taken to further it.[58]

The chief actor in the rescue mission was to have been the Ministry of Foreign Relations, and this is where the problem lay. When the Jewish leaders inquired at the ministry two weeks later, it was found that the president's instructions had indeed been forwarded but had not been carried out. After another month of waiting, a delegation of Jewish activists approached the minister of interior. It was then mid-April 1943, and all eyes were focused on the island of Bermuda where the United States and Great Britain were discussing measures to save the Jews of Europe. When the Jewish activists returned with the news that the minister of interior had promised his assistance and would remind the president of his commitment, hopes ran high that action would soon be taken. However, another month passed and there was still no progress. On May 21, representatives of the DAIA and Soprotimis met with the deputy minister of foreign relations, Roberto Gache, who expressed sympathy for their cause. Within a few days, Gache reported that the minister had instructed Argentina's ambassadors in Europe to arrange for the children's passage. The Jewish press was triumphant over this news, but the truth of the matter was that only the ambassador in Vichy, Ricardo Olivera, had been contacted and asked for his advice on how to proceed. His response, received on June 7, was that the Argentine embassy in Berlin should negotiate with those in power, that is, the Nazi occupiers. It was now over six months since Argentina's verbal agreement to take in the children, but nothing of substance had yet been done.[59]

Meanwhile, changes were taking place in Argentina's political arena. On June 4, 1943, Castillo was overthrown by a group of military officers, among them Pedro Pablo Ramírez, his minister of war, in order to prevent the corrupt election of an extremely conservative candidate who enjoyed Castillo's backing. This candidate was a supporter of the Allies; with his elimination, it seemed that the Nazi sympathizers in Argentina had gained the upper hand. Yet, at this stage the junta was composed of officers with a wide spectrum of political beliefs, united by their opposition to the corrupt government. Within two days of the coup, Ramírez was named president, Congress was dissolved, and the state of emergency that had been declared on the eve of the war was extended until further notice.

Despite the change of government, an official request to free one thousand Jewish children from the concentration camps in Europe was forwarded to the Nazis on June 24. On the orders of the German foreign minister, it was ignored. On its heels came a similar request from the French government at Vichy, submitted at Argentina's urging. Vichy was advised by the Germans not to reply right away. Meanwhile, the German

Foreign Ministry had received other petitions to release Jewish children, among them a British request submitted through Switzerland to allow five thousand children to emigrate to Palestine. As far as the Germans were concerned, all this was part of Action Juive, a comprehensive scheme devised by international Jewry to rescue thirty to fifty thousand Jews. The foreign minister ordered all the appeals to be handled as a unit, and since most involved emigration to Palestine, German–Arab relations played an important role in whether they were considered.

On July 21, 1943, the Foreign Ministry drew up a list of its decisions on the rescue of Jews. Emigration to Palestine was categorically rejected. The Nazis regarded Palestine as the lebensraum (living space) of the Arabs, and, as they later put it, "the government of the Reich cannot lend a hand in allowing a people as noble and courageous as the Arabs are to be forced from their homeland, Palestine, by the Jews." However, they agreed to release Jews if the British government was prepared to absorb them in the British Isles. This would set the stage for negotiations in which Jewish survivors would be exchanged for Germans held by the Allies. The Nazis consoled themselves with the thought that increasing the Jewish population in Great Britain would stir up anti-Semitism there.

The same conditions were to be presented to Argentina. The release of one thousand children would require a commitment to settle them on Argentine soil and prevent them from emigrating to Palestine. Argentina would also be obligated to use its influence with the Allies so that Germans in South and Central America could return to their homeland. It was further suggested that "a request should be submitted to the Reichsführer-SS so that the objects, who may eventually be needed for an exchange, will not be sent for the time being to the eastern territories." Germany's willingness to negotiate with Argentina thus opened up the possibility that a certain number of Jewish children would be taken off the death list and perhaps rescued. The situation had not changed by the end of October, when a revised copy of the Foreign Ministry document was approved by the Reichsführer-SS.[60]

Were the Germans genuinely prepared to free the children if their demands were met? Rudolph Levy, a Turkish Jew living in Germany who had fled to the Netherlands, convinced the Nazis that he was the citizen of a neutral country. In January 1944, he was sent to a transit camp in Bergen-Belsen together with other Jews whose lives were spared because they had visas to Palestine and were useful for prisoner exchange. In July,

284 of them were liberated and, contrary to Nazi policy, permitted to emigrate to Palestine. It was thus quite conceivable that vigorous diplomatic intervention on the part of Argentina, even in the second half of 1943, might have achieved the children's release. However, no such intervention took place. When the Argentine ambassador in Vichy, Olivera, inquired if he should continue his efforts to arrange exit permits, he received a negative reply. On September 21, 1943, the foreign minister of the military junta informed him that securing permission to leave was now up to the applicants themselves.

There was not a single international body that could press Argentina to exploit its capability to save human lives. Following the deliberations in Bermuda, an attempt was made to revive the Intergovernmental Committee established at the Évian Conference. Cárcano, the Argentine ambassador to Great Britain, attended a meeting of the committee in early August 1943. The rescue of the children was on the agenda but was scheduled for discussion only in January 1944, to determine whether the United States, Canada, and Argentina still stood by their commitment to take in the children if the Nazis released them. Forceful action to compel the Nazis to give them up, which the Nazis themselves expected and were prepared for as a basis for negotiation, did not even enter the minds of these "intergovernmental" bureaucrats seemingly in charge of saving the Jews.[61]

The Nazis were also willing to consider the release of Jews with Argentine citizenship. In principle, they were prepared to allow any neutral nation to evacuate their Jewish countrymen. Arrangements were to be made by the end of March 1943, although an extension was possible. Once the time was up, however, these Jews would be treated as any others and deported to the "East." In January 1943, the Argentine ambassador in Vichy requested the repatriation of twelve to fifteen Argentines living in France. He was told he had three months to arrange for their departure, but more time would be granted if necessary. Six months later, the ambassador had not yet submitted a list of names. Although the German repatriation offer was still open, the ambassador made no further contact in this regard.[62]

In March 1943, the German Foreign Office offered Luís H. Irigoyen, secretary of the Argentine embassy in Berlin, the opportunity to evacuate Argentine Jews from German-occupied lands. From Irigoyen's reply, the Germans concluded that "in Buenos Aires there was absolutely no understanding on this matter." Nevertheless, Eichmann was advised to leave the

Argentine Jews alone for the time being, to avoid confrontation with Argentina or other neutral countries. Meanwhile, Irigoyen was asked to handle the repatriation of six Argentine Jews living in Salonika. Eberhardt von Thadden, Eichmann's correspondent in the Foreign Office, stated that it was inconceivable for them to remain in Greece after it had been "cleansed" of all its Jews.[63] Seven Argentine Jews in the Netherlands, as well as an unspecified number in Belgium, were in the same situation. The Germans exercised notable caution in all these cases and were prepared to oversee the Argentines' swift departure; however, the Argentine embassy failed to respond as anticipated by making the necessary arrangements.

The largest group of Jews with Argentine papers resided in Kraków, Poland. At the end of July 1943, when the Polish Jewish community had been all but decimated, Eichmann's deputies informed the Foreign Office that several dozen Jews from enemy countries had been found in Kraków—six from Palestine and fifty-nine from Argentina. The papers of sixteen were forwarded to Berlin, and Irigoyen was called to Thadden's office to look them over. He immediately pronounced them forged. In his report, Thadden concluded that "the Argentine embassy has, of course, no interest in the bearers of these counterfeit documents."[64]

No concentrated effort was made in 1943 to repatriate Jewish Argentines, and the events in early 1944 changed the situation entirely. After the discovery of a broad German spy network in its midst and attempts to buy arms from the Nazis, Argentina succumbed to pressure from the United States and other Latin American countries and relinquished its neutrality on January 26, 1944. This move might have been expected to end Argentina's potential for rescuing Jews, but this was not so. When Eichmann's bureau ordered the incarceration of all Jews of foreign nationality in the Netherlands, Argentines included, the German foreign minister cabled Ernst Kaltenbrunner, chief of the Reichssicherheitshauptamlt, and urged him to reconsider lest the Allies encourage the persecution of "Germans of the Reich" living in Argentina, and lest arrest of one hundred Jews cause hardship to eighty thousand Germans.[65] These fears were soon proved baseless. Neither the Allies nor Argentina showed much concern for the Jewish Argentines detained by the Nazis. However, the Germans still regarded them as good "bargaining material," and Argentina thus was still in a position to save Jewish lives long after its relations with Germany were severed.

Jews possessing Argentine passports and other documents were sent to the transit camp for foreign nationals in Bergen-Belsen. An inmate of the camp who arrived in January 1944, and was eventually released in exchange for Germans, recalls meeting thirty-five Eastern European Jews with Argentine citizenship. From the sources at our disposal it is difficult to ascertain whether Argentine papers were helpful to other Jews, but we do know that Argentina's handling of the protection of such Jews was lethargic and pursued with reluctance. In Argentina itself there was no one to press for action. Until October 1943, the Immigration Department was part of the Ministry of Agriculture; thereafter it was attached to the Ministry of the Interior and a special committee was appointed to formulate immigration policy. The new immigration commissioner, like his predecessors, refused to admit anyone desiring to settle in Argentina to escape persecution. The gradually emerging fact that European Jewry was on the verge of extinction did not soften Argentina's position. In late November 1943, Argentina flatly refused to take in seventy-nine Jews who were allowed to leave France by virtue of their Spanish citizenship but were forced out of Spain by the government of General Francisco Franco. The immigration commissioner claimed that he was prevented by law from allowing them into Argentina.[66]

The years of Argentine neutrality constituted a critical period in the history of the Holocaust. Given Argentina's position in international politics and its rapid industrial development during the war, its objective possibilities for the rescue of Jews were greater than those of any other Latin American nation. The records of the Immigration Department show how little this capacity was exploited. In 1942, 3,373 transatlantic passengers entered Argentina, 2,325 of them traveling first class. Of the 1,849 passengers who declared their religion, sixty were Jews. The following year, the number of transatlantic passengers dropped to 1,852. Of the 834 who stated their religion, only twenty-six were Jews. While it is true that the immigration figures of the Jewish organizations were higher— approximately thirteen hundred Jewish arrivals in 1942 and 524 in 1943— most of these reached Argentina by way of bordering countries such as Paraguay and Bolivia. Soprotimis secured a total of 115 entry permits in 1942, but as we have seen, very few of the applicants were able to make use of them.[67]

Faced with the combination of Nazi restrictions on Jewish movement, the difficulty of traveling during wartime, and, above all, Argentina's closing gates, the only activity left to Soprotimis in 1943 and 1944 was to plan postwar immigration.

Argentines and the "Jewish Question"

In January 1944, just as Argentina broke off relations with Germany, President Roosevelt ordered the establishment of the War Refugee Board in Washington. This board was empowered to rescue Jews using every possible means, even those previously ruled out during the war. US embassies all over Latin America were asked to report on the prospects for absorbing Jewish refugees in their host countries. The reply of the US embassy in Buenos Aires was: "The consensus of persons active in Jewish rescue and relief work is that so long as the present regime remains in power, no assistance whatsoever can be expected from the Argentine Government in refugee matters."[68]

The authors of this report were referring to the military junta, yet we have seen that previous administrations were no less indifferent to the plight of the Jews. When the Congress took a vote in December 1938 on whether to discuss "actively cooperating with other governments to ease the arrival of Jewish emigrants and their settlement in this country," a House majority, forty-five delegates, came out in favor and thirty-five came out against. According to House rules, the proportion was not large enough to bring the issue to the floor. This was obviously official government policy: The Argentine delegation took a similarly hard line on refugee absorption at the Eighth American Convention, held that month in Lima, Peru. Argentina thus emerged among Latin America's opponents to Jewish aid.[69]

Argentina's ambassador to Germany between 1936 and 1939, Eduardo Labougle, followed the emergence of the Nazi regime with unconcealed horror. He was particularly angered by its hostility to the Catholic church and its attempts to foster ties with German expatriates and their offspring in Argentina. His reports describe the totalitarian brutality of the Nazis and their persecution of the Jews, but for all his sympathy with the victims he did not call upon his government to take action. Although critical of the Nazis and openly supportive of the democratic powers, Labougle was not committed to intervention on behalf of the refugees.[70]

An ability to combine hatred of the Nazis with insensitivity and active dislike of the Jews was clearly demonstrated by Labougle's elderly colleague, Tomás Le Breton, who was Argentina's representative at the Évian Conference and its ambassador to Great Britain in 1940–1942. In his shifting attitude toward the Jews, Le Breton reflected the turn of mind of many Argentine liberals of the time. He was born in Buenos Aires in 1868, the year Sarmiento became president, and studied law in 1885–1891 as the first large waves of immigration commenced. Like many of his peers, he joined the newly founded Radical movement, where he met Alvear and other upcoming young leaders of the first rank. By the time Le Breton was appointed minister of agriculture in 1922, he had behind him many years of distinguished service in the Radical party, both as a member of Congress and ambassador to the United States. His liberal views on immigration, which came to the fore in 1924, seemed to bode well for the Jews. In early 1940, when the leaders of the JCA appealed to him for an entry permit for the relative of a Jewish colonist in Argentina, they addressed him as "a man familiar with our project and its methods of operation" who would surely grant the necessary permit in light of the "long-standing relationship between us." However, the power invested in Le Breton personally to decide the fate of individual refugees exposed his real attitude at that time toward Jewish immigration.[71]

In May 1941, Herbert Emerson, chairman of the Intergovernmental Committee, took on the case of twenty German Jewish children residing in England who wished to join their families in Argentina. Le Breton refused to issue them visas. Lord Winterton, sixth Earl Winterton, a friend of Le Breton's and a "former colleague at the Évian Conference," where he headed the British delegation, tried to persuade the ambassador to change his mind. Winterton later wrote: "I have never met an Ambassador of a neutral country who was more pro-Ally." However, when the real issue came up, Winterton found Le Breton steadfast in his refusal: "He said that the vast majority of the refugees were Jews, and that there were already too many Jews in the Argentine, their number having increased by immigration very largely during the last two or three years." Le Breton maintained that much of this immigration was illegal and argued that "the permanent resident Jewish population was much alarmed at the increase in the general Jewish population, because they fear that it may create a serious amount of antisemitism." When Winterton explained that the immigrants in question were only minors who would be cared for by their relatives, Le Breton "replied that these were exactly the people whom the Argentine Government did not want to have in the country, as they would eventually grow up and would help to increase the Jewish population by propagation. In fact, he said emphatically that he would only grant visas to them *if we were prepared to have them sterilized before they went there* [emphasis added], a task which I told him it was quite beyond our powers to effect."

Lord Winterton failed in his attempt to secure visas for the twenty children. In the process, however, a surprising similarity came to light between the views of the seventy-three-year-old Le Breton, a representative of Argentina's liberal period, and the country's nationalist anti-Semites. Both, it seems, were guided by their fear of the "Jewish threat" to Argentina.[72]

Jew-hatred was then widespread in the Argentine Ministry of Foreign Relations. Throughout its records, we find only one halfhearted attempt to utilize Argentina's influence on behalf of the Jews. On September 11, 1942, a clerk in the German Foreign Ministry wrote that the Argentine chargé d'affaires had come to the office with a list of German Jews living in the Netherlands who had been invited to join their relatives in Argentina. The diplomat acknowledged that Argentina had no right to make such a request, but he was acting on the orders of his minister, whose colleague, Interior Minister Miguel J. Culaciati, "a German supporter," was interested in bringing them over. The clerk intimated that there was little hope for a positive reply, and there seems to have been no further mention of this issue.

On the other hand, the archives of the Argentine Ministry of Foreign Relations contain a wealth of material on the poor treatment of Jews. A careful survey of the records of the Argentine consulates in Marseilles, France, in Spain, and in the countries bordering Argentina demonstrates that the ministry and its employees did their utmost to detect and prevent the infiltration of Jews into Argentina. When Paraguay instituted a law barring entry to "members of the Semitic race," the Argentine Ministry of Foreign Relations adopted a particularly strict interpretation of this law and insisted on checking the truthfulness of statements in which refugees declared they were Catholic before granting transit visas—even after the Paraguayan government had issued entry visas on this basis.[73]

When Argentina finally declared war on Nazi Germany on March 27, 1945—after the defeat of the Third Reich—the issue of "enemy aliens" arose. Fears that German survivors of the Holocaust living in Argentina would be harassed by the police and threatened with the confiscation of their property proved well founded. The appeals of the DAIA to Colonel Juan D. Perón, the government strongman, and to the minister of the interior brought no relief. Despite the optimism of Moshe Goldman, president of the DAIA, in his report on April 2, 1945, the issue was not resolved and required further action by the organization throughout 1945 and the first quarter of 1946. Only on April 11, 1946, more than a year after Argentina's declaration of war, was the DAIA informed that the Ministry of Foreign Relations would "investigate with utmost attention requests for exclusion from the law . . . in the case of all those able reliably to prove ties to the land [Argentina] and no past affiliation with Nazi institutions." The victims of nazism thus ended up having to prove to those who had preserved their neutrality that they were not their own victimizers.[74]

The Final Tally

What, then, was the total volume of Jewish immigration and rescue through Argentina during the Nazi era?

The official figure for immigrants who declared themselves Jewish in the years 1933–1945 was 24,488. Yet, this does not include first-class passengers, except for 1944 and 1945, or those who declared themselves Catholics or Protestants in the hope of better treatment. Indeed, a closer look at some of the Immigration Department's files reveals quite a few "Catholic" immigrants with typically Jewish names.[75] The Jewish organizations, particularly Soprotimis and the JCA, were in a better position to estimate the true volume of Jewish immigration. According to Simón Weill, the author of a comprehensive socioeconomic survey of the Argentine Jewish community in 1936 and a JCA director in Buenos Aires, the total number of immigrants, including illegals, was 39,441. Approximately 40–50 percent were German-speaking and the remainder, East Europeans. This knowledgeable estimate refers only to arrivals; a large number, especially of those reaching Argentina at the beginning of the period, reemigrated.[76] When the war broke out, their previous connection with Argentina might have been helpful in saving a certain number of lives: Some of the Jews who had reemigrated might have returned to Argentina, and others could have claimed protection by showing their Argentine papers. However, such protection was extended to only a few individuals and the total rescue count could hardly be affected thereby. The only sizable rescue operation—the plan to bring over one thousand Jewish children from France—never materialized. Thus, Argentina's only real contribution to the rescue of the Jews was through immigration.

The number of Jewish immigrants during the thirteen years of the Nazi era contrasted sharply with the official figure for Jewish immigration in 1920–1930, which reached 75,505, but also reflected the lower rate of immigration in general during these years. Indeed, between 1933 and 1945, arrivals exceeded departures by only 124,398 persons. This, of course, included transatlantic passengers of all three categories, rather than just immigrants, and excluded those arriving via the neighboring countries, but it provides a striking illustration of the poor volume of immigration. The fact that 97,888 persons, or 78.7 percent of this surplus of arrivals, entered the country in 1933–1938 indicates the drastic impact of the decree of July 1938. This is even more significant given the fact that Argentina's economic recovery was felt much more toward the end of this thirteen-year period than in the early years.[77]

This economic recovery was largely due to the commencement of domestic production to replace imports. After a temporary crisis caused by the outbreak of the war, Argentine products competed successfully with US products on the Latin American market. When the United States entered the war, Argentina's local industry surged ahead all the more.[78] The demand for manpower was certainly great enough for Argentina to have relaxed its immigration policy and created a situation wherein Jewish and Argentine immigration needs would converge, yet this step was not taken because of the conservative attitudes of the ruling class on the subject of immigration. The traditional link between immigration and rural colonization was too deeply rooted to be suddenly replaced by the legitimization of urban immigration. While Foreign Minister Carlos Saavedra Lamas was well pleased with his pact with the "Nordic" nations in 1937, the idea was to provide Argentina with farmers. Urban immigration was merely tolerated, if not actually outlawed.

The fate of Jewish immigration must be understood in the context of this general policy; the fact that it was presented as a refugee problem only aggravated the situation. The demand for special consideration based on Jewish suffering was rejected by the Argentine government when it was first raised in 1933, and the term *refugee* was never accepted as a valid category for immigration. The same attitude was taken to Spanish refugees who escaped after the defeat of the Republic. The Socialists and Radicals intervened on behalf of both Jewish and Spanish refugees in Congress and in extraparliamentary frameworks, but the governments of Justo, Ortiz, Castillo, and, of course, the military junta were more willing to listen to the nationalists than to the liberals and Socialists of the opposition. An apparent deviation from this line occurred in November 1942, when President Castillo authorized the children's rescue from France through immigration. However, Argentina's diplomatic influence on the Germans, which was necessary for this operation, was pursued in such a reluctant and bureaucratic manner that it produced no results.

Argentina's rigid immigration policy, its stubborn refusal to introduce greater flexibility even for humanitarian reasons, and its indifference to Jewish suffering—all these were behind its failure to use its economic and diplomatic potential to save more Jews. To what extent did Jewish and international organizations try to change this situation?

Until 1937, spontaneous Jewish immigration to Argentina lagged far behind the actual immigration opportunities. Before Argentina began to restrict the flow of newcomers, neither the JCA nor the emigration societies in Europe had created any incentive for the Jews to choose Argentina through developing a large-scale colonization program or at least disseminating favorable information about the country. The Jews began to show more interest only after the Anschluss of Austria in March 1938, but, by this time, the JCA had lost practically all its influence with the Argentine authorities and required international assistance to keep the new, retroactive immigration laws from being enforced in the case of colonists whom they had already selected. By June 1940, the staff members of the JCA office in Paris were themselves refugees.

Argentina's major Jewish organization, the DAIA, was occupied with mobilizing the Jewish masses in response to acts of global anti-Semitism such as the onset of persecution in Germany and the Kristallnacht atrocities. It also organized a boycott of German products and supported the massive fund-raising effort on behalf of the victims of nazism and their resettlement in Palestine. Immigration was not its central concern. While it led the campaign to save the French children, it never organized a public demonstration on the issue of immigration. This was left to Soprotimis, with its handful of sympathizers and activists, and to the German-speaking Asociación Filantrópica. These organizations did their best to help the new immigrants, and Soprotimis's discreet contacts with the Immigration Department enabled many Jews to obtain entry permits. Nevertheless, the Argentine Jewish community did not participate directly in these endeavors, and no international Jewish organization called upon it to reorder its priorities and place immigration on a higher rung.

If the Jews had exerted greater political pressure after 1938, would the Argentine government have changed its policy? The answer might be inferred from the few cases in which non-Jewish international agencies pleaded on behalf of the immigrants. The high commissioner for refugees, James McDonald, did his best to influence Argentine policy in 1935, with very meager results. A much less insistent President Roosevelt appealed for Argentina's help in solving the refugee problem at the Évian Conference in July 1938; Argentina's response was to limit immigration even more that same month. The British government in 1938–1939, and Emerson and Winterton in 1941, all representing the Intergovernmental Committee of which Argentina was a member, intervened on behalf of small groups of Jews; they succeeded only in the case of colonists who had already undergone selection. Argentina's policy proved to be immune to pressure, at least to the kind exercised on these occasions.

Ambassador Le Breton's insensitive response to Lord Winterton was more than just a negative reply; it was a denial of the Jews' legitimate right to live in Argentina. This was the freely expressed view of the country's nationalists, and these same feelings, although less explicit, found their way into Argentina's immigration policy.

In spite of the attempts to delegitimize Jewish existence, Argentine Jews continued to cultivate their Jewish identity and to fortify their institutions. The Ashkenazic burial society, known after 1940 as the Asociación Mutual Israelita Argentina (AMIA), became a multiservice communal organization housed along with the DAIA and other institutions in a large, modern building. Welfare societies such as Ezrah expanded their membership, as did many of the flourishing cultural, educational, and recreational organizations, some of which moved into their own buildings during World War II. The economic prosperity attained during these years is attested to by the balance sheets of the two major Jewish banks, the Banco Comercial and Banco Israelita del Río de la Plata, which were founded in 1917 and 1921 respectively as very modest credit cooperatives. The assets of the Banco Comercial increased from 578,548 pesos (US

$189,524) in 1933 to 9,159,187 pesos ($1,845,576) in 1945; the Banco Israelita dispensed loans totaling 6,628,399 pesos ($2,171,372) in 1933, compared with 111,042,812 pesos ($22,375,126) in 1945, after a merger with six smaller credit institutions. The Sephardic communities also consolidated and modernized their communal and educational institutions.[79] But the greatest strides of all were made by the new central European Jewish community.

Within the span of twelve years, the German-speakers grew from a handful of isolated individuals into a prominent and tightly knit organizational entity. In 1937, the Asociación Filantrópica Israelita was joined by the Jüdische Kultur Gemeinschaft (German Jewish Cultural Organization). The establishment of an Orthodox congregation, Ahdut Israel, was followed in 1939 by a Conservative congregation, Nueva Comunidad Israelita, introducing styles of prayer and worship that differed from the modern French liturgy used by the Congregación Israelita. It was not long before a Reform congregation was established, too, further widening the religious pluralism of Argentine Jewry.

The Zionist movement, Theodor Herzl, and the Bar Kochba sports association soon took the lead ideologically, expressing their views through *Die Jüdische Wochenschau,* a German-language weekly that began to appear in Argentina in 1941. Although the German Jews were willing to cooperate with their non-Jewish countrymen in order to perpetuate German language and culture among their offspring, there was little love between them politically, save for a small minority, mostly members of the German left, who dreamed of a return to the homeland together with other anti-Nazi Germans. However, that the relationship between the German Jews and the Jews from Eastern Europe was not devoid of cultural and spiritual tension did not prevent political and sometimes social cooperation between them, and the ability of the German immigrants to band together and organize themselves was greatly admired and respected.[80]

Although the legal position of the German Jewish refugees was still under debate when the war ended, Argentine Jewry, now more diversified and affluent than ever before, looked forward to contributing to the search for a home for the survivors of the Holocaust.

6

The Survivors,
1945–1950

W hen a new era dawned for the world with the Allied victory in Europe, Argentina was under military rule and had immense reserves of gold in its coffers. How did the domestic and international postwar developments affect Argentina's immigration policy? Did they also influence the opportunities for Jewish immigration? How effectively did the survivors of the Holocaust and the local Jewish community lobby for Jewish immigration, and what can be deduced about the status of the Jews in Argentina from the government's response? These are some of the basic questions that must be asked about the crucial years following the Holocaust.

The Displaced Persons

On April 30, 1945, after the Soviet and Allied armies had descended on Berlin and the Third Reich lay smouldering among the ruins, Hitler committed suicide in the bunker outside his office. When the cease-fire went into effect on May 8, the war-torn nations could heave a great sigh; not so the Jewish people.

As the concentration camps were thrown open, the consequences of the assault on the Jews that had begun six and a half years before the outbreak of World War II emerged in all their horror. Greeting the liberators were mountains of corpses, rows of walking skeletons, scenes of monstrous brutality that were captured on film and have been etched ever since in the minds of the human race. These shocking images are a dramatic reminder that the Nazis and their machines of destruction ground to a halt just short of accomplishing their aims.

The Allied forces found over 10 million "displaced persons" (DPs) in Germany and Austria. Among this enormous population, one could find citizens of nearly every European country. Most of them were victims of the Nazis—forced laborers, detainees, and prisoners of various kinds—but many others were Nazi collaborators who had voluntarily joined the German war effort or had fled their home countries when the Nazi defeat became imminent. Among them there were only seventy-five thousand Jewish survivors, and their number dwindled further in the first weeks after the war as many thousands succumbed to hunger and disease. The first solution proposed by the Allies—repatriation—was acceptable for the millions of non-Jews who had been brought to Germany against their will. A small number of Jewish exiles from Western Europe were also anxious to return to their countries in search of relatives and property. But for the Jewish survivors from Eastern Europe, repatriation was out of the question.

Of the more than 3 million Jews who had lived in Poland before the war, only eighty thousand were still alive. In the Fascist countries of southeastern Europe, the number of survivors was higher. However, liberation did not bring an end to the Jew-hatred in these countries. When the Jews went back to seek out relatives and reclaim belongings, the contempt of their murderous dispossessors burned more fiercely than ever. In Poland, the vale of death for so much of European Jewry, more Jewish blood was spilled on July 4, 1946, when a classical medieval blood libel in the town of Kielce triggered off a pogrom that left forty-one dead.

As the Jews fled for their lives, the number of DPs in Germany continued to swell. Toward the end of 1945, it was believed that the DP camps were sheltering 100,000 survivors; by the summer of 1947, there were close to a quarter of a million in Germany, Austria, and Italy. With the help of emissaries from Palestine and US Jewish funding, the survivors established a clandestine Zionist organization that resettled Jews in Palestine using an efficient network of escape routes and absorption points.[1] Officially, however, the gates of the Holy Land had been closed to Jewish immigration since the publication of the White Paper in May 1939, and the

British government had no intention of changing its policies. In June 1946, it rejected the recommendation of the Anglo-American Committee of Inquiry that 100,000 Jews be admitted into Palestine at once. Even the intervention of the president of the United States was to no avail. Finding a home for hundreds of thousands of survivors was thus the key concern of the Jewish people in the years 1945–1947. All the countries that had absorbed immigrants in the past, including Argentina, were called upon to open their doors once more.

The Peronists and Jewish Immigration

The victory of the Allies strengthened the democratic spirit in Argentina. On August 6, 1945, the state of emergency in effect since 1941 was officially repealed, and on September 19, tens of thousands of citizens took part in the Marcha de la Constitución y de la Libertad, parading through the streets of Buenos Aires to demand that Congress be reconvened. The return to constitutional rule was further stimulated by infighting and rivalries in the military junta. Juan Domingo Perón, who was concurrently vice-president, minister of war, and minister of labor, was popular among the workers but disliked and envied by his colleagues. On October 9, he was stripped of all his posts and, four days later, imprisoned on the island of Martín Gracía at the mouth of the Río Uruguay. By October 17, however, he had been brought back and set free at the demand of the raging crowds who demonstrated in central Buenos Aires, and the date that had been set for the general elections was pushed up to February 24, 1946.

A stormy election campaign commenced in the final months of 1945. Perón, supported by the labor unions, lower classes, nationalists, and Catholic loyalists, was set against a broad spectrum of political parties, ranging from the Conservatives to Socialists and Communists. The students and their leaders, many of whom were Jewish, were largely opposed to Perón, as was the Jewish community in general. On the other hand, he enjoyed the support of the Arabs, represented in Argentina by a group of former Syrians and Lebanese.[2] To his opponents, the successful colonel represented the last vestiges of fascism. This claim was strengthened by the "Blue Book," attesting to Perón's close ties with the Axis powers, that was compiled by Spruille Braden, a former US ambassador to Argentina who was now head of Latin American affairs at the State Department in Washington. However, this only poured oil on the nationalist fire. Using the campaign slogan "Perón o Braden!" Perón was able to secure the votes of those Argentines who were more enraged over the US bid to influence the elections than by the accusations against Perón. In Argentina's first democratic presidential elections since 1928, Perón won 56 percent of the vote, and, on June 4, 1946, the third anniversary of the military coup, he became president of Argentina.

In the months after the war, immigration was brought up frequently. In August 1945, Argentina's leading newspapers, *La Nación* and *La Prensa,* called for renewed immigration in the Argentine tradition to meet the needs of the economy as determined by the employers' Unión Industrial Argentina. From the opposite side of the political spectrum, the Communists proclaimed the importance of "developing immigration and measures to promote natural increase." The Socialists were of a similar opinion. Nonetheless, immigration policy did not figure prominently in the election campaign of any political party.[3]

La Tribuna, which supported the new government, took the opposite approach. According to this newspaper, past experience had shown the folly of promoting immigration. When the gates were thrown open in the beginning of the century, the country had been flooded with foreigners to the point of losing its independent character. "Only now are we seeing the reaction to this, in the revolution endorsed this very moment at the polls," claimed the leading article on May 4, 1946. Earlier, the paper had declared: "We prefer the assimilating immigrant over the one who adapts under pressure. There are too few of us Argentines and we will not consent to having our place taken from us in our own home." *La Tribuna* was also against taking in war victims: "The Republic cannot be transformed into an immense sanatorium for nervous diseases." On the other hand, it protested the negative attitude of the liberal newspapers toward German and Italian immigrants. Regarding them as a "fifth column" was not in keeping with the Argentine "love of liberty" and belief in "Christian charity," the newspaper charged. The editors of *La Tribuna* were not unaware of the gravity and complexity of the immigration problem, but they firmly believed that Perón's administration could handle it. "We know that the solution lies in the hands of talented, diligent, and patriotic men," they declared. Special praise was reserved for the head of the Immigration Department, Santiago M. Peralta.[4]

"Doctor of Philosophy and Letters, Department of Anthropology of the University of Buenos Aires"—this was title Peralta went by in his book on the Jews of Argentina, *La Acción del Pueblo Judío en la Argentina,* published in 1943. Written during the period when the fate of Eastern European Jewry was becoming public knowledge, this book was and remains one of the most vicious anti-Semitic tracts ever published in the Republic of Argentina. As befitted an "anthropologist," Peralta opened with a characterization of the "Jewish race" and its uniqueness among the Semitic peoples. Using the classical stereotypes, he depicted the Jews as merchants, as wanderers, as members of a mystical brotherhood, and, above all, as seeking to rule the world. After some fifty pages of "scientific" theory about Jews in general, he came to the point—the Argentine people as the victims of the Jews. "Before this defenseless nation looms the Jewish giant: solid; organized around one idea; directed by one hand; lord over the lives of all as it regulates finance and agricultural wealth, the principal source of national life."

According to Peralta, the Jews not only dominated the economy but also determined immigration policy. A population of less than 14 million, practically no natural increase, and immigration on hold—these were sufficient in Peralta's opinion to arouse the concern of any politician. Yet, the government of Argentina was indifferent to the demographic future of the country, and the Jews were to blame:

> The immigration office has been in their hands for a long time. . . . It is they who instated ignorant, barbaric leaders and brought about the cessation of European immigration so that they would remain the only settlers. . . . This strange resolution coincided with the fall of the Jewish regime in Germany. . . . They needed a new homeland for the "persecuted" from Germany, and the place was our country. When General Justo rose to power, there were ninety thousand Jews [in Argentina]; by the time he stepped down, there were 500,000 . . . and the slow, silent tide of poor Jewish immigrants continues as the Argentines find excitement in Negro music, tropical dancing, and [North] American cinema.

To counter this "Jewish conspiracy," Peralta proposed that all the ignorant and ineffectual leaders be removed—and he be appointed in their place. Indeed, when the war was over and the survivors were desperate for somewhere to go, it was the scientific anthropologist Santiago Peralta who was appointed by the junta to guard Argentina's gates as commissioner of the Immigration Department.[5]

Benjamín Mellibowsky, the elderly secretary of Soprotimis, attempted to reason with Peralta. He and Haim Shoshkes, the HIAS emissary visiting Argentina at the end of 1945, tried to obtain permission for relatives of the first, second, and third degree (parents, children, spouses, siblings, aunts and uncles, and cousins) to join their kin in Argentina. They also pushed for the admission of Jewish craftsmen and industrialists. Peralta made no promises, but his cordial manner led Mellibowsky to believe that he had agreed "not to make any unfavorable decisions on applications of our coreligionists without first consulting with me." Whether this was a projection of Mellibowsky's own desires or an attempt by Peralta to disguise his real views in this preelection period, it was not long before the bitter truth came out.[6]

On March 30, 1946, one of Peralta's most cherished dreams came true: the Oficina Etnográfica was created for the "ethnographic and anthropological study of the diverse currents of possible immigration in order to establish the capacity for adaptability and assimilation of each of them in our people." This information was to be used by the Immigration Department in deciding which immigrants to admit and how to organize their geographical dispersion across the Republic. Peralta did not need this research; he already knew whom he would choose. In his book, *La Acción del Pueblo Arabe en la Argentina,* published at that time, he described the similarities and common origins of the Argentines and the Arabs; the colonial founders of Argentina, he said, came from Andalusia. In what was certainly a new turn in the policies of the Immigration Department, the Arabs were declared desirable immigrants.[7]

The Jews, however, were not. In mid-May 1946, the SS *Jamaica* reached the port of Buenos Aires carrying seventy Jewish passengers with visas issued by Argentine consuls in Europe. Peralta refused to admit them, charging that the visas had been granted improperly. This episode drew attention to a treatise he had written, "Concepts Regarding Immigration," in which he presented his racist ideas and declared his intentions of implementing them in Argentina's immigration policy. After Perón's inauguration in June 1946, a storm of protest erupted. The Committee Against Racism and Anti-Semitism demanded an investigation of Peralta's allegation that the visas of the Jewish passengers were invalid. The morning newspapers accused Peralta of obstructing immigration and damaging the country's good name. *Gobernantes,* a prestigious weekly, reported on the commissioner's racist inclinations and remarks against foreigners in general, which renewed interest in his book on the Jews. According to this weekly, which was quoted in other papers, "the permanency of an anti-Semite at the head of the immigration office is an insult to the country." Certain newspapers began to carry advertisements saying: "Today it is exactly [so many] days since, voicing a real popular desire, we demanded the resignation of the director of immigration, Doctor Santiago Peralta. What is he waiting for?" Protest also came from international circles, which were already in tumult over Perón's election.[8]

Racist and anti-Semitic allegations against Perón and his followers were not new. On that great day for Peronism, October 17, 1945, when mass demonstrations brought Perón back from exile, the Jews of Buenos Aires were already being harassed by his supporters. During the election campaign, he was accused of anti-Semitism by the democratic camp, and this image was reinforced by his open backing of various nationalist elements. Perón denied these charges in public statements and newspaper interviews, and his journalist friends tried to prove that many Jews had voted for him, yet Perón refused to remove Peralta from his post.[9]

The range of action open to the Jewish organizations was very limited. In early August 1946, Jedidio Efron, the president of Soprotimis, met with Peralta to discuss Jewish immigration. The Jewish colonies in Entre Ríos, with which Peralta was familiar from his work as educational inspector in 1918–1919, were cited as an example of the Jewish contribution to the Republic. Peralta promised that Jewish farmers would be treated more liberally, but, on the whole, he responded with "scientific anthropological" arguments. Peralta's meeting with HIAS representative Shoshkes yielded similar results. In the second week of November, a delegation of ten Jewish leaders met with President Perón. Among the issues discussed was the freeze on Jewish immigration. The Immigration Department refused to permit family reunification even in the case of first-of-kin; Jews seeking to immigrate to Paraguay and Bolivia were denied transit visas, as were those who entered Argentina legally from neighboring countries. The president listened to the complaints, asked for a full report on individual cases, and promised that the matter would be investigated.[10]

This meeting was part of a government effort to improve relations with the Jewish community—not through policy changes but through occasional acts of goodwill that were usually politically motivated and highly publicized. One such gesture was the president's order on February 14, 1947, to release forty-seven Holocaust survivors detained aboard the *SS Campaña*. This group had left Europe with Brazilian visas that had expired by the time they reached Rio de Janeiro. When Peralta refused to admit them into Buenos Aires, DAIA president Moshe Goldman appealed directly to Perón, who was about to meet with a group of supporters interested in organizing a Jewish Peronist association. Perón signed the order to release the *Campaña* group, and that week the Organización Israelita Argentina (OIA) was born. Openly encouraged by the president and his wife, the OIA soon began to compete with the DAIA over political representation of the Jews of Argentina. Thus we see that behind Perón's so-called humanitarian gesture, political motives were clearly at work.

The release of the *Campaña* passengers was celebrated by the Jewish institutions and news media for many days. Accompanied by a delegation of Jewish leaders from the DAIA and other organizations, the immigrants visited the presidential mansion to thank Perón personally, although only the minister of interior was there to receive them. The event was hailed by the Jewish press as a turning point in the attitude to Jewish immigration. In fact, it remained an isolated humanitarian-political act.[11]

Peralta's intransigence made it necessary to appeal separately on behalf of each group of immigrants, however small. On March 27 and April 1, 1947, the chairman of the DAIA asked Perón to admit twelve Jewish refugees with Paraguayan visas who were temporarily kept from entering that country by the political unrest there. Despite the fact that they possessed Argentine transit permits, the Immigration Department would not allow them to disembark, and had ordered their return to Europe. The following month, another fourteen refugees were detained on board for nearly three weeks while hundreds of Ukrainian and German fellow passengers entered Argentina with no difficulty. After meeting with a group of Soprotimis activists and an HIAS delegate from the United States, Peralta finally agreed to house them at the government-run immigrants hostel, but only to prevent the affair from stirring up US public opinion. On the same occasion, Peralta promised greater leniency in providing Jewish travelers with transit permits, although he later denied this.

Argentina's attitude to Jewish immigrants became an issue at the United Nations after the interception of a confidential government memo in which its consuls were instructed to withhold visas to Jews. In addition, a Jewish businessman who had approached the commissioner about his brother's immigration was advised by Peralta to pack up his bags and leave Argentina while he and the Jewish community were still able. A delegation of HIAS and Soprotimis officials complained to Foreign Minister Atilio Bramuglio about these official manifestations of anti-Semitism and were promised that President Perón would be informed. By the end of June 1947, Peralta had been dismissed and a new immigration policy was introduced in Argentina.[12]

Immigrants: Supply and Demand

Argentina's demographic problems were further aggravated by the industrialization process that had been set in motion long before Perón. The Perón administration favored accelerating this process and granting priority to the urban sector over agriculture. Agricultural exports and the prices of meat and grain were government-controlled, and farmers were paid in local currency at rates much lower that those on the international market. Agriculture and cattle raising were thus employed to finance industrialization. Aside from the large balance of profits shifted from one sector to another, this policy also intensified migration from rural areas to the city. The result was intersectoral competition for manpower, which was heightened by the development plans of the Perón government. According to one estimate, postwar Argentina was already 50 percent short of the annual manpower increment required by the national economy; further development would tip the scales entirely. The only solution was immigration, and Perón acknowledged this.[13]

At a labor union meeting four days before his taking office, Perón had declared his intention of bringing 2 to 3 million immigrants to Argentina within a short span of time. In his address before Congress a few days later, he cited "directing immigration and intensifying it as much as possible" as one of his goals. This would be accomplished, he stated, with the help of "healthy elements with an affinity to our culture and to the bases of our social structure."

These ideas were worked into a five-year plan outlining the activities of the Perón government for 1947–1951. A new immigration and colonization law was drafted on October 25, 1946, to replace the law dating from 1876. Its principles were spontaneity, selectivity, and directedness. In an effort to settle the apparent contradictions among these terms, the legislators claimed that without hindering "freedom of immigration," they would "establish rules of preference with regard to those currents of immigration more able to adapt to the Argentine character." In this spirit, the third clause of the proposed law stated that

> in no case will immigration be restricted or prohibited on the basis of origin or credo of any kind, but preference will be given to immigrants whose origin, habits, customs, and language will facilitate assimilation with the ethnic, cultural, and spiritual characteristics of Argentina, and who will dedicate themselves to farming, cattle raising, or craftsmanship. Also, preference will be given to immigration consisting of workers and technicians whose skills or expertise are appropriate or required by the country.

Thus we see that Perón and his supporters were not discriminating, as it were, against "undesirable" immigrants; they were only granting priority to the desirables, who now included those with urban-industrial professions.

This policy was acceptable not only to the supporters of the new government, but also to many of its political opponents. When asked for its opinion on the proposal, the conservative and highly influential association of Argentine landowners, the Sociedad Rural Argentina, was openly supportive.[14]

By this time, steps were already being taken to renew the flow of immigration. The first target was Italy, which had suffered greatly in the war. In early 1946, Argentina's ambassador in Rome was instructed to report on the prospects of emigration from Italy. On the basis of this report, the Delegación Argentina de Inmigración en Europa (Argentine Delegation for Immigration in Europe) was established and dispatched to negotiate with the Italian government in December 1946. By February 21, 1947, the two countries had reached an agreement. Argentina would accept laborers, craftsmen, technicians, or farmer-settlers registered for immigration with the government of Italy and would also supply updated information through the delegation on the number of workers required in the various professions. The Comisión de Recepción y Encauzamiento de Inmigrantes (Commission for the Reception and Direction of Immigrants), in collaboration with observers appointed by the Italian government, would handle the absorption of the newcomers and protect them from exploitation. Approved candidates were exempt from the $49 tax on Argentine visas and eligible for travel loans.

Although nearly 100,000 applications had accumulated by the time the agreement was signed in February, the first group set out for Argentina only in June. The bureaucracy and personal documentation required of each immigrant slowed the process considerably, and, early on, it was discovered that many applicants had falsified their occupations. Nevertheless, there were thousands of immigrants among the 38,510 Italian passengers who entered Argentina in 1947. Although slight changes were introduced in the agreement a year later, Italians continued to arrive in large numbers—373,327 over the next four years. Even after subtracting the 115,272 who later left the country, the Italian community in Argentina was augmented by 296,565 persons, which represented half of the total surplus of arrivals over departures during these five years. And, on October 18, 1948, Argentina signed an agreement with Spain, another preferred source of immigration, which brought 140,000 Spaniards into Argentina during the next five years.[15]

In opening its doors to immigration from Italy, Argentina became a haven for Ukrainians, Croats, and Yugoslavians living in Italy who were unable or unwilling to be repatriated after the war. They were all anti-Communist, and a large percentage were Nazi collaborators. With the help of ethnic organizations in Buenos Aires and the Catholic church in Rome, hundreds of Ukrainians and thousands of Croats joined the Italians leaving for Argentina. The US State Department also intervened on behalf of some fifteen thousand Yugoslavians who could not return to Tito's Yugoslavia because they had fought under the promonarchist General Dragoljub Mihajlović or were suspected of collaborating with the Nazis. These people did not fit into the category of refugees handled by the international relief agencies, and their presence on Italian soil was the responsibility of the US and British occupying forces. Argentina was asked by the United States to take in five thousand of them. Likewise, the British government requested that Argentina absorb a group of Polish soldiers who had fought to liberate Italy under the anti-Communist General Władysław Anders. Argentina complied in both cases, thereby bringing into the Republic thousands of newcomers, many of them openly anti-Semitic.

Perón's willingness to cooperate with the Allies signified a thaw in the strained relations that had existed between Argentina and the United

States during the war. As the Soviet Union and the United States grew further apart, Washington toned down its denunciation of Perón as a dictator and a Nazi sympathizer, and welcomed Argentina as a new partner in the fight against communism. Perón took advantage of this state of affairs, which tied in well with his hatred of communism, to change his country's immigration policy. A presidential order in October 1948 declared that no native of Russia or its satellites would be admitted into Argentina. So strictly was this order followed that even the intervention of the Vatican in certain cases was of no avail.[16]

Although Perón opened Argentina to mass immigration and envisaged his country's rehabilitation through the help of the Allies, Argentina did not join the International Refugee Organization that took over the work of the United Nations Relief and Rehabilitation Administration on July 1, 1947. Argentina had initially agreed to sit on the board of directors but then withdrew because it feared it might lose control over its own immigration policy. The truth was that Argentina refused to accept immigrants it considered "undesirable." As we see from a comprehensive report on the history of the International Refugee Organization, no overall resettlement plan was devised for Argentina: "Migration to the Argentine Republic remained on an individual basis, the documentation for each application being completed in accordance with normal consular procedure." Even so, 32,712 refugees had been resettled in Argentina by the time the International Refugee Organization closed its doors in 1952.[17]

Perón sought to improve relations with the United States but, at the same time, to assure Argentina's hegemony in South America. He believed this could be accomplished by taking in scientists, technicians, military personnel, and police experts from the collapsed Third Reich. When the war was over, key Nazi figures were vigorously courted by the victors, and the competition became even fiercer with the eruption of the cold war. Argentina may not have attracted the top people, but it is undeniable that many Nazis found a secure niche there. The extent of this phenomenon and how it affected Perón's administration require further investigation. However, the fact that thousands of Fascists from Italy and elsewhere were free to settle in Argentina indicates that, unlike the Jews, they were not regarded as *indeseables*.[18]

The Comisión de Recepción y Encauzamiento began its work by questioning Argentine industrialists about the number and type of workers they needed for their factories. The Jewish industrialists were particularly excited. On May 16, 1947, the Jewish Chamber of Commerce and Industry called together representatives of the major Jewish organizations and newspapers to discuss the possibility of bringing over Jewish immigrants to work in Jewish-owned factories. It was decided to hold an employment survey among the factory owners and to obtain a list of candidates for immigration from the world Jewish organizations, primarily HIAS. HIAS's representative in Argentina, Mark Turkow, was initially skeptical, but when Perón issued a new presidential order later that month, he, too, became enthusiastic. The order signed on May 29, 1947, seemed to herald a fundamental change in Argentina's policy and fresh prospects for Jewish immigration. The preamble stated that "since the reasons for the decrees of 1932 and 1938 regarding the restriction of immigration have disappeared . . . the president of Argentina, in a general accord with his ministers, declares: The Immigration Department *may* [emphasis added] permit the entry into the country of foreigners with any family relation whatsoever to residents of Argentina, regardless of how long they have lived here and the place where the immigration process began." The immigration organizations were authorized to handle the applications of relatives and of "technical experts, artisans, skilled workers, and contracted colonists regardless of nationality." All these "invited" immigrants were exempt from paying consular fees, thereby removing the financial barriers on immigration that had been in effect since 1932.

At long last, it seemed as if Soprotimis's demands had been met. Greatly encouraged by the fact that this order bore the signatures of the president and his cabinet and that Peralta was gone, the Jews rushed to the offices of Soprotimis and the Immigration Department to apply for their relatives. The directors of Soprotimis met with the new immigration commissioner, Pablo Diana, in early September, personally submitting these applications. On September 26, Soprotimis and the DAIA asked the Comisión de Recepción to recognize them as authorized immigration agents. They promised to cover all the expenses involved in bringing over the immigrants and maintaining them until they were settled, preferably in the provinces.[19]

Their hopes were soon dashed. The Comisión de Recepción refused to recognize them because "this committee grants the authority in question only to Argentine shipping companies owning vessels that fly the national flag." The DAIA tried to bring its grievances before Perón, but Goldman, who had enjoyed personal contacts with the president since 1943, was denied an interview. The Jewish community wrote letters to protest the "obstacles that have impeded the entry of Jews for years," and another meeting was arranged with the immigration commissioner—all to no avail. Only six hundred Jews entered Argentina in 1947 according to HIAS and Soprotimis records, compared with an official immigration total of 116,095. When the immigration total doubled in 1948 (reaching 219,096 according to the official figures), there were no more than 680 Jewish entries, including travelers on their way to other countries. It is apparent that it was not only Peralta who was to blame for locking the gates to Jews. The administration as a whole, from the president down, was responsible for keeping the Jews out of Argentina.[20]

Legal Versus Illegal Immigration

The failure of the DAIA and Soprotimis to eliminate discrimination against the Jews in Argentina's immigration policy led to ever-increasing attempts to enter the country illegally. As before, the neighboring countries, and especially Paraguay, were used as a cover. There were various agents in Buenos Aires and Paraguay who helped Jews in Argentina and elsewhere obtain visas for their relatives. However, the Argentine immigration service did not grant transit visas easily. Transit passengers reaching the port of Buenos Aires were denied permission to disembark until their destination was confirmed. After reaching this destination, however, they would return to Argentina by stealing across the border. When tighter control was introduced in the northern provinces, dozens of these border-crossers found their way to jail. The result was that the legalization of all immigrants who lacked the requisite papers, both longtime residents and new arrivals, became a more urgent and pressing issue.

Handling the day-to-day affairs of the illegal immigrants was now almost exclusively in the hands of Soprotimis. After its breakaway from HIAS in November 1945 and the dismantling of HICEM, the JCA was much less involved in Soprotimis's activities. Its interest flagged all the more after the war, when candidates for agricultural settlement in Argentina became increasingly hard to find, and the few who met the requirements of the JCA were refused visas by the Immigration Department. HIAS, which took over HICEM's duties, continued to maintain close ties with Soprotimis and contribute small sums to its budget.

On the other hand, both HIAS and Soprotimis found themselves competing with private agencies that arranged visas and public organizations such as the Joint Distribution Committee that provided travel loans. The president and founder of Soprotimis, Max Glucksman, died in October 1946, and its secretary general, Benjamín Mellibowsky, retired soon after. In 1947, the society underwent a period of reorganization with the goal of bringing together all the bodies involved in immigration. As a result, the communal organization that had developed from the Ashkenazic burial society, now known as the AMIA, also became involved in immigrant absorption. The Asociación Filantrópica of the German Jews and other landsmanschaften operated alongside it, offering aid to Holocaust survivors from their hometowns. Yet, Soprotimis remained the only major organization that brought immigrants to Argentina. In the course of 1948, it was to play a central role in the lives of the Jewish illegal immigrants.[21]

In early February 1948, about a year after the release of the *Campaña* passengers, the DAIA met with Perón to find a solution for nine Jewish immigrants who had been living in Argentina illegally for some time and were now under custody at the immigrants hostel prior to their expulsion from the country. No progress was made at this meeting, and in the coming months, the Jewish community's preoccupation with Israel's War of Independence pushed the problem of illegal immigration temporarily aside. Perón, who had not kept his promise to support the UN partition plan for Palestine on November 29, 1947, was now pressed into recognizing the State of Israel. The improvement in his attitude to the Jewish community was noticeable after May 15, 1948, when the Jewish state became a fact. In June, the chairman of the DAIA reported that he and the delegates of the OIA and Soprotimis had met twice more with the president. Perón had promised that "the group of coreligionists detained at the immigrants hostel over the past few months, after having entered the country without the required legal documents, will be set free." He also pledged "to regulate the status of all those who have entered the country in the same manner" and empowered the OIA to handle the administrative aspects. All those at the meeting were highly impressed with Perón, and, of course, the OIA in particular. Giving this organization administrative responsibility also furthered Perón's own interests: It drew his Jewish supporters into the limelight. The DAIA was hardly enthusiastic about this assignment of duties, but Soprotimis proceeded to forge close ties with the Peronist organization.

A group of volunteers leaving to fight in Israel's War of Independence, 1948 (Archives of Kibbutz Mefalsim)

On August 20, 1948, after a month of preparations by the OIA and other major Jewish organizations, the Jewish community held a tribute in honor of General Perón and his wife, Evita. Despite the festivity of the occasion, a protest against the discriminatory treatment of Jewish immigrants was included in the remarks of the DAIA chairman, Ricardo Dubrowsky.[22]

By early September, no solution for the illegal immigrants was yet in sight. One hundred twenty immigrants sat in jail in the town of Posadas in northern Argentina, and others were on trial in Buenos Aires. However, a proposal then being debated in Congress offered a glimmer of hope. Clause 42 of this proposed law, involving the issuing of identity cards and establishment of a national population registrar, stated that illegal aliens who appeared before the authorities within ninety days would be pardoned and granted identity cards. The law was ratified by Congress on September 24 and became effective when the president and minister of interior affixed their signatures on October 14.[23]

Was the inclusion of Clause 42 a special gesture toward the Jewish community or merely an administrative measure to facilitate government control over the inhabitants? The sources at our disposal do not answer this question. The Jewish community, however, was clearly overjoyed at the prospect of a general pardon for thousands of refugees. In its annual report for 1948, Soprotimis cited "two basic events that characterize this past year. One with capital importance for Jews as a whole, and the other of particular interest to our community in Argentina: the establishment of the State of Israel . . . and the legalization of thousands of Jewish immigrants without documentation . . ."

The moment the law was passed, Soprotimis, with the help of other organizations, braced itself to handle the hundreds of Jews who submitted legalization requests. After the presentation of a passport, character references, and proof of employment or means of livelihood, the applications were forwarded to OIA and then to the Immigration Department along with the required fee. To simplify the procedure, the immigration authorities agreed to accept character references issued by Soprotimis itself, on the basis of two letters of testimony. Within ninety days, Soprotimis was able to legalize the status of six thousand immigrants.

The period of amnesty was scheduled to end on January 12, 1949, but was extended on January 20 when it became clear that many illegal immigrants had not yet registered. In March, however, just as the Jewish community was planning another tribute to Perón for recognizing the State of Israel, the difficulties resumed. Illegal immigrants were again detained for long periods of time, and Soprotimis's special privileges ceased to be honored. With thousands of undocumented immigrants still living in Argentina, the OIA pushed for further extensions of the amnesty agreement, on July 8 and again on October 4. The Jewish institutions worked tirelessly to locate the immigrants in question, and, according to Soprotimis records, another four thousand were helped to legalize their status. By the end of March 1950, the final date, they had been joined by hundreds more.[24]

In marked contrast to this liberalism toward illegal immigrants, the attitude toward legal Jewish immigration remained as uncompromising as ever. In its annual report for 1948, which was so enthusiastic about the legalization, Soprotimis wrote:

> In respect to the possibilities for Jewish immigration to Argentina, this past year was not very generous in meeting our expectations. Lamentably, despite the lack of any official regulation espousing racial discrimination, it is still impossible to obtain entry permits even for first-of-kin. . . . The few permits that were somehow secured were not approved by the consular agents in Europe. Practically speaking, the aspiration for Jewish immigration to Argentina has been, and continues to be, blocked.[25]

Argentina and the Survivors

Unlike the United States, Canada, and the United Kingdom, all of which had suffered from the transition to a wartime economy, Argentina was not hurt by the war. On the contrary, it flourished in many sectors. When the guns fell silent, Argentina did not face years of rehabilitation or readjustment to a peacetime economy but rather a severe manpower shortage brought on by tremendous momentum in growth and development. In the five years between 1947 and 1951, 598,939 immigrants settled permanently in Argentina—compared with 126,925 in the fourteen-year period between 1933 and 1946. The number of Jews, however, was extremely small. In the five years after the Holocaust, 1945–1949, Jewish sources recorded the legal immigration of no more than one thousand to fifteen hundred Jews.[26]

On the positive side, illegal immigrants were pardoned in large numbers. According to Soprotimis, nearly ten thousand Jews had taken advantage of the opportunity by the end of 1949, and several hundred more did so during the first quarter of 1950. Soprotimis and the OIA were lavish in their praise of Perón, virtually ignoring the fact that the pardon was equally advantageous for the government, and that many non-Jewish immigrants, including Nazis and Nazi collaborators, were pardoned, too. We do not know precisely how many of the Jews who benefited from the amnesty agreement settled in Argentina after the Holocaust. The only figures available for these years are Simón Weill's estimates for the total number of Jewish immigrants, both legal and illegal. According to Weill, eight hundred Jews entered Argentina in 1945, five hundred in 1946, five hundred in 1947, two thousand in 1948, and one thousand in 1949, bringing us to a total of forty-eight hundred. Assuming that fifteen hundred of these entered the country legally, then the remaining thirty-three hundred were illegals.[27]

This was a far cry from the number of Jewish DPs Argentina was capable of absorbing and demonstrated the limited success of the Jewish organizations in changing the situation. As the demand for immigration surged dramatically, the DAIA, whose main efforts were devoted to combating anti-Semitism and supporting the struggle for Jewish independence in Palestine, made an attempt to tackle this issue, too. However, many of its plans, such as bringing over one thousand young Holocaust survivors to compensate for the futile attempt to rescue one thousand children from France, ended in failure.[28]

In the interval between the Holocaust and the establishment of the State of Israel, Argentina was not the only country that remained unmoved by the misery of the survivors. From these other countries, General Perón might have gained the "moral support" he needed to persevere in his discrimination against Jewish immigrants, and this prevented any pressure upon him on their part to change his policies.

Earl G. Harrison was sent to Europe by US President Harry Truman to report on the plight of the DPs. His account of the shocking conditions he found there, which was published in the United States at the end of September 1945, helped to improve the lot of Jewish survivors in US-occupied zones. On the other hand, his recommendations for a permanent solution achieved relatively little. His first proposal, that the British government permit the resettlement of 100,000 Jews in Palestine, was rejected. The second, that the United States absorb tens of thousands of immigrants, was accepted only in part. On December 22, 1945, Truman issued a special order to admit thirty-nine thousand DPs. Although this order remained effective for a year and a quarter, only 14,688 visas were granted to Jews. Around this time, broad sectors of the US public began to press for the absorption of 400,000 DPs—a figure equal to nearly half the United States's unfilled immigration quota during the war. To minimize resistance to the idea, the emphasis was on the non-Jewishness of the population in question and the fact that Jews would account for no more than 20 percent. After long deliberations, Congress passed a bill on June 18, 1948, that permitted 200,000 immigrants to the United States over a two-year period. When the Displaced Persons Law was presented to the president for signing, he remarked on the discrimination against the Jews that was evident in certain clauses.[29]

The Canadian attitude toward the immigration of Jews was just as negative as that of the United States, if not more so. Canada's reluctance to accept Jewish immigrants, which was obvious even before World War II, continued in the years after the war. Despite its efforts, the Canadian Jewish Congress obtained only two thousand entry permits for Jews from 1945 to 1948. "None is too many" seemed to be the slogan of the Canadian immigration officers when dealing with the survivors of the Holocaust, just as it had been when the rescue of Jews prior to the Holocaust was still possible.[30] Let us bear in mind, then, the immigration norms of the United States and Canada when considering the assertion of George Messersmith, the US ambassador to Argentina, that "Perón and his associates in the government . . . are against any Jewish discrimination"—a statement made while Peralta was still in office.[31]

Although based on anti-Jewish sentiment, Argentina's immigration policy was not accompanied by any government action against the established Jewish community. On the contrary, Perón's official relations with Argentina's Jews were correct and, in the case of the Peronist Jewish organization, OIA, even warm. When he addressed Jewish audiences, he praised the spirit of Jewish national solidarity, and he certainly respected the Jews' international connections, which he tried to enlist for the furtherance of his own aims. Yet, this did not transform the Jewish community into a genuine and wholly legitimate Argentine entity. Increasing the number of Jews through immigration was not allowed, and the perpetuation of their individuality through Jewish institutions, culture, language, and so on was tolerated only in the sense that these phenomena were tolerated in other foreign communities "resident" in Argentina. Perón's positive attitude toward the Zionist cause did not contradict this stance but rather complemented it.[32]

Both Argentina's need for immigrants and the Jewish need for a home were acutely felt during the postwar years, but the paths of Jewish and Argentine history were not destined to meet. The nationalists in Argentina had created an identity—*argentinidad*—that ruled out the kind of pluralism that would have allowed the Jews to be considered a legitimate part of the nation. This was not a new ideology, but, merged now with Peronist populism, it became the official line and gained a much wider influence than ever before. It caused the Jewish immigrants to be regarded as *indeseables*.

7

Conclusion

Less than a quarter of a million Jews entered Argentina during the 140 years we have studied, and many of them eventually reemigrated. This was definitely a meager share in the wave of cross-continental migration that took place during this period and was estimated to involve over 5 million Jews.[1]

The Three Actors

Why did so few Jews make Argentina their home? The answer to this critical question may be found in the interplay between the three principal actors in the immigration drama, namely, the host society, Argentina; the Jewish immigrant; and the Jewish organizations called upon to assist this process.

The need for immigration was felt in the Argentine Republic from its earliest days and effectively expressed in the Immigration and Colonization Law of 1876. During the 1880s, an aggressive and very costly campaign was launched to bring immigrants to the country. Despite the severe economic crisis in 1889–1891, this open door policy continued, and millions of immigrants settled in Argentina before the flow was temporarily checked by another economic crisis and the outbreak of World War I in 1914.

The Jewish immigrant came onto the stage rather late. During the first decades of the nineteenth century, very few Jews crossed the ocean; until 1880, intercontinental Jewish migrants numbered about 200,000, and they headed almost exclusively for the United States. Only a trickle reached the shores of South America. Later, when the pogroms in Russia unleashed the first large wave of Jewish emigrants, it was still the United States that attracted them, although many settled in Germany, Great Britain, and France. Argentina was discovered by the Jewish passengers of the *SS Weser* in 1889, at the very end of the brief period during which Argentina introduced a lavish free-tickets policy to attract immigrants. It was as a direct result of this policy, and of the intervention of Jewish organizations and communal leaders in France and Germany, that this discovery took place and the historical paths of the Jewish people and Argentina converged.

Now that the three actors were on the stage, Baron de Hirsch appeared and moved the plot forward with his colonization project and the institutionalization of the JCA. The creation of an economic basis for Jewish immigrants and the systematic transfer of organized groups of settlers to their new home, as was done by the JCA in Argentina, was a unique phenomenon in the history of modern Jewish migrations. Only the work of the Zionist Organization after World War I, and especially after the establishment of the State of Israel, could compare. Yet, the scope of the JCA's immigration activities, both during the baron's lifetime and after his death, was limited to populating the colonies at a rate determined by the organizational capabilities of the JCA, regardless of Argentina's immigration potential. Noncolonists who chose to settle in Argentina had nowhere to turn for assistance. The JCA did not make use of its authoritative position to establish programs for the economic absorption of Jewish immigrants aside from farmers. Without encouragement to come, and only partial and sporadic assistance to remain, the number of Jews who made Argentina their permanent home before World War I was thus far below the number Argentina was able and prepared to receive.

The political consequences of the emerging proletariat were already felt by Argentina's ruling class before the end of the nineteenth century. Another source of irritation was the linguistic and cultural pluralism that began to "invade" the capital and some of the provinces. Opposition to this social, ethnic, and cultural melee mounted but was not strong enough to change the open door policy in any radical manner. The Red scare, or fear of a worldwide proletarian revolution, was shared in the 1920s by both Argentina and the United States. Unlike the United States, however, Argentina did not shut its doors; entry was just made more difficult through the introduction of increasingly rigid bureaucratic regulations that made clearer Argentina's already existing priorities, namely, that immigration was meant first and foremost to provide farmers, and that urban immigrants were not wanted. This was the basis for the agreement reached by Juan Ramos and the JCA in 1924. Other types of immigration, particularly the reunification of families, were constantly being curbed through new and tortuous decrees.

Opposition to immigration gained the upper hand during the 1930s, based on the traumatic experiences of the Great Depression and reinforced by growing nationalism and xenophobia. While couched in general terms, Argentina's immigration policy in July 1938 clearly discriminated against the Jews, the formula being that "forced" emigrants—that is, refugees— were not real immigrants as conceived in Argentine law.

Of course, the potential Jewish emigrant in Europe was not aware of the undercurrents in Argentina that were working to change this country's immigration policy. His choice was influenced by the immigration options still open to him, by his personal connections with relatives and *landsleit,* and by the information he gathered about the life in the host countries. Exactly what the multitudes considering emigration in the 1920s heard about Argentina is hard to say, but we do know that Argentina was given low priority by thousands of emigrants heading for the United States who were stranded when the US Congress introduced new immigration laws in 1924. Was it Argentina's reputation in Eastern Europe as a den of white slave trade that deterred some of the potential immigrants? Was it, as Louis Oungre claimed, the biased coverage of the dispute between the colonists and the JCA in the Polish and Lithuanian Jewish newspapers? While Argentina's image as reflected in the Jewish press in Europe and the United States requires further study, there is no doubt that the Jewish establishment refrained from any explicit encouragement of immigration to Argentina.

As we have seen, the role of the third actor in our triangle, the Jewish organizations, was quite limited. Even after the dispute between Halfon and the Central Committee for the Relief of the War Victims was resolved, and Soprotimis came into existence, immigrant absorption remained a secondary issue pursued by a handful of activists. Funding was commensurate with this low status, and the immigration congress in 1928 did little to improve the situation. The JCA refused to consider agricultural settlement as a means of expanding immigration, boycotting the discussion of this issue at the congress. In this way, it flung away the main opportunity afforded by Argentina's immigration policy for bringing in more Jews. HICEM, the international organization devoted to emigration, did not see its task as the encouragement of emigration to Argentina or any other country; its goal was to assist those who had made the decision to emigrate, wherever they wished to go. Throughout the 1920s, Jewish immigration to Argentina thus remained a personal enterprise involving the immigrant and his close relatives.

As Hitler rose to power in Germany and tens of thousands of Jews crossed the borders, the Jewish organizations modified their stance. They approached the Argentine authorities on behalf of potential immigrants, and a new welfare organization, Hilfsverein der Deutschsprechender Juden, later renamed the Asociación Filantrópica, opened its doors. But increased immigration did not become a major priority for Argentine Jewry, and the colonization policies of the JCA remained as they were. There was no acceleration in the pace of settlement, and the proposal to introduce small farms in the vicinity of the urban centers, which might have suited the German Jewish immigrants better, was repeatedly rejected. Thus, the colonization scheme of the JCA was a solution only for a few hardy individuals who could endure the rough life and isolation involved in pioneering. From the outset, the JCA refused to be a partner to fictitious authorizations of settlement. Consequently, the role it played in augmenting immigration was limited to its support of Soprotimis on a local level, and HICEM on an international level.

Although a large proportion of Jewish emigrants became refugees, in 1933–1935 they were not fugitives who would go to Argentina at any cost. It was only in 1936, and especially during 1938–1941 that the dikes set up by the Argentine government began to overflow, and illegal immigration attained significance. The Jewish organizations now employed their limited resources to help these de facto immigrants legalize their status.

The only difference after the Holocaust was that the Argentine authorities dropped their mask and adopted a more explicitly anti-Jewish policy. Whereas urban immigration was no longer curbed, the bias against Jewish immigrants continued. Thus we see that though one of the players, Argentina, tried to leave the stage, the other two—the Jewish immigrant through illegal immigration and the Jewish organizations through their efforts to assist him—kept the act going.

In the fifty years preceding the Nazi era, the volume of Jewish immigration to Argentina was determined by the lack of interest of the Jewish emigrants and the lack of encouragement by the Jewish organizations. During the Holocaust era and the postwar years, it was Argentine immigration policy that drastically limited the number of Jewish arrivals.

Why did the Jewish establishment act as it did and why were the Argentines so negative toward the Jews?

Ideologies and Legitimacy

Although migration was a basic and vital facet of modern Jewish history, it did not occupy a central position in Jewish ideology. Revolutionary socialists, the Bund included, fought for a solution of the Jewish problem in their home countries. This was also true of the liberal, emancipated Jews in France, Great Britain, and Germany, who were the principal supporters of the Jewish philanthropic organizations. After the death of Baron de Hirsch, the JCA adopted this attitude, too. While the Zionists recognized the importance of mass migration for the Jews, and Ber Borochov and his socialist-Zionist followers turned spontaneous emigration into a cornerstone of their Zionist thinking, they dedicated themselves to resettlement in Palestine—not to emigration to other parts of the world. Only territorialists, and particularly those with socialist beliefs such as Latzky-Bertholdi, pushed for a worldwide organization to encourage and aid Jewish migrants. Their supporters were very few.[2]

Most of these ideologies also found their adherents among the Jews of Argentina, who tirelessly devoted themselves to a variety of causes. Immigration to Argentina, however, was not a top priority in any of these ideological associations and was shunted aside.

The attitude to the Jews in Argentina was very much bound up with the Argentines' ideas on national identity. When the conflict between liberals and clericalists that had emerged during the writing of the Constitution in 1853 flared up again in 1883–1884 over the issue of the public education law, the supporters of a liberal, nonreligious school system gained the upper hand. The Catholic loyalists who demanded that Catholic dogma be incorporated in the curriculum may have been vanquished, but they did not vanish. When the military junta came to power sixty years later, in December 1943, the Catholic loyalists finally had their way: The teaching of Catholicism was introduced in all public schools. In their view, Argentina was a Catholic nation by virtue of its history, national identity, and population. The Peronist bloc in Congress, which was democratically elected in 1946 and not yet transformed into a docile group of supporters, reconfirmed this stance in a majority vote on March 14, 1947.[3] For a substantial part of the Argentine nation (possibly a half or more), non-Catholics and, particularly, non-Christians could never be regarded as full Argentines. Although they were not to be harassed or molested, their presence in Argentina was merely tolerated; they were only residents—not legitimate members of the nation.

Even the liberals were opposed to the preservation of ethnic distinctions, Jewish or otherwise. Sarmiento, a leading advocate of mass immigration, spoke out in 1881 against the inclination of Italian immigrants to transmit their language and culture to their offspring. His support of the liberal, secular public school was explicitly aimed at bringing about the disappearance of ethnicity by merging the immigrants and preventing them from achieving cultural-ethnic consolidation.[4] This view was officially expressed in a report on the national census in 1895, which enthusiastically supported the biological fusion of foreigners and Argentines to create "a new, intelligent, and vigorous race."[5]

And so we see that Argentina's attitude to Jewish immigration was closely bound up with its self-image as a Catholic society and its expectation that immigrants would integrate completely. This had an important bearing on the degree to which Argentina was disposed to grant legitimacy to the Jews. In 1910, the now-retired immigration commissioner, Juan Alsina, and the young writer and educator Ricardo Rojas spoke out against the de facto social and cultural pluralism that had been created by immigration. Like others in Argentina, they upheld the "melting pot" theory, in which foreign groups and cultures would combine to form a united whole. The Jews, however, demonstrated that they were indissoluble. They were endogamic, they preserved their linguistic, religious, and cultural distinctiveness, and they were insistent on passing on their heritage to the younger generation. Moreover, they were densely concentrated in the center of Buenos Aires and Argentina's three major provinces, and thus highly visible.

As Argentine nationalism grew stronger, the estrangement from the Jews grew, too, although not necessarily to the point of the overt anti-

Semitism that was common among the extreme nationalists. When Perón blended nationalism and populism, with its latent Catholic overtones, anti-Jewish feeling was brought into the mainstream. Through the spiritual revival of the caudillo Juan Manuel de Rosas, populist-Catholic beliefs were further disseminated. The notion of a "Catholic republic" gained currency, perhaps not in the clericalist sense of 1853, but in the sense of a national identity.

Under these circumstances, the Jewish community could claim legitimacy only as a *colectividad extranjera*. This type of legitimacy Perón was willing to grant lavishly. However, strengthening the community through massive immigration was not in line with his thinking, hence the restrictions on the entry of Jews and the bureaucratic red tape introduced to deter potential immigrants.

The Outcome

In their espousal of the melting pot theory, Sarmiento and Rojas overlooked or refused to recognize the fact that while some immigrants were willing to abandon their traditions and identity, many others were not. For groups such as the Jews, immigration signified a meeting rather than a fusion of cultures, and the intention was to keep them both.

The first budding of the Jewish community in 1862 proved that ancestral memories and mores were still strong enough to induce some of the more sensitive Jews to seek an organized expression of their Jewish identity. The majority of the Jews living in Buenos Aires at the time did not share these feelings, and the newborn community might not have outlived its founders if mass immigration in the late 1880s had not assured its continuity. The diverse Jewish needs of these newcomers led to the creation of a ramified institutional network in the cities and colonies, with an intellectual elite and religious functionaries drawn from the body of new settlers. The colonies, with their large tracts of land, almost exclusively Jewish population, and independent educational, religious, and economic institutions, represented a phenomenon of quasi-autonomy that was unique in the whole of the Diaspora.

Nonetheless, even before World War I, acculturation set in. The children of the colonists, who attended high schools and universities in the urban centers, acted as one of the bridges into Argentine society. Literary periodicals such as *Juventud* and *Vida Nuestra* were early expressions of the creative encounter between the Jews and Spanish culture. Even manifestations of anti-Semitism, such as the pogrom during La Semana Trágica in January 1919 and other incidents during the 1930s, which dealt shocking blows to the Jews of Argentina, did not dampen the prevailing optimism with regard to successful integration or sever the cultural contacts with Argentine society. When the Nazis declared war on the Jewish people, with its local repercussions in the form of creole anti-Semitism, the Jews of Argentina emerged strengthened in Jewish identity and created the DAIA, their political representation in Argentina. Their organizational ties with world Jewry, particularly through the Zionist Organization, which had existed since the birth of the community, intensified during the Holocaust period, and as their financial status improved, they became firm supporters of global Jewish causes. Thus we see that though the Jewish community came into existence during the liberal period of Argentine history, it was in the nationalistic and populist periods that it achieved consolidation.

Epilogue

The second half of the 1950s marked a decisive change in the character of immigration to Argentina. The number of immigrants from Europe dropped drastically, and, beginning in 1965, Europeans leaving the Republic outnumbered those who arrived. But the overall immigration balance remained positive because of the tide of newcomers from Paraguay, Bolivia, Chile, Uruguay, and Brazil. All told, 1,559,013 immigrants from these neighboring countries settled in Argentina during the thirty-year period from 1955 to 1984, close to 1 million from Paraguay and Bolivia alone. Indoamericans began settling in all parts of the country, many of them illegal immigrants who had crossed the border to find work. A large proportion were smuggled in by Argentine bosses who took advantage of their fragile status and employed them under deplorable conditions. In order to solve this problem, the government repeated the measure taken by President Perón in 1948: It offered amnesty to the illegals. During four periods of amnesty declared between 1958 and 1985, 516,277 persons legalized their status in Argentina. In the 1980s, a new, "exotic" group of immigrants made their appearance: Koreans who had left their homeland, with its stable currency and high living standards, hoping to make a profit in Argentina where devaluations were frequent and prices low.[1]

No Jewish immigration of note reached Argentine shores during this period. There were only two more stimuli of Jewish immigration to Argentina: the exodus from Communist Hungary following the unsuccessful revolution of 1956, and the exodus from Egypt after the Sinai campaign of October 1956. The fallout from these events was quite small. The Argentine national census in 1960 showed that only 35.4 percent of the 833 North African Jews identified had arrived in Argentina between 1940 and 1960. Furthermore, only 299 of all the North African Jews in the country (including those who had immigrated before World War II), hailed from Egypt. Even if we assume that the figures for the Jewish community are incomplete, the Sinai campaign in 1956–1957 did not add much.[2] A careful reckoning based on the 1960 census gives us a mere 2,094 Jewish newcomers between 1955 and 1960, compared with a total overseas immigration to Argentina of 84,048.[3]

Jewish immigration declined even more in later years, and no longer constituted a factor of importance in the size of the Jewish community. A demographic study based on the 1960 census has shown that Argentina's Jewish population reached a peak of 310,000 that year and has been declining ever since.[4] Of the persons identified that year, 113,881 were immigrants and the remainder were native-born. With immigration practically at a standstill for twenty years, most of the foreign-born were elderly. It was their children and grandchildren who accounted for the overwhelming majority of the Jewish population. In this respect, the Argentine Jewish community was consolidated as never before.[5]

With the maturation of the second and third generations, the financial standing of the Jews steadily improved. Perón's allocation of greater resources to industry naturally resulted in priority being given to the urban sector, to which most Jews belonged. On the other hand, his policies drained the agricultural sector. Migration to the cities increased, and large numbers of Jews left the colonies. Nevertheless, according to the 1960 census, 2.3 percent of all the Jews in the work force (who declared their Jewishness) were employed in agriculture. In the provinces, 10.9 percent of all Jewish males were farmers. Such a proportion of Jews in rural occupations was probably unheard of anywhere else in the West. As time passed, many of the Jews who remained in the colonies prospered and bought up the lands of those who moved to the cities, pursuing large-scale farming and cattle raising with the help of hired laborers. Jews also maintained their position of leadership in the agricultural cooperatives, which were now mostly non-Jewish. In this way, the colonization scheme of Baron de Hirsch continued to leave its imprint on Argentina.[6]

The organized Jewish community also gained in wealth and prestige. The organizations consolidated in the 1930s and 1940s became more active, public buildings multiplied, Yiddish newspapers and publishing companies flourished, and an increasing number of Jewish publications were put out in Spanish. The immigrant generation still retained key roles in leadership, and greater centralization was introduced through the nationwide umbrella organization, Va'ad Ha-Kehilot (the Communities' Committee), which was initiated in 1952 by the Ashkenazic community of Buenos Aires to promote the educational and religious interests of all sectors of the population. In the late 1950s and early 1960s, non-Orthodox religious movements such as the Conservative movement and, to a lesser extent, the Reform movement made their appearance in Argentina as local branches of the movements in the United States.[7]

North American influence may have spread through the work of organizations such as the American Jewish Committee, but Jewish life in Argentina was more profoundly affected by the establishment of the State of Israel. The Israeli embassy in Buenos Aires became a focus of interest, and the Zionist parties, which had played a role in the life of the community from its earliest days, achieved new dominance. Every split and new alliance formed by the political parties in Israel quickly registered itself in Argentina. When Adolf Eichmann, the chief executioner of the Holocaust, was captured in Argentina by the Israeli secret service in May 1960, Argentine Jewry was subjected to one of the most trying tests of a Jewish community in the Diaspora: how to resolve the conflict between its Jewish and civil loyalties. In order to bring Eichmann to trial and keep him from escaping with the help of pro-Nazi Argentines, Israel had indeed violated the sovereignty of the Argentine Republic. Yet, the Jewish community wholly justified and defended the action of the Jewish state, with the support of the progressive elements in Argentina who were indignant over Eichmann's use of the country as a shelter. The response from both nationalists and the more conservative strata in Argentina was a fierce condemnation of the Jewish state and its defenders, again raising implicit questions about the legitimacy of Jewish existence in Argentina.

As the bonds with the State of Israel tightened and greater emphasis was placed on Jewish education and community life, the Jews also became increasingly active in Argentine society and politics. During the presidency of Arturo Frondizi (1958–1962), the first Jew was appointed to a cabinet post and two others were elected governor in the provinces. As long as the two centrist-radical parties were in power, the phenomenon of Jews in politics was not unusual, although they did not represent the Jewish community and, in some cases, even emphasized their detachment from it. This contrasted sharply with the policy of the military governments that took over Argentina in 1966–1973 and again in 1976–1983 with the backing of conservative elements. The Jews were dismissed from nearly all positions of importance, and no new Jewish appointments were made. It became clear that for large sectors of the population, Argentine nationalism was inextricably bound up with symbols and values inspired by Catholicism. The Jews were not considered by them full-fledged members of the nation, and a permanent Jewish presence was deemed unacceptable—even if no legal action was taken to deprive them of their individual rights.

Rejected by the right, many Jewish students joined Marxist organizations as well as the Peronist left wing despite the Catholic element in Perón's populism. Some of them became involved in the underground activities that plagued Argentina during Perón's third term (1973–1974) and particularly during the presidency of his widow and successor, Isabel (1974–1976). This did not win the Jews any admiration from the right, and least of all from the anti-Semites. In the years leading up to the military coup in March 1976, anti-Jewish outbursts became more frequent in Argentina, and the Peronist right joined in willingly. The murderous Triple A (Alianza Anticomunista Argentina), a clandestine organization responsible for the assassination of many Jews who were members or suspected sympathizers of the left, flourished under the sponsorship of José López Rega, who was Perón's longtime personal secretary and minister of welfare, and later éminence gris in Isabel's regime. More and more, Jews were made to bear the brunt of the battle between right and left. When the army took over in March 1976, many anti-Semites, both military personnel and civilians, reached the top echelons of the federal and provincial governments. In the "dirty war" (La Guerra Sucia) against the forces of the left, an inordinate number of Jews were among the victims and *desaparecidos*.

During the 1970s and 1980s, the older generation of Jewish immigrants, which had conducted communal affairs for years, stepped down and handed the helm to the younger generation. The best indicator of the change of guard was the Yiddish press, which all but disappeared in the 1980s. The younger generation found itself constantly scrutinized with regard to its Jewish and Argentine identities. Rejected by Argentine nationalists and the military regime, and linked with the Jewish people and the State of Israel in the minds of their compatriots, many intellectuals and young people became more open to Judaism and Zionism. When military rule ended in December 1983, and Radical leader Raúl Alfonsín was elected president, many Jews found a niche in the new administration. Their Jewish and Zionist affiliations were known to all and there was no attempt to disguise them. So numerous and distinguished were the Jewish appointments, which included minister of finance and deputy minister of education and culture, that opponents soon nicknamed the Alfonsín government La Sinagoga Radical (the Radical Synagogue).

All the while, the Jewish community of Argentina was growing smaller—the joint product of intermarriage, assimilation, and emigration. As soon as Israel was established, even before the end of the War of Independence, Argentine Jews began leaving the country to settle in the Jewish state. The first kibbutz of former Argentines was founded in April 1949, and many others have been founded over the years. Demographic studies have shown that forty-five hundred Jews left Argentina between 1955 and 1959, although not all went to Israel. Until 1950, there had been more Jews entering Argentina than leaving, but then the tide turned.[8] In the early 1960s, as the economic crisis in Argentina worsened and anti-Semitic incidents became more frequent, the number of departures for Israel increased substantially; 1963 marked a peak year in this respect. The violence and terror that raged in Argentina from 1976 to 1978 and continued on a lower key until 1983 gave rise to a new category of emigrant: the Argentine Jewish refugee.

In the course of these dramatic events, there were rumors that Argentines were leaving the country in the millions. In the Jewish community it was said that over ten thousand Jews had fled to Spain, and thousands more to Mexico and Venezuela. When democracy was restored, a panel of government experts was appointed to ascertain how many Argentines had fled and how they could be brought home. It was found that a total of 547,000 Argentines had departed since the 1950s and had not returned by 1984; the majority had left Argentina after 1970. This was a far cry from the figure of 2.1 million that had appeared in the newspapers, based on a survey that was later proved groundless. The number of Argentines living

Hundreds of Jewish emigrants boarding the *SS Flaminia* in 1962 on their way to settle in Israel
(Central Zionist Archive)

in Venezuela, Mexico, and Spain was also lower than assumed. According to a census in Venezuela in 1981, there were 11,541 Argentines in the country; Venezuelan immigration records show that no more than 22,707 Argentines had applied for local identity cards by 1985. On the basis of a Mexican census in 1980, it was estimated that 8,376 Argentines were living in Mexico in June 1982. In 1980, there were 13,077 Argentines in Spain. The proportion of Argentine Jews in these countries, however substantial, could not have been anywhere near the rumored figures. According to a census in 1980, there were 68,887 Argentines living in the United States; again, the number of Jews is open to speculation.[9] On the other hand, there is no question about how many Argentines emigrated to Israel: a total of 39,900 from the establishment of the state until 1983. This figure undoubtedly represents the largest core of first-, second-, and third-generation Jewish Argentines living outside Argentine borders.[10]

Thus we see that over the last century, Argentina went from being a country of absorption to a country of exodus. For tens of thousands of Argentine Jews, Rabbi Shmuel Mohilewer's blessing to Colonel Goldsmid in 1892 was prophetic: The road their fathers took to Argentina did indeed lead them to Zion. Among those who have remained in Argentina, a large proportion have personal, family ties with the State of Israel, perhaps more than any other Jewish community in the West; yet the majority have made Argentina their permanent home. Although Argentine Jews have suffered from frequent economic and political upheavals along with their countrymen, and the legitimacy of their presence has been denied by many, there is no doubt that the Jewish community has become a deeply rooted factor in the social and cultural landscape of the Argentine Republic.

Notes

The following abbreviations are used, for the convenience of both author and reader, throughout the notes:

ACA   *Asambleas Constituyentes Argentinas,* edited by Emilio Rav-
               ignani. Vols. 1–6. Buenos Aires, 1937–1939
AI   Les Archives Israélites, Paris
AIU Archives   Archives of the Alliance Israélite Universelle, Paris
AJA   Anglo-Jewish Association, *Annual Reports.* London
AJYB   *American Jewish Yearbook*
AYS   *Argentiner IWO* (Yivo) *Shriftn.* Buenos Aires
AZDJ   *Allgemeine Zeitung des Judentums*
BO   *Boletín Oficial de la República Argentina*
BPRO   (British) Public Record Office. Kew
Bul. Inf.   Informatsie Bleter fun der Emigratsie Farainigung (Bulletin
               d'Information de l'Association pour l'Emigration), pub-
               lished by HIAS-JCA-Emigdirekt
Cong. Actas   Minutes of the Congregación Israelita de la República Ar-
               gentina. Buenos Aires
CNCD   Congreso Nacional (de la Nación Argentina), Cámara de
               Diputados (House of Representatives) Diario de Sesiones
CNCS   Congreso Nacional (de la Nación Argentina), Cámara de
               Senadores (Senate) Diario de Sesiones
CZA   Central Zionist Archives, Jerusalem

DAIA Actas	Minutes of the Delegación de Asociaciones Israelitas Argentinas. Buenos Aires
DAIA Arch.	Archives of the DAIA
EJ	*Encyclopaedia Judaica.* Jerusalem, 1971
FORUS	United States, Department of State, Foreign Relations of the United States, Diplomatic Papers
HVGB	Hilfsverein der Deutschen Juden, *Geschäftsbericht* (Annual report). Berlin
HVKB	Hilfsverein der Deutschen Juden, *Korrespondenzblatt des Centralbüreaus für jüdische Auswanderungsangelegenheiten* (Information Bulletin). Berlin
ICJ	Institute of Contemporary Jewry, Oral History Division, The Hebrew University of Jerusalem
Id. Ts.	*Di Idishe Tseitung—El Diario Israelita.* Buenos Aires
JC	*The Jewish Chronicle.* London
JCA(BA)	Archives of the Jewish Colonization Association, Buenos Aires (now at the Central Archives for the History of the Jewish People, Jerusalem): includes Cop. Ext. (Copiador Exterior), bound volumes of Correspondence sent abroad and Cop. Int. (Copiador Interior), bound volumes of correspondence within Argentina
JCA Conseil	Séances du Conseil d'Administration, Procés Verbaux (Minutes of the Central Council of the JCA)
JCA(Lon)	Archives of the JCA, London
JCA(Lon) Session	Mimeographed and bound documents, presented to the members of the council at each of their meetings
JCA Rapport	*Rapport de l'Administration Centrale* (Annual published reports)
JJS	*Jewish Journal of Sociology*
JSS	*Jewish Social Studies*
MFA Argentina	Archives of the Ministry of Foreign Relations, Argentina
MFA Arg. Memoria	Argentina, *Memoria del Ministerio de Relaciones Exteriores y Culto* (Ministry of Foreign Relations and Religion)
MFA Germany	Archives of the Ministry of Foreign Relations, Germany
MFA Madrid	Archives of the Ministry of Foreign Relations, Spain
MFA Paris	Archives of the Ministry of Foreign Relations, France
MI	*Mundo Israelita.* Buenos Aires
Min. Agr. Memoria	Argentina, Ministry of Agriculture, *Memoria . . . Presentada al H. Congreso de la Nación* (Annual report)
MSA	Museo Social Argentino, *Boletín Mensual del Museo,* Buenos Aires

Sop. Actas	Minutes of the Sociedad de Protección a los Inmigrantes Israelitas (Soprotimis)
Yad Vashem	Archives, Jerusalem
Yivo(BA)	Archives of Yivo, Buenos Aires
Yivo(NY)	Yivo Archives, New York
YHH	HIAS-HICEM Files at the Yivo Archive, New York
ZO Protokoll	(Zionist Organization), *Stenographisches Protokoll der Verhandlungen des . . . Zionisten-Kongresses* (Minutes of the Zionist congresses)

Chapter 1. The Beginnings, 1810–1876

1. Jacinto Oddone, *La burguesía terrateniente argentina*, p. 15.

2. Declaration of May 26, 1810; facsimile in José C. Ibáñez, *Historia argentina*, p. 140.

3. Mariano Moreno authorized this escort in the name of the provisional government on July 19, 1810. See the document printed in Boleslao Lewin, *La Inquisición en Hispanoamérica*, p. 279.

4. "Sesiones de la Asamblea General Constituyente de 1813–1815," ACA, vol. 1, p. 30.

5. Ibid., pp. 34–38, session of April 29, 1813.

6. Ibid., "Conferencias secretas realizadas por el Congreso General Constituyente en las que se despacharon los tratados con la Gran Betaña y con la República de Colombia, febrero a junio de 1825," vol. 3, pp. 1267–79; "Sesiones reservadas del Congreso General Constituyente de las Provincias Unidas del Río de la Plata en Sud América de 1825–1827," vol. 3, pp. 1283–93; Emilio Ravignani, "El tratado con la Gran Bretaña de 1825 y la libertad de cultos."

7. Emilio Ravignani, "El Congreso Nacional de 1824–1827," pp. 112–13.

8. "Congreso General Constituyente de la Confederación Argentina, Sesión de 1852–54," ACA, vol. 4, pp. 515, 530, 535; Juan Bautisti Alberdi, *Bases y puntos de partida para la organización política de la República argentina*, pp. 307–32; Antonio Sagarna, "La organización nacional, la Constitución de 1853," pp. 184–97.

9. Boleslao Lewin, *Los judíos bajo la Inquisición en Hispanoamérica*, p. 90; also see Salvador Canals Frau, "La inmigración europea en la Argentina," p. 89, citing Registro Nacional, vol. 1, p. 177.

10. José Antonio Wilde, *Buenos Aires desde 70 años atrás (1810–1880)*, pp. 77–80, 85–89, 147–50, 189–92.

11. See Roberto Schöpflocher, *Historia de la colonización agrícola en Argentina*, pp. 24–31, on the colonization scheme of William Parish Robertson; see José Panettieri, *Inmigración en la Argentina*, pp. 9–14, on additional schemes.

12. Panettieri, *Inmigración*, pp. 16–17.

13. Domingo Faustino Sarmiento, *Facundo: Civilización y barbarie*, pp. 31–48.

14. Alberdi, *Bases y puntos*, p. 17. Alberdi frequently changed his views and contradicted himself, but continued to be regarded as the "father of immigration" among his contemporaries and later generations. Also see Ricardo Levene, *Historia de las ideas sociales argentinas*, pp. 99–102 on "Alberdi se contesta con Alberdi."

15. Alberdi, *Bases y puntos*, p. 233.

16. Ibid., pp. 87–89, 237–38.

17. Ibid., pp. 108, 121–26, 129.

18. See Clauses 16/64 and 104 of the original draft approved in 1853. These clauses are identical to Clauses 16/67 and 107 in today's version, which has been slightly revised. See appendix in Alberdi, *Bases y puntos*, pp. 307–32; "Congreso General Constituyente de la Confederación Argentina, Sesión 1852–54," ACA, vol. 4, pp. 515, 530, 535.

19. Clauses 14, 16, 17, 18, and 19 refer inclusively to all inhabitants of the nation. Clause 20 refers specifically to foreigners, and Clause 21 to military service. Also see "Congreso General Constituyente de la Confederación Argentina, Sesión 1852–54," ACA, vol. 4, pp. 514–15.

20. Lázaro Schallman, "Proceso histórico de la colonización agrícola en la Argentina," pp. 166–79; Schöpflocher, *Colonización agrícola*, pp. 42–45. Also see Ezequiel Gallo, *La pampa gringa*.

21. Panettieri, *Inmigración*, pp. 46–48; Donald Steven Castro, *The Development of Argentine Immigration Policy*, pp. 180–84.

22. *Opiniones de la prensa nacional*, pp. 49–91: law proposals of President Avellaneda and Minister of the Interior Simón de Oriondo presented to Congress on August 5, 1875. Also see CNCS, August 5, 1876, pp. 503–13.

23. CNCS, August 5, 1876, pp. 503–13, clauses 12–18, 50, 88, 91.

24. See *Opiniones*, pp. 3–38; CNCD, September 20, 1875, p. 1190; CNCS, August 5, 1876, pp. 519, 525, August 8, 1876, pp. 554–55, August 10, 1876, pp. 571–73, 579–82.

25. Boleslao Lewin, *La colectividad judía en la Argentina*, pp. 33–36, 63–65; Bernard David Ansel, "The Beginnings of the Modern Jewish Community of Argentina, 1852–1891," pp. 27–35, 42, 49–66.

26. AZDJ, September 28, 1846, pp. 586–87.

27. José Toribio Medina, *La Inquisición en el Río de la Plata*, pp. 274–76; Lewin, *Inquisición*, pp. 188–95, 199–202, 285–91.

28. Alberdi, *Bases y puntos*, pp. 121–23.

29. See "Congreso General Constituyente de la Confederación Argentina, Sesión de 1852–54," ACA, vol. 4, pp. 509, 512, 525.

30. See AZDJ, December 20, 1870, p. 1004, letter from Buenos Aires dated

October 1870 in which the author estimates a Jewish population of five hundred. Ansel, "Beginnings," p. 46, sets the number of Jews at three hundred.

31. See Miguel Navarro Viola, "La primera boda judía en la Argentina." Also see detailed analysis of this episode in Ansel, "Beginnings," pp. 100–109.

32. See Victor A. Mirelman, "Jewish Life in Buenos Aires before the East European Immigration (1860–1890)," p. 198, who bases his account on oral testimony cited by Yosilevits in *Di Yiddishe Hofnung*, September 1909, pp. 2–7. Also see reservations in Ansel, "Beginnings," p. 115.

33. See Lewin, *Colectividad judía*, pp. 42–44. Figures for membership in the Congregación Israelita are derived from a letter dated May 22, 1892, written by Achille Levy, chairman of the congregation, to Alliance Israélite; in Victor A. Mirelman, "A Note on Jewish Settlement in Argentina 1881–1892," p. 3.

34. See Alcibíades Lappas, *La Masonería argentina a través de sus hombres*, pp. 72–81; and Esteban F. Rondanina, *Liberalismo, Masonería y Socialismo en la evolución nacional*, pp. 148–81.

35. See Carlos Heras, "Presidencia de Avellaneda," pp. 197–204.

Chapter 2. The Formative Years, 1876–1896

1. See *Registro Nacional de la República Argentina*, 1878–1881, vol. 8, p. 512.

2. See *L'Union Française*, August 22 and 26, 1881; *El Nacional*, August 25 and 26, 1881; and Mirelman, "Jewish Settlement," p. 7.

3. On Spain's offer and its practical importance, see Haim Avni, *Spain, the Jews and Franco*, pp. 14–18.

4. For a partial translation of this pamphlet and further information on this episode, see Mirelman, "Jewish Settlement," pp. 4–6. Also see Lewin, *Colectividad judía*, pp. 77–80, who presents the document almost in full.

5. In early 1882, General Gregorio Luperón, former president of the Dominican Republic, proposed to Baron Edmond de Rothschild and the Alliance Israélite that Jewish immigration and settlement be directed to his country. This proposal was seriously considered by the alliance and reported in the Jewish newspapers; see Mark Wischnitzer, *To Dwell in Safety*, p. 65 and the sources he cites. The fact that immigration to Argentina was not seriously considered seems to indicate either mishandling of the issue by Bustos or the disinterest of the alliance and other Jewish organizations in proposals not brought directly before them by top government officials.

6. It is difficult to calculate the precise number of Jews who left Russia in the 1880s. Neither do we know how many entered the United States, since the US immigration services did not keep a separate count for the Jews until 1898. See

Samuel Joseph, *Jewish Immigration to the United States, 1881–1910*, p. 93, Table 4; cf. Wischnitzer, *To Dwell in Safety*, p. 289, and Wischnitzer, *Visas to Freedom*, p. 326.

7. JCA(Lon), no. 304, 'Kogan's letter to Paris, May 15, 1893. Also see Aaron Pavlovsky, *Problemas de inmigración*, pp. 5–6; Bernard David Ansel, "European Adventurer in Tierra del Fuego"; and Boleslao Lewin, *Popper* on Julio and Max Popper.

8. On the "unclean" in Argentina, see Victor A. Mirelman, "The Jewish Community Versus Crime," and Edward J. Bristow, *Prostitution and Prejudice*. Also see JC, August 5, 1887, p. 7, letter signed "Resident" in response to a letter from an English Jew in Córdoba, ibid., May 13, 1887, p. 6. Between 1886 and 1888, a total of 2,385 Russian immigrants entered Argentina, although only 120 appear in the records for 1881–1885. For immigration data, see Argentina, Ministry of Agriculture, *Resumen estadístico del movimiento migratorio en la República Argentina 1875 a 1924*, p. 16.

9. See Castro, *Immigration Policy*, pp. 119–27, 161–63.

10. See *Ha-Tsfirah*, June 3, 1888, p. 1; *Ha-Melitz*, June 21, 1888, p. 1322, August 31, 1888, pp. 1937–38, November 27, 1888, p. 2520. Also see Yaacov Rubel, "Argentina, ¿sí o no?" pp. 274–75.

11. See José Mendelson, "Génesis de la colonia judía de la Argentina—1884–1892," pp. 97, 325; Ansel, "Beginnings," p. 237. Ansel states that according to government records a group of forty-five arrived on November 3, 1888 on the *SS Río Negro*.

12. The figures here are derived from Ansel, "Beginnings," pp. 257–60, who examined the original passenger list submitted to the immigration authorities by the captain. See also Mendelson, "Génesis de la colonia," pp. 317–23.

13. *Ha Tsfirah*, August 15, 1889, p. 807, June 16, 1890, p. 518, June 18, 1890, p. 527. Heading the delegation was Eliezer Kaufman, a farmer from a village near Kamenetz Podolsk who served as leader throughout the journey. Also see Castro, *Immigration Policy*, pp. 136–41, 168–72.

14. These data are based on the testimony of Zalman Aleksenitser. See Noe Cociovitch, *Génesis de Moisesville*, pp. 260–61. Compare with Yisroel David Fingerman, "Di geshikte fun der idishe kolonizatsie in Argentine" (Id. Ts., April 10, 1927, p. 11). Also see Zosa Szajkowski, "Di onhoyben fun der yidisher kolonizatisie in Argentine," p. 32, fn. 22, appendix to agreement. Simmel relays similar information in *Di Juedische Presse*, July 18, 1889, pp. 293–94.

15. *Ha-Tsfirah*, July 8, 1889, p. 574; also see Szajkowski, "Yidisher kolonizatisie," pp. 12–13, 38–39, fn. 22, and pp. 42–43, fn. 32–33; Haim Avni, *Argentina ha-aretz ha-yeuda*, p. 45.

16. See Ansel, "Beginnings," p. 262 with regard to 43,168.50 pesos that the immigration department paid to the shipping agency on September 4, 1889, for eight hundred passenger tickets for the *SS Weser*. Also see Alejandro E. Bunge, "Ochenta

y cinco años de inmigración," p. 33; and Juan A. Alsina, *La inmigración europea en la República Argentina,* p. 127.

17. See Szajkowski, "Yidisher kolonizatisie," p. 11; JC, November 8, 1899, p. 13; *Ha-Tsfirah,* December 4, 1889, p. 1045. On the order to cease issuing free tickets to Jews, see *La Nación,* August 17, 1899, leading article.

18. See MFA Paris, Argentine, Correspondance Politique, vol. 61, pp. 190–92, 202–203, reports of the French ambassador on July 3, 1889, August 11 and 22, 1889.

19. See Hassan's remarks in JC, October 11, 1889, p. 6; there is another eyewitness description in *Ha-Tsfirah,* November 21, 1889, p. 999.

20. See Szajkowski, "Yidisher kolonizatisie," pp. 41–42. Also see MFA Paris, Argentine, Correspondance Politique, vol. 61, p. 72, report of French ambassador on the organizing of the Belgians and the steps taken by the British to protect the immigrants.

21. See *Ha-Melitz,* May 9, 1890, p. 2; *Ha-Tsfirah,* June 19, 1890, p. 531.

22. See *La Nación,* November 30, 1889, leading article; letters of Henry Joseph and David Hassan in JC, December 20, 1889, p. 8 and January 10, 1890, p. 8.

23. See Szajkowski, "Yidisher kolonizatisie," p. 43, fn. 35, alliance resolutions; AJA decision, JC, January 10, 1889, p. 8; *Ha-Tsfirah,* February 20, 1889, p. 110. Also see Rubel, "Argentina, ¿sí o no?" p. 286. The number of Russians, both Jews and non-Jews, who officially entered Argentina in 1890 was only 318, compared with 1,334 in 1889. See Argentina, Ministry of Agriculture, *Resumen estadístico,* p. 16.

24. The number of Russian Jews entering the United States doubled in 1891—43,457 compared with 20,981 in 1890. See Joseph, *Jewish Immigration,* p. 93, Table 6.

25. Avni, *Argentina ha-aretz ha-yeuda,* pp. 27–33; Theodore Norman, *An Outstretched Arm,* pp. 16–18; Kurt Grunwald, *Türkenhirsch,* pp. 68–71.

26. Baron de Hirsch's article originally appeared in *North American Review* 416 (July 1891). Also see Avni, *Argentina ha-aretz ha-yeuda,* pp. 44–50.

27. Avni, *Argentina ha-aretz ha-yeuda,* pp. 52–56, 58–66. I quote Hirsch from Conference de Londres, *Exposé,* in ibid., pp. 328–32. See also JCA(Lon), no. 302, confidential letter to Löwenthal, dated October 10, 1881.

28. See Avni, *Argentina ha-aretz ha-yeuda,* pp. 63–67, 113–17, 122–23; also see AJA, vol. 22, 1892/93, pp. 10–12, vol. 25, 1895/96, pp. 15–18.

29. Marcos Alperson, *Kolonie Mauricio,* pp. 13–36; Isaac Rülf, *Die russische Juden,* pp. 51–52; Lázaro Schallman, "Dramática historia de los pampistas o Stambuler."

30. Avni, *Argentina ha-aretz ha-yeuda,* pp. 225–29, 315–17; US dollar calculated at 3.55 pesos (paper) per one dollar.

31. Ibid., pp. 189–96.

32. Ibid., pp. 239–48.

33. See JCA(Lon) Session, November 8, 1902, vol. 1, Sonnenfeld's report on his visit to Argentina, June–September 1902, appendix.

34. Joseph, *Jewish Immigration*, p. 93; Lloyd P. Gartner, "Notes on the Statistics of Jewish Immigration to England, 1870 to 1914"; Rülf, *Russische Juden*, p. 55.

35. David Gurvitz et al., *Ha-aliyah, ha-yishuv ve-ha-tnuah ha-tiv'it shel ha-okhlusiah be-eretz yisrael*, pp. 19, 21; and Roberto Bachi, *The Population of Israel*, p. 79, Table 8.1. Also see Avni, *Argentina ha-aretz ha-yeuda*, pp. 302–307, on the role of Palestine in the Argentine colonization effort.

36. Cociovitch, *Génesis de Moisesville*, pp. 59–66.

37. JCA(Lon), no. 308, letter of Congregación Israelita to Baron de Hirsch, February 18, 1894.

38. MFA Paris, Direction Politique, 7, 15, 29, reports of the consul on February 4, April 1, and May 21, 1891. Also see MFA Madrid, Correspondencias Embajadas Argentina, 1889–1896, no. 1353, and reports of the ambassador on April 15, 1890; and Great Britain, Foreign Office, *Accounts and Papers*, p. 139.

39. *Ha-Tsfirah*, June 3, 1888, p. 1.

40. An agreement to bring over German-Russians was signed on August 3, 1877, and approved by Congress on October 5. See JCA(Lon), no. 312, appendix to Yehoshua Lapine's report dated July 1893. Also see report of French ambassador on October 12, 1885, MFA Paris, Argentine, Correspondance Politique, p. 58. On the Société Patrie, see MFA Paris, Correspondance Consulaire et Commerciale, vol. 18, p. 288, report dated February 9, 1895; on the celebrations of the Italians, see ibid., p. 235, report dated September 22, 1889. See MFA Madrid, Correspondencias Embajadas Argentina, Leg. XB 1353, on the declarations of support conveyed by the large, wealthy Laurak-Bat society to the Spanish ambassador on November 4, 1893

41. See *El Argentino*, February 12, 1891; and Avni, *Argentina ha-aretz ha-yeuda*, pp. 77–83.

42. Victor A. Mirelman, *En búsqueda de una identidad*, pp. 31–40, 113–28.

Chapter 3. The Avalanche, 1896–1914

1. See Jakob Lestschinsky, "National Groups in Polish Emigration," p. 108, Table 8; also see Wischnitzer, *To Dwell in Safety*, p. 289, and cf. Bachi, *Population of Israel*, p. 79, Table 8.1. According to Bachi, immigration to Palestine in 1948–1975 totaled 1,569,875.

2. Based on Salo W. Baron, *Steeled by Adversity*, p. 153. See also Canada in EJ, vol. 5, pp. 104–105, and vol. 15, p. 186.

3. All the statistical data are based on Mario Rapoport, "El modelo agroexpor-

tador argentino, 1880–1914," pp. 181, 200, 203. Also see James R. Scobie, *Revolution on the Pampas,* epilogue.

4. Carl Solberg, *Immigration and Nationalism,* pp. 13–14.

5. La Ley de Residencia (Law 4144), BO, November 23, 1902, p. 1. This law remained a source of controversy for many decades. See CNCD, May 3, 1948, p. 190, and Carlos Sánchez Viamonte, *Biografía de una ley antiargentina,* on the enforcement of the law during the Perón era (1946–1955).

6. See JCA(Lon) Session, November 11, 1911, p. 135, and Louis Oungre's report on his visit to Argentina in February–September 1911, p. 130.

7. Min. Agr. Memoria, 1898, p. 203. Also see JCA(BA), Paris correspondence, file 8, Sonnenfeld letter, May 2, 1901, no. 581; JC, July 12, 1901, p. 5.

8. JCA(BA), Cop. Ext., vol. 7, pp. 302, 406, 840, letters dated February 2, March 16, and December 7, 1905, and vol. 8, pp. 81, 127, 136, letters dated April 12, 1906, May 3 and 10, 1906. These and many other letters allude to the close relationship between the directors of the JCA and the immigration commissioner. Also see JCA Rapport, 1905, pp. 54–56.

9. JCA(BA), Paris correspondence, file 13, letters 970, 973a, 975, dated September 26, 1907, October 3 and 17, 1907, and appendices. Also see JCA(Lon) Session, January 4, 1908, letter of Davíd Veneziani, confidential, no. 1359a, dated October 31, 1907.

10. See Juan A. Alsina, *La colectividad israelita al ex director de inmigración . . . ,* and *La inmigración en el primer siglo de la independencia,* pp. 203–25.

11. See José Panettieri, *Los trabajadores,* pp. 137–46; JCA(Lon) Session, January 22, 1910, no. 1527, letter from Buenos Aires, dated November 25, 1909, and March 12, 1910, letters 1536, 1539, dated January 6 and 20, 1910. On the remarks of the chief of police and the repercussions for the Jewish community, see Rabbi Halfon's report on the Jewish community dated May 3, 1910, JCA(Lon) Session, September 24, 1910, pp. 181, 186.

12. JCA Conseil, vol. 1, pp. 6–7, October 14, 1896; vol. 2, p. 95, May 11, 1901, p. 117, October 11, 1901; vol. 5, p. 61, January 22, 1910. Also see Zionist Organization, *Stenographisches Protokoll,* VII *Zionisten Kongresses,* pp. 222–25; HVGB, no. 5, 1906, pp. 154–55.

13. JCA Conseil, vol. 4, p. 193, resolution on June 27, 1908, and p. 206, resolution on October 31, 1908; vol. 6, p. 70, resolution on December 14, 1912, and p. 91, resolution on February 1, 1913.

14. On the Saint Petersburg committee see ibid., vol. 1, pp. 13–14, meeting of October 14, 1896; vol. 3, p. 51, resolution on October 31, 1903; vol. 4, p. 212, resolution on December 12, 1908. Also see Wischnitzer, *To Dwell in Safety,* p. 126, on JCA support of the IRO; HVGB, no. 10, 1911, pp. 148–49; and Hilfsverein der Deut-

schen Juden, *Festschrift Anlässlich der Feier* . . . , p. 45 on the JCA's "substantial participation" in the immigration budget.

15. JCA Rapport, 1896, p. 11; JCA(BA) Cop. Ext., vol. 7, p. 70, letter 1171 dated September 14, 1905.

16. On the expulsion of Chasanowitch, see JCA(Lon) Session, January 22, 1910, letters 1528a and 1530a from Buenos Aires, dated December 2 and 9, 1909.

17. Ibid., May 23, 1910, letter 1542 from Buenos Aires, dated February 3, 1910.

18. See MFA Paris, Correspondance Commerciale, Rosario, vol. 1, p. 185, consul's report on February 15, 1897.

19. JCA(Lon), file 313, letter from colonists sent to Baroness Clara, Colonel Goldsmid, and Sir Samuel Montagu. Also see JCA(Lon) Session, November 8, 1902, p. 72, table in Sonnenfeld report.

20. JCA(Lon) Session, November 8, 1902, Sonnenfeld report on the faults of the administrators, pp. 72, 81–83, 100–103. On those who left the colonies, the JCA imposed a worldwide ban: No other colony under JCA's control in Palestine, the United States, Canada, or Argentina would accept them.

21. JCA(Lon) Session, July 9, 1899, p. 44, November 11, 1899, pp. 52–53, letters 579 and 774, dated May 27 and October 3, 1899. Also see Cociovitch, *Génesis de Moisesville*, pp. 232–56.

22. On the position of the committee in Saint Petersburg, see JCA(BA), Paris correspondence, file 8, letters from Feinberg, February 14 and March 6, 1901, undated appendix to Sonnenfeld letter 578 of April 18, 1901, and response of Hirsch and Cazés, appended to Sonnenfeld letter 601 of August 14, 1901.

23. Ibid., file 7, letter 539 dated July 26, 1900, and file 8, letter 615 dated November 14, 1901; ibid., copies of letters to Paris, vol. 5, letter 832 dated August 24, 1900.

24. JCA(Lon), file 385, requests from Kishinev; JCA(Lon) Session, July 25, 1903, Auerbach report dated July 20, 1903, Cazés report dated July 19, 1903, and October 31, 1903, Cazés report to council. Also see JCA Conseil, vol. 3, p. 47, resolutions on October 31, 1903.

25. See JCA(BA), Paris correspondence, file 9, letters 716 and 719 dated October 19 and November 5, 1903; file 10, letter from Saint Petersburg dated April 3, 1904, and letter from Paris to Saint Petersburg dated November 29, 1904.

26. On the colony of Baron Hirsch see, e.g., Gregorio Verbitzky, *Afán de medio siglo,* and Morton D. Winsberg, *Colonia Baron Hirsch.* These works do not sufficiently examine the autonomous beginnings of the colony. See JCA(BA), Paris correspondence, file 10, letter 780 dated September 22, 1904, and file 11, letter 820 dated September 27, 1905. On the information circulating in Russia that anyone possessing 2,000 rubles (or 3,000 by another account) would be accepted as a colonist, see JCA(BA), Paris correspondence, file 13, letter 941 dated April 11, 1907. The JCA directors in Buenos Aires intervened after the colony suffered a severe

agricultural crisis in 1912. Their investigation showed that no fewer than twenty-five landowners had leased their farms and left the colony. Some had returned to Russia or emigrated to the United States; see JCA(BA), Cop. Ext., vol. II, pp. 921–1002, letter 1773 dated November 7, 1912.

27. On real estate holdings, see JCA Rapport, 1908, p. 15 and 1913, p. 12. An offer of thirty-five thousand hectares in La Pampa, near the Bernasconi railway station, was rejected by the JCA in 1906. In mid-1908, the association changed its mind and purchased the land at the cost of 40 pesos per hectare.

28. Ibid., 1913.

29. See JCA(BA), Paris correspondence, file 10, letter 761 dated June 6, 1904, and file 12, letters 890 and 897 dated July 26 and August 2, 1906. Conditions were particularly bad in the colonies of Narcisse Leven in La Pampa, Montefiore on the northern border of Santa Fe, and Dora in Santiago del Estero.

30. Figures based on JCA Rapport, 1901–1913. The information in the hands of the colonial directors was not always up to date because not all the immigrants who reached the colonies registered at the JCA offices.

31. JCA(Lon) Session, May 12, 1901, pp. 216–22, 227–30, 258–66. Also see JCA(BA), Paris correspondence, file 12, letters 881 and 883 dated April 26 and May 10, 1906, and JCA Rapport, 1906, p. 21.

32. JCA Rapport, 1908, p. 45; JCA(Lon) Session, May 23, 1910, p. 130, no. 1545, report from Buenos Aires dated February 17, 1910.

33. JCA(Lon) Session, December 17, 1910, pp. 123–29, 148–49, 160–61, 170–73, letters of Nandor Sonnenfeld, and February 11, 1911, pp. 22–24, 129–48, final report and outline for council debate; JCA Conseil, vol. 5, February 11, 1911, p. 129. Cazés and Oungre were dispatched to report on the educational and administrative problems in the colonies; their reports also relate to the problems of the immigrants. See JCA(Lon) Session, September 18, 1911, pp. 25–44, 105–15; see also JCA(BA), Cop. Ext., vol. 13, p. 252, Veneziani letter 2070 dated August 24, 1916 on the sixty-two units containing 104 apartments built by the JCA, which were of such poor quality and so overcrowded that they soon became dirty ghettos that "we are ashamed to present to visitors."

34. JCA(Lon) Session, May 3, 1913, pp. 134–36, protocols from the general meeting of the settlers' cooperatives on January 3, 1913.

35. See JCA Rapport, 1905, p. 44, on the 126,000 francs sent out of the colonies to support relatives in Russia; ibid., 1909, p. 21, on the flour distributed to hungry immigrants in the colony of Clara by the local cooperative. Identification with the settlers was borne out by the fund-raising campaign in 1911 on behalf of the starving colonists of Narcisse Leven in La Pampa. See *Der Jüdischer Kolonist*, 2d year, no. 8 onward; the problems of the immigrants were never aired in this periodical— not even in letters to the editor. See JCA Rapport, 1910, p. 17 and 1911, p. 8, Sidi's

remarks. On the review procedures for the annual report, see JCA Conseil, vol. 4, p. 117, July 6, 1907.

36. JCA Conseil, vol. 1, pp. 125, 188, resolutions on March 2 and December 17, 1899, and vol. 2, pp. 10, 231, resolutions on January 28, 1900 and December 27, 1902; in each case, aid was extended to five–twelve immigrants. See also L. Benchimol, "La langue espagnole au Maroc."

37. JCA Conseil, vol. 2, pp. 32, 44, 55, 66, 69, 76, resolutions from April 28, 1900, to January 5, 1901; also see JCA(BA), file 9, August 1902, various letters on the subject of Romanian immigrants.

38. JCA(Lon) Session, May 12, 1901, pp. 216–22, Buenos Aires letter 870 dated March 14, 1901; and ibid., March 19, 1905; pp. 130–35, letter 1119 dated February 2, 1905. JCA(BA), Paris correspondence, file 8, letter 596 dated July 18, 1901, on the remarks of one JCA employee in Buenos Aires, published in the JC on July 12, 1901.

39. JCA Conseil, vol. 3, p. 172, resolution on April 15, 1905, and p. 222, resolution on December 16, 1905. Also see JCA(BA), Paris correspondence, file 11, confidential letter 797 dated January 5, 1905, on the reduced spending on immigration and absorption that accounted for 4,000 pesos out of an overall budget of 668,772.

40. JCA Conseil, vol. 3, p. 165, resolution on March 19, 1905; JCA(BA) Cop. Int., vol. 12, pp. 231ff., letters to the president of Ezrah in May–June 1905.

41. See Yivo(BA), Division 36, invitation to attend the general assembly and report of activities between April and July 1905. See also Ezrah, *Libro del cincuentenario,* pp. 51–53; Cong. Actas, vol. 2, p. 13, session on April 5, 1905, Brie's announcement on the establishment of the organization; and JCA(BA), Paris correspondence, file 12, letter 920 dated December 27, 1906, on the cessation of activities of Shomer Israel.

42. See Mirelman, *En búsqueda de una identidad,* pp. 135–37 on the Hoffman incident. See also JCA(BA), Paris correspondence, file 13, letter 942 dated April 18, 1907, and file 14, letter 1005 dated April 15, 1908, on the trial; JCA(Lon) Session, October 31, 1908, Buenos Aires letter 1408 dated June 4, 1908 on Hoffman's suicide.

43. See Pinie Wald, *In gang fun tseiten,* pp. 357–75, and supplementary information in Wald, *Yidisher arbeter klas un sotsiale bavegung in argentine,* pp. 1–16. Also see JCA(BA), Cop. Ext., vol. 8, p. 136, letter dated May 10, 1906.

44. See Mirelman, *En búsqueda de una identidad,* pp. 382–86. Cf. JCA(Lon) Session, September 24, 1910, pp. 179–81, 189, Halfon report on May 3, 1910. The Ashkenazic burial society that had been in existence for sixteen years was about to purchase its first cemetery, and the Ezrah society had just begun to implement its plan to found a hospital.

45. On the early Zionist movement, see Silvia Szenkolewski, "Di tsionistishe bavegung in argentine fun 1897–1917." Figures for the Jews from Morocco and the Turkish Empire are based on a survey by Halfon; see JCA Rapport, 1909, pp. 303–306.

46. JCA(Lon) Session, September 24, 1910, pp. 207–208, 232, Halfon report on May 10, 1910, and directors' reply on May 12, 1910; February 11, 1911, pp. 144–45, Sonnenfeld report on January 3, 1911; and November 11, 1911, p. 135, Oungre report in September 1911.

47. JCA(BA), Paris correspondence, file 18, letter 1242 dated April 18, 1912.

48. JCA(Lon) Session, February 1, 1913, pp. 123–24, 133, 137–40, letters dated December 19 and 26, 1912, and appendices.

49. Ibid., February 1, 1913, p. 24, remarks on agenda; JCA Conseil, vol. 6, p. 85, resolution on February 1, 1913, and p. 111, resolution on June 28, 1913; JCA(Lon) Session, May 3, 1913, pp. 35–38, letter 1799 dated February 27, 1913, June 28, 1913, p. 23, remarks on agenda and letters dated May 8 and 22, 1913, and pp. 87ff.

50. See Cong. Actas, vol. 2, pp. 327–28, session on May 8, 1913. JCA director Davíd Veneziani was a member of the Executive Committee; he was absent from this meeting.

51. Bristow, *Prostitution and Prejudice,* pp. 145, 236–48; Mirelman, "Community Versus Crime." Also see JCA(Lon) Session, November 30, 1901, pp. 67–72, report of the Association for the Protection of Girls and Women in London; a similar report was submitted to the JCA every year.

52. The population census of 1960 found that one-third (34–36 percent) of all the Turkish, Syrian, and African-born Jews were immigrants who had come to Argentina before 1919. These were older people, of the first generation of immigrants who had arrived forty–sixty years before the census. See Margalit Bejarano, "Los sefardíes en la Argentina," pp. 144–46.

53. This figure is based on the routine reports of the JCA administration in Buenos Aires, which were sent to the directors in Paris beginning in January 1905. Their source was the government Immigration Department. See JCA(BA), Cop. Ext. vol. 7, p. 302, report of February 2, 1905, which offers data for 1901–1904. For annual figures, see Haim Avni, *Argentina y la historia de la inmigración judía,* pp. 536–37.

54. JCA(Lon) Session, January 1, 1910, p. 128, report from Santa Fe on October 29, 1909, and May 23, 1910, p. 156, report on the census in the province of Buenos Aires on February 6, 1910. Also see Eugene Sofer, *From Pale to Pampa,* pp. 101–15.

55. See Mirelman, *En búsqueda de una identidad,* pp. 44–50.

56. See Panettieri, *Trabajadores,* pp. 66–77. From the research relating to 1897 cited by Panettieri, we see that on the average the 134,722 workers in Buenos Aires worked only 256 days a year. Also see Hertz Brusilowsky, "Der onteyl fun idishe arbeyter in di argentinishe arbeyter organizatsies," pp. 568–71.

57. See Panettieri, *Trabajadores,* pp. 71–76; James R. Scobie, "Buenos Aires as a Commercial Bureaucratic City, 1880–1910," pp. 1045–48. Also see JCA(Lon) Session, September 24, 1910, p. 172, Halfon report on May 3, 1910.

58. JCA(BA) Cop. Ext., vol. 9, p. 229, letter of March 26, 1908.

59. Calculation based on Jakob Lestschinsky, "Jüdische Wanderungen im letzten Jahrhundert." For a detailed, landmark discussion of Jewish reemigration from the United States in earlier years, see Jonathan D. Sarna, " The Myth of No Return."

60. Argentina, Directive Commission of the Census, *Tercer censo nacional levantado el 1°. de junio de 1914*, p. 109. The number of immigrants cited for 1895–1914 was 3,389,645. This refers to all three categories of overseas passengers arriving at the port of Buenos Aires (including first-class passengers who, according to the immigration law, were not immigrants but excluding those arriving from Montevideo, by riverboat). See Argentina, Ministry of Agriculture, *Resumen estadístico*, pp. 33–34. These figures were quoted again in Congress on July 14, 1938; see CNCD, July 14, 1938, p. 619.

61. Preferential immigrants included those from Britain, France, Switzerland, Belgium, the Netherlands, Sweden, and Denmark. According to the 1914 census, there were 161,984 such immigrants in Argentina. See Edgar W. Collins, "Desarrollo y distribución de la inmigración," p. 846; and Solberg, *Immigration*, p. 135.

62. See Ricardo Rojas, *La restauración nacionalista*, pp. 128–29. Also see Solberg, *Immigration*, pp. 132–47, who writes extensively on this subject, and Gladys S. Onega, *La inmigración en la literatura argentina*, p. 80.

63. See Alsina, *Inmigración en el primer siglo*, pp. 203–209. Two large groups in the 1914 census were 93,634 Russians and 64,349 " Turks." There were also 38,123 Austro-Hungarians, although not all of them could be considered "exotics."

64. See Buenos Aires, General Directory of Municipal Statistics, *Censo general de población*, pp. 220–21, 230–35.

65. Educational statistics based on JCA Rapport, 1910.

66. Rojas, *Restauración*, pp. 125–28. JCA(Lon) Session, September 24, 1910, pp. 174–230, Halfon reports on May 3 and 5, 1910. Also see Haim Avni, *Emantsipatsia ve-khinuch yehudi*, pp. 36–45.

67. See Buenos Aires, General Directory of Municipal Statistics, *Censo general de población* [1909], vol. 1, p. 93. Overall population estimate based on Alsina, *Inmigración en el primer siglo*, p. 25. In 1895, 10,474 of the 26,750 Protestants in Argentina lived in the capital. If the ratio of Buenos Aires to the provinces remained the same, the total number of Protestants would still be less than 90,000. See Argentina, Directive Commission of the Census, *2° censo de la República Argentina*, p. clxxviii, Table 19.

68. Alsina, *Inmigración europea*, p. 350; and Rojas, *Restauración*, pp. 127–28.

69. Many studies have been devoted to this fundamental issue in Argentine history. See, e.g., Scobie, *Revolution*, pp. 73–91. For a contemporary account, see detailed reports of the Italian immigration commissioner who spent eighteen months traveling across the Republic in 1905–1907: V. Tomezzoli, "L'Argentina e l'emigrazione italiana," pt. 1, pp. 1747, 1764, 1772, 1819, pt. 2, p. 1878.

70. See Solberg, *Immigration*, pp. 51, 53, 84–90. With regard to Buenos Aires, see Argentina, Directive Commission of the Census, *Tercer censo*, vol. 2, p. 6.

71. See Avni, *Argentina ha-aretz ha-yeuda*, pp. 291–94 on the government colony of Yerúa in Entre Ríos. Also see Tomezzoli, "Argentina e l'emigrazione," pt. 1, p. 1753 on a colony in the Córdoba region. On the colony of Moisesville, see Argentina, Ministry of Agriculture, *Informes y estudios de la División de Estadística y Economía Rural*, p. 31, and Hugo Miatello, *La chacra santafecina en 1905*, p. 57.

72. See Argentina, Directive Commission of the Census, *Tercer censo*, vol. 2, pp. 3–7. In the absence of more-concrete data, we can only guess the religion of these property owners.

73. See Enrique Dickman, *Recuerdos de un militante socialista*, pp. 185–88; Pinie Wald, "Yiden in der tragisher vokh," p. 6; JCA(Lon) Session, September 24, 1910, pp. 184–88, Halfon report on May 3, 1910.

74. A total of 38,904 registered Jewish immigrants attempted to settle in the provinces in 1910–1914; this represented 41.24 percent of all registered Jewish immigrants who arrived in these years. Fifty-four and a quarter percent of them went to JCA colonies. This calculation is based on the weekly reports submitted by the JCA administration in Buenos Aires.

75. See Ira Rosenswaike, "The Jewish Population of Argentina," p. 200; and Bronislav Bloch, "Hitpatkhut ha-okhlusiah ha-yehudit be-argentina, 1900–1960," pp. 85–86, tables 25, 26. Bloch attempts to reconstruct a demographic picture of the time, based on the 1960 census. Also see Bachi, *Population of Israel*, p. 32, who claims that the Jewish community in Palestine numbered only ninety-four thousand souls—81,900 in the city and 12,100 in rural areas.

Chapter 4. The Last Chance, 1914–1932

1. Ricardo M. Ortiz, *Historia económica de la Argentina*, vol. 2, pp. 5–6, 322–29; Adolfo Dorfman, *Historia de la industria argentina*, pp. 323–54. Unemployment in Argentina reached 14.5, 17.7, and 19.4 percent in 1915–1917, compared with 6.7 percent in 1913.

2. Ezrah, *Libro del cincuentenario*, pp. 95–120.

3. On the early fund-raising on behalf of war victims, see CZA, L6/34, no. 1, letter of Solomon Liebschutz to Zionist Executive in Copenhagen; cf. Mirelman, *En búsqueda de una identidad*, p. 316. Also see *Berikht funm yudischen kongres*.

4. Wald, *In gang fun tseiten*, p. 415; Schallman, "Historia del periodismo judío en la Argentina," pp. 156–59.

5. Mirelman, *En búsqueda de una identidad*, pp. 193–99 Also see Manuel G. Morgenstern, *De la Legión Judía a Medinat Israel*.

6. *Berikht funm yudischen kongres*, pp. 36–37. Marcos and Manuel Bronstein, "La

inmigración israelita," refuted the anti-Semitic attack of Francisco Stach published in MSA, vol. 5, no. 55/56, July–August 1916, pp. 361–89. See also Cong. Actas, vol. 3, pp. 162–70. These textbooks *(La Argentina, La Tierra)* were already in circulation in 1910.

7. MSA, vol. 8, no. 85/90, pp. 25, 27, 89, 90, 119, 181.

8. One of them was Tomás Amadeo, the founder and secretary general of the Museo. See ibid., pp. 36, 54, 84, 141.

9. International Labour Office, *Emigration and Immigration,* pp. 214–20. William S. Bernard, ed., *American Immigration Policy,* pp. 18–54. Bernard cites the following data: An annual quota for Polish immigration was introduced in 1921; the number of Polish immigrants dropped from 30,977 to 5,982 in 1924 and went up to 6,524 in 1927. The quota for Romanian immigrants dropped from 7,416 to 603, and then to 295.

10. Avni, "Argentina."

11. *Vida Nuestra 2,* no. 7 (January 1919):145, and no. 8 (February 1919):170. Also see *La Prensa,* January 26, 1919, p. 4, for a detailed report on the presidential interview.

12. International Labour Office, *Emigration and Immigration,* pp. ix–xv, 163–220.

13. Oscar A. Natale, ed., *Aspectos jurídicos, económicos y sociales de la colonización con inmigrantes,* pp. 15–28, esp. Clauses 5, 10–17. The contents of the order and one of the circulars sent to the consuls can be found in HVKB, April 1924, pp. 5–6. Also see MI, May 31, 1924, article by Marcos Satanowski.

14. MI, April 19, 1924, p. 1.

15. Ibid., July 12, 1924, p. 1, interview with Juan Ramos, and March 1, 1924, p. 1. Also see editorial on May 17, 1924, p. 1, wherein Ramos's approach is presented as "cold" and "scientific" compared with Le Breton's. On the conference in Rome, see Miguel Ángel Cárcano, "La Conferencia Internacional de Roma y la política inmigratoria argentina," pp. 52, 55.

16. MI, January 8, 1924, p. 1, and February 7, 1925, p. 1; HVKB, no. 5–6, 1925, pp. 8–9.

17. JCA(Lon) Session, January 14, 1922, pp. 120–30, Halfon letter dated November 23, 1921; and Sop. Actas, November 10, 1921.

18. JCA(Lon) Session, May 13, 1922, pp. 103–107, letter dated February 24, 1922. Also see JCA Rapport, 1922, p. 137, and 1923, p. 268; and *Der Imigrant* 1 (February 1923):3–4.

19. JCA(BA), Paris correspondence, file 24, memorandum to Argentine ambassador Alvear on April 1, 1921 (appendix to Paris letter no. 1370); also see JCA(Lon) Session, October 6, 1923, pp. 123–24, Halfon letters dated June 3 and August 13, 1923. This change of heart with regard to special privileges seems to have been very

sudden. On May 8, 1923, all the privileges were still in force. See JCA(Lon) Session, July 7, 1923, pp. 126–27, letter no. 104, dated May 8, 1923.

20. This memorandum, dated April 24, 1924, was made public. See MI, May 24, 1924, p. 1, and the appeal to Minister of Agriculture Le Breton, June 29, 1923.

21. JCA(Lon) Session, October 11, 1924, pp. 112–17, revised and final draft of resolution no. 1783, dated August 8, 1924, and signed by Juan Ramos, and circular no. 2765 sent by Louis Oungre to the members of the board on October 2, 1924. Also see MI, October 11, 1924, p. 1, exchange of letters between the JCA and Juan Ramos. Cf. Jacob Latzky-Bertholdi, *Di drom-amerikaner lender un di idishe eynvanderung,* p. 9.

22. JCA(Lon) Session, January 14, 1922, pp. 120–22, Halfon letter dated November 23, 1921, and May 3, 1922, pp. 107–13, Halfon letter dated February 22, 1922.

23. José Mendelson, "A yovel idish lebn in Argentine," p. 89.

24. JCA(Lon) Session, October 6, 1923, p. 113, Halfon letter dated March 6, 1923, and October 11, 1924, p. 112, Oungre circular dated October 2, 1924. See memorandum of Central Committee to Ramos dated April 4, 1923, and resolution 2299 of the Immigration Department, dated April 13, 1923; my thanks to Yosef Rubin of Tel Aviv who provided access to this important document. See testimony of Yosef Rubin, ICJ, pp. 24–27.

25. JCA(Lon) Session, July 7, 1923, pp. 125–30, letter of Soprotimis dated May 8, 1923, and October 6, 1923, pp. 120–28, Halfon letters dated June 1 and 3, 1923. Also see Satanowski, MI, May 31, 1924, p. 5.

26. *Der Imigrant* 1 (February 1923):1–9; JCA(Lon) Session, October 6, 1923, pp. 41–42, remarks on agenda, and pp. 107–19, Soprotimis letter dated May 30, 1923, and Oungre's circular to board of directors on August 3, 1923; ibid., pp. 129–35, Soprotimis letter dated August 13, 1923; Soprotimis, *Di arbeyt fun di yohren 1922–1927 mit statistishe tabelen,* pp. 22, 40.

27. For text of agreement, see MI, June 8, 1924, p. 1. Poalei Zion leader Marcos Regalsky, editor of *Di Idishe Tseitung,* Matias Stoliar, journalist Yosef Mendelson, and others joined the board. However, the positions of president, secretary, and treasurer remained in the hands of Soprotimis activists. Emigdirekt—Vereinigtes Komitee für Jüdische Auswanderung (the United Committee for Jewish Emigration)—with headquarters in Berlin, was formed in October 1921 at a conference called by HIAS and the World Conference for Jewish Relief. This was a partial and late realization of Latzky-Bertholdi's idea, dating from 1907, regarding the formation of a Jewish democratic congress systematically to organize Jewish emigration.

28. It was originally believed that ten thousand emigrants were affected by the new law. An Emergency Committee on Jewish Refugees, headed by Louis Marshall, was formed in New York on June 22, 1924. In July 1925, it established the

United Evacuation Committee together with the JCA and Emigdirekt. See AJYB, vol. 27, 1925–1926, pp. 441–45; Wischnitzer, *To Dwell in Safety*, pp. 155–56; JCA Rapport, 1926, pp. 283–303.

29. See JCA Rapport, 1925, p. 293; statistical report of Soprotimis in MI, January 29, 1927, p. 7, and MI, May 29, 1926, p. 8 (four-year report) and November 12, 1927, p. 2. Four thousand thirty-eight immigrants, or 52 percent of all those registering with Soprotimis, did so during the two years prior to its merger with the Central Committee; 3,778 immigrants, or 48 percent, registered during the three and a half years following the merger. Also see Liga Israelita Argentina Contra la Tuberculosis, *Boletín Especial (1916–1966)*:29.

30. Yivo(NY), Argentina, placard of Idisher Arbaiter Imigratsions Komitet. Also see ICJ, testimony of Andor Glick on the assistance offered by the Association of Hungarian Speakers.

31. See Wischnitzer, *To Dwell in Safety*, p. 157; JCA Rapport, 1927, pp. 114, 117.

32. Id. Ts., March 14, 1928, p. 7, and the honorary issue of April 1928, articles of Levi Mas and Shmuel Horowitz, pp. 38, 91.

33. Ibid., May 29, 1928, p. 5; A. L. Schussheim, "Der ershte idisher imigratsie kongres in drom amerike," p. 57; Id. Ts., May 30, 1928, p. 5; and MI, June 2, 1928, p. 4. Calculation of pesos in US dollars is based on the table in Norman, *Outstretched Arm*, pp. 307–308.

34. MI, August 3, 1929, summary of activities for year after the congress and partial data, and March 2, 1929, p. 3; Id. Ts., July 15, 1929, p. 6, and August 1, 1929, p. 5.

35. JCA Conseil, vol. 7, pp. 28, 50, sessions on December 23, 1917, and April 11, 1919, budgets for 1918–1919. Also see ibid., p. 88, session on January 5, 1920, budget for 1920; cf. ibid., vol. 8, p. 215, session on January 23, 1926, budget for 1926. Calculation of US dollar equivalency based on Norman, *Outstretched Arm*, pp. 307–308.

36. JCA, *Conditions d'installation des agriculteurs dans les colonies de la JCA*, pp. 3–4; JCA Rapport, 1926, pp. 308–309. Also see JCA(Lon) Session, October 27, 1928, vol. 3, pp. 55–61. The turnover during this period was very high. In 1926, for example, the JCA settled 158 new families in the colonies, but actual growth was only sixty-nine families because eighty-seven families left that year; see JCA Rapport, 1926, p. 4.

37. Id. Ts., April 24, 1928, p. 6, leading article, May 30, 1928, p. 85, and June 3, 1928, p. 8, Oungre's letter to the immigration congress and Regalsky on May 30, 1928. Also see MI, April 14, 1928, p. 1, leading article, June 2, 1928, p. 4, and June 9, 1928, p. 2; and Schussheim, "Idisher imigratsie kongres," p. 55.

38. See detailed report to members of the board with cover letter dated October 12, 1928, in JCA(Lon) Session, October 27, 1928, vol. 3, pp. 53–72. Also see JCA Conseil, vol. 9, p. 78, session on October 27, 1928.

39. See Dorfman, *Industria argentina,* p. 366. On grain prices, see JCA Rapport, 1931, p. 1.

40. See Marysa Gerassi Navarro, *Los nacionalistas,* pp. 32–67; Tulio Halperin Donghi, "Crónica del período," pp. 23–32; and Collins, "Desarrollo y distribución," pp. 836–37. It was claimed that the higher fee was not for the visa itself but for the consular endorsement of accompanying medical certificates and proof of integrity. See Bul. Inf. 1/24 (March 15, 1931):2, and 4/27 (November 15, 1931):1; and MI, December 27, 1930, p. 1.

41. See Bul. Inf. 1/24 (March 15, 1931):3, and 1/26 (July 1, 1931):2; and MI, March 7, 1931, p. 1. Also see Sop. Actas, vol. 2, p. 277, meeting of Jewish organizational representatives on February 25, 1931.

42. See Sop. Actas, vol. 3, sessions on November 12 and August 31, 1931, and passim. On the departure for Birobidzhan, see MI, February 6, 1932, p. 1; Id. Ts., April 1, 1932, p. 6.

43. Sop. Actas, vol. 2, p. 272, sessions on May 27 and February 18, 1931. On suburban settlements, see session on September 30, 1931; the decision was reached despite the opposition of Isaac Starkmeth. See ibid., August 3, 1932, on the cutback in HICEM support.

44. Min. Agr. Memoria, 1932/33, pp. 315–19, the order and explanatory circular. Also see Sop. Actas, session on December 7, 1932, p. 15; Id. Ts., November 28, 1932, leading article.

45. All general immigration figures are based on CNCD, July 14, 1938, p. 819, which includes three passenger categories. The number of Jewish immigrants varies slightly in some of the sources. Cf. Wischnitzer, *To Dwell in Safety,* p. 291; JCA, *Le Baron Maurice de Hirsch et la Jewish Colonization Association,* p. 38; and Simón Weill, *Población israelita en la República Argentina.* Figures for 1900–1914 as listed in Avni, *Argentina y inmigración,* app. 1, Table 1, col. 9.

46. See HICEM, *Four Years of Jewish Migration, 1927–1930,* pp. 3, 47; and, with slight variations, JCA, *Hirsch et la JCA,* p. 38. Also see Rosenswaike, "Jewish Population," p. 211, who states that 66,065 immigrants remained in Argentina in 1920–1930.

47. See Francis Korn et al., *Buenos Aires,* p. 144, and map on p. 93 showing location of these slums. The "Jewish quarters" were full of them.

48. See HVKB, April 1924, p. 5, and May–June 1925, p. 10; quotation is from the March–April 1927 issue, p. 7. Also see Latzky-Bertholdi, *Drom-amerikaner lender,* p. 6; and Emigdirekt, *Der tsveyter idisher emigratsie tsuzamenfor . . . ,* p. 18.

49. JCA Rapport, 1927, p. 119; and remarks of Isaac Kaplan, a longtime Zionist and leading figure in the settlers' cooperatives, on the eve of the immigration congress, in Id. Ts., March 19, 1928, p. 7.

50. On JCA's activities in Europe, see JCA Rapport, 1930, pp. 98–216.

51. Margalit Bejarano, "Ha-kehilla ha-sefaradit shel Buenos Aires," pp. 160, 166,

and introductory chapters. Also see Soprotimis reports in MI, November 12, 1927, p. 2, and September 6, 1930, p. 4.

Chapter 5. The Closing Gates, 1933–1945

1. According to the Reichsvereinigung der Juden in Deutschland, the central organization of German Jews established in July 1939, there were 522,700 Jews in 1933, but this may have included "racial" Jews and converts. See Yehuda Bauer, *American Jewry and the Holocaust*, pp. 26, 461 n. 13.

2. Sop. Actas, March 29, 1933, p. 53, and July 5, 1933, meeting to discuss the plight of the unemployed; Id. Ts., July 14, 1933, p. 6.

3. Min. Agr. Memoria, 1932, pp. 313ff., report proposals and law interpretations. Also see Sop. Actas, May 17, 1933, p. 56, on the meeting with the deputy minister; and *La Prensa*, May 30, 1933, MI, June 3, 1933, and Id. Ts., May 31, 1933, p. 4, on the rejection of the proposal.

4. Sop. Actas, May 17, 1933, and July 5, 1933; JCA(Lon) Session, September 16, 1933, p. 44, remarks of director general.

5. JCA(Lon) Session, September 16, 1933, pp. 44–48, 80.

6. See *Filantropía* 109 (April 1943):1–4; Asociación Filantrópica Israelita, *Diez años de obra constructiva en América del Sud, 1933–1943*, pp. 21–25, 43. Also see Sop. Actas, May 7, 1933, and June 7, 1933; and cf. Asociación Filantrópica Israelita, *Libro aniversario*, pp. 1–24. Anti-Semitism was rampant among the Germans in Buenos Aires. On April 5, 1933, fifty-one German organizations celebrated Adolf Hitler's rise to power, singing the "Horst Wessel Lied" at Teatro Colón, the Argentine opera house. See Ronald C. Newton, *German Buenos Aires, 1900–1933*, pp. 170–71, 181. On the relations between the German Jews and the anti-Nazi Germans in Argentina, see David Bankier, "Die Verhältnisse zwischen jüdischen Flüchtlinge und deutschen Exilierten in Lateinamerika."

7. On the scope of immigration, see Min. Agr. Memoria, 1934, p. 475. On the number of applicants to the relief organizations, see Asociación Filantrópica Israelita, *Diez años de obra*, pp. 46–47, 78. The Jewish immigration total includes 1,962 immigrants who were officially registered as Jews and an additional hundred who, according to JCA director Simón Weill, either concealed their religion or entered illegally; see JCA(Lon), file 539, report appended to letter no. 317 of May 10, 1940.

8. See Werner Rosenstock, "Exodus 1933–1939," p. 379. These figures are still accepted by researchers. See Avraham Margaliot, " The Problem of the Rescue of German Jewry . . ." pp. 247–58; Shaul Esh, "Beyn haflayah le-hashmadah," pp. 74–77, 80.

9. Min. Agr. Memoria, 1934, pp. 458–62, esp. Clauses 2–4, 9, 17.

10. James G. McDonald, *Draft of an Interim Report on the Mission to South and*

Central America . . . , pp. 16–34, annex 1; Haim Avni, "Latin America and the Jewish Refugees," pp. 47–50.

11. See McDonald, *Report on the Mission,* pp. 9–13; in his view, another factor influencing Argentina's policy was the desire of the ruling class to protect its vast property holdings. Also see *Criterio* 8, no. 376 (May 16, 1935):1, leading article, and nos. 422 and 425 (April 2 and 23, 1936).

12. JCA(Lon) Session, December 18, 1935, vol. 3, pp. 2–4, Aronstein report on May 30, 1935, and vol. 4, pp. 184–86, 252–53. Also see Sop. Actas, March 17, 1935, p. 138.

13. JCA(Lon) Session, May 4, 1935, resolutions, p. 187, and material for meeting on October 26, 1935, pp. 65, 86, 219; ICJ, testimony of Noy-Meir, pp. 5ff., on how these young people fared in Avigdor.

14. See Id. Ts., January 9, 1936, p. 5; MI, February 1, 1936, editorial. Also see JCA(BA), Soprotimis, Letter book 1, pp. 1, 26, standard JCA letters of approval; and CZA, Z4/17063, data on colonization in Argentina amassed by the representative of Keren Hayesod, Abraham Mibashan, on January 26, 1939.

15. Asociación Filantrópica Israelita, *Diez años de obra,* pp. 166–69, testimony of two young people who remained on the farm in 1943. See Jedidia Efron, "Informe presentado a la dirección general de la JCA en Buenos Aires," p. 35, for a historical eyewitness account, report on Río Negro. For legal reasons, the farm was managed by Fomento Agrícola Adolfo Hirsch. Also see ICJ, testimony of Juan Waldeck.

16. Sop. Actas, July 18, 1935, pp. 153–58, February 4, 1936, and March 3, 1936.

17. In a careful review of MI and Id. Ts., 1934–1936, no encouraging statements were found with regard to immigration to Argentina. See ZO Protokoll . . . Wien, November 15, 1937, pp. 22–26, on the convention in Vienna; JCA(Lon) Session, December 18, 1937, vol. 2, pp. 223–24, on the interorganizational meeting held from November 30 to December 1, 1937. Also see Hilfsverein der Juden in Deutschland, *Jüdische Auswanderung Korrespondenzblatt über Auswanderunges und Siedlungswesen,* pp. 34–38, letters from Argentina in 1935–1936.

18. See BPRO, FO 371/19763, documents 452–64: text of order issued on October 17, 1936, internal correspondence, and instructions to ambassador.

19. See BPRO, FO 371/20598–2, agreements with the Netherlands, Switzerland, and Denmark; and reports of British ambassador. Also see Canals Frau, "Inmigración europea," pp. 98, 101, 111, which gives immigration totals by country of origin.

20. See Sop. Actas, October 28, 1936, p. 20, and March 31, 1937, p. 39, on the difficulty in obtaining entry permits. See also Bul. Inf., October–November 1936, pp. 2, 8–9; and Id. Ts., March 17, 1936, p. 3, DAIA response to police commissioner's report identifying Jews with Communists.

21. On the scope of immigration, see JCA(Lon) 539, appendix to letter no. 317,

Simón Weill to JCA Paris, May 10, 1940; Wischnitzer, *To Dwell in Safety*, p. 291. See also Asociación Filantrópica Israelita, *Diez años de obra*, pp. 46, 78. The lists of the two organizations should not be combined because many immigrants may have registered with both.

22. On the memorandum submitted by the Polish League of Nations Federation on the Jewish question, January 1938, see Nathan Feinberg, *Ha-agudot ha-yehudiot lema'an hever ha'leumin*, pp. 172–91. See Emanuel Meltser, "Ha-diplomatiah ha-polanit u-b'ayot ha-hagira ha-yehudit be-shanim 1935–1939," p. 211; and Leny Yahil, "Madagascar—Phantom of a Solution for the Jewish Question" on Poland and the Madagascar affair. On anti-Semitism in Romania, see Bela Vago, *The Shadow of the Swastika*, pp. 21–72.

23. See José Blanco, "Industria," pp. 226–36, who quotes census totals for 1935, 1941, and 1946. Also see Ruth Sautu, "Poder económico y burguesía industrial en la Argentina, 1930–1954." The figures quoted by Felix J. Weil, "La industrialización argentina en los años '40," p. 372, Table 6, are somewhat different yet indicate the same phenomenon of accelerated and impressive growth.

24. See *La Luz*, March 11, 1938, p. 1; MI, March 5, 1938, p. 1, April 2, 1938, p. 1, April 16, 1938, p. 1, and June 4, 1938, p. 3. Also see JCA memorandum to minister of agriculture on May 27, 1940, pp. 6–14, quotations from report of Doctor Domingo Borea, the official appointed in June 1938 to investigate JCA activity, in Ministry of Agriculture, file 03475/38. My thanks to Yosef Rubin of Tel Aviv for allowing me access to this important document.

25. See statements of Le Breton, Intergovernmental Committee, *Proceedings of the Intergovernmental Committee, Évian, July 6–15, 1938*, pp. 21–22; and statements of representatives of the technical subcommittee, in BPRO, FO 371/22530, documents 154–55. The order was officially published in BO, August 6, 1938, p. 10118, and was signed by President Ortiz and his ministers of foreign affairs and agriculture.

26. See CNCD, August 9 and 10, 1939, quotation from confidential circular; and Id. Ts., August 26, 1938, p. 8.

27. JCA(BA), Soprotimis, Letter book 2, p. 893, Weill letter dated August 31, 1938.

28. BPRO, FO 371/22534, report of conversation with Robert T. Pell, deputy director of the Intergovernmental Committee, on September 6, 1938; and ibid., instructions to the British ambassador and his reply. Also see JCA memorandum to minister of agriculture on May 27, 1940, pp. 1–2 (see note 24 above).

29. See *Criterio* (August 4, 1938):1; Comité Contra el Racismo y el Anti-semitismo, *Actas del primer congreso contra el racismo y el antisemitismo*, pp. 41–42, 135, 220, 226.

30. See Juan Solari's call to investigate the legality of the orders, in CNCD, September 19, 1938, pp. 134–38; also ibid., December 15, 1938, pp. 447–52, and January 17, 1939, pp. 549–53. Esp. see the demands of Leonidas Anastasi and Bernar-

dino Horne on June 1, 1939 for reports by the ministers of agriculture and the interior, and the debate on September 10, 1939, pp. 836ff. In direct contrast, Reynoldo Alberto Pasto of the Partido Demócrata Nacional and Vicente Solano Lima of the Conservative party openly questioned the legitimacy of the Jewish presence in Argentina. Also see Comité Contra el Racismo y el Antisemitismo, *Tierra sin hombres,* pp. 20–21; Id. Ts., August 30, 1938, p. 6; and *La Fronda,* August 2, 1939.

31. Id. Ts., September 6, 1938, p. 6; and Sop. Actas, July 14 and October 12, 1938, pp. 107–17.

32. Id. Ts., November 20, 1938, pp. 7, 10, 12, and November 21, 1938, pp. 4, 6. The DAIA protested to the president and minister of the interior over this "census" of closed Jewish businesses; see DAIA Arch., November 22, 1938.

33. See Elvira Rissech, "Inmigración judía a la Argentina 1938–1942"; Nelida Giuvicich et al., *El fenómeno inmigratorio,* "Conferencia de ministeros de hacienda," pp. 93–94.

34. JCA(Lon), file 539, report on immigration in 1939 appended to letter 317 by Simón Weill, dated May 10, 1940; and Id. Ts., June 14, 1939, p. 6. For details of the *Monte Oliva* affair, see *Critica* (November 17 and 21, 1940). The intermediary, attorney Faustino E. Jorge, did not deny his professional contacts with the Immigration Department and admitted having been paid 950 pesos per family. There is no definite information regarding the other forty-four persons, who may have been returned to their ship. See Elvira Rissech, "Final Report," pp. 110–13.

35. Id. Ts., July 13, 1939, p. 5, and May 20, 1939, p. 5; Sop. Actas, March 1, 1939, pp. 129–31, July 4, 1939, pp. 146–48, and August 22, 1939, pp. 149–52.

36. Legalization cost 162 or 192.50 pesos depending on the circumstances. Forty thousand pesos were forwarded for the purpose of moving the orphanage; see MI, August 19, 1939, p. 7, and April 27, 1940, p. 12, article by Mibashan.

37. Figures for Jewish immigration are according to JCA(Lon), file 539, report on immigration in 1939, appended to letter no. 317 by Simón Weill, dated May 10, 1940; and Min. Agr. Memoria, 1938, vol. 1, pp. 411–12.

38. German imports were boycotted by the Committee Against Racism and Anti-Semitism in 1934, and later, by the DAIA; see, e.g., Id. Ts., May 5, 1939. The riots in Palestine in 1936–1938, and especially the White Paper of May 1939, caused an uproar among Argentina's Jews.

39. José Alfredo Martínez de Hoz, "Agricultura y ganadería," pp. 191–96.

40. JCA(Lon), file 539, resolution no. 9045 signed by the minister of agriculture on September 12, 1939 (Exp. 3457/38).

41. Ibid., letter no. 539 from Buenos Aires, dated January 20, 1940, and letters from Paris, no. 466 dated February 17, 1940, no. 477 dated April 5, 1940, and no. 485 dated May 16, 1940.

42. Ibid., letters from Buenos Aires, no. 531 dated January 5, 1940 and no. 556

dated February 27, 1940, on encouraging the young people to remain in the colony. On September 4, 1940, the director of the JCA notified the immigration commissioner of the cancellation of entry permits for three members of the Oppenheimer family whose son had left the colony of Ungre-Cohen after settling there in June 1938; see JCA(BA), Soprotimis, Letter book 5, p. 3.

43. JCA(Lon), file 539, letter no. 569 from Buenos Aires, dated April 19, 1940. Also see memorandum (see note 24 above) to minister of agriculture on May 27, 1940, pp. 1–5, 30–34.

44. See Sop. Actas, July 18, 1940, p. 175; JCA(BA), Soprotimis, Letter book 5, p. 53, letter to immigration commissioner on December 3, 1940, p. 88, letter dated February 5, 1941, p. 199, letter dated July 30, 1941, and p. 235, letter dated March 18, 1942. In these last two letters, the JCA requested a permit for Alfred Jacques Bronschweig, one of its employees in Argentina for fourteen years; the request was rejected.

45. BO, August 28, 1940, p. 11534, order 68518 on July 27, 1940; Id. Ts., July 30, 1940, p. 3; and Sop. Actas, August 6, 1940, pp. 178–82, February 17, 1941, pp. 7–8, and September 20, 1941, pp. 32–34. On the request of the Reichsvertretung der Juden, see Sop. Actas, July 18, 1940, p. 175; and DAIA Actas, session 28, August 13, 1940, p. 37.

46. Sop. Actas, February 17, 1941, pp. 190–92. The report of inspector Enrique J. Plate was published in *Critica* (November 16, 17, 18, and 21, 1940). Maspero Castro took office on November 16, 1940. See also Rissech, "Inmigración judía," p. 104.

47. MI, January 25, 1941, p. 1; Rissech, "Inmigración judía," p. 112, mentions thirteen Jews who were rejected (their names are given in the final report, p. 117). According to MI, February 1, 1941, p. 3 ("De semana a semana"), they were finally allowed into the United States.

48. YHH, series 1, 17/XIII, letter of Mellibowsky to HIAS director on March 26, 1946, detailing restrictions imposed in June 1941. Also see Sop. Actas, June 24, 1941, pp. 22–27, September 24, 1941, pp. 32–34, and February 28, 1942, pp. 41–47. After the abolishment of the "advisory committee" to the immigration commissioner, an "immigration council" was established in September 1941 with the power to approve or bar the entry of immigrants.

49. See Sop. Actas, February 17, 1941, p. 190, February 24, 1942, pp. 54–56; and MI, February 14, 1942, p. 12. Also see Min. Agr. Memoria, 1940, vol. 2, pp. 295–96. The estimated Jewish immigration here follows Weill, *Población israelita* (handwritten addenda), and Wischnitzer, *To Dwell in Safety*, p. 291; also AJYB, vol. 47, 1946, p. 656.

50. See BPRO, FO 371/3670, ambassador's letter no. 103, dated April 19, 1943; and MI, April 26, 1941, p. 15, Soprotimis's call to the public; Sop. Actas, February 17, 1941, p. 3, report on 1940, and February 24, 1942, p. 60, report on 1941.

51. Rissech, "Final Report," pp. 123–28, referring to SS *Cabo de Buena Esperanza* and SS *Cabo de Hornos,* which arrived in Buenos Aires on October 1 and 24 respectively. See also Bauer, *American Jewry,* p. 202; JCA(BA), Soprotimis, Letter book 5, dozens of notifications from the end of 1941 and 1942 regarding immigrants with entry permits who could not reach Argentina.

52. Dotación Carnegie para la Paz Internacional, *Conferencias internacionales americanas,* p. 180.

53. MFA Arg. Memoria, report on 1942–1943, pp. 7–12, 23–36; Hiroshi Matsushita, "A Historical View of Argentine Neutrality during World War II"; Mario Rapoport, *Gran Bretaña, Estados Unidos y las clases dirigentes argentinas, 1940–1950,* "Conclusiones," pp. 291–99.

54. Leonardo Senkman, "La problemática de los refugiados centro europeos y su enmigración a la Argentina, 1933–1945," pp. 63–72.

55. Donald A. Lowrie, *The Hunted Children,* pp. 218–28; Sop. Actas, October 13, 1942, p. 104; DAIA Actas, session 79, October 22, 1942, p. 101; MI, November 28, 1942, pp. 1, 4; and Senkman, "Problemática de los refugiados," pp. 407–408.

56. DAIA Actas, session 81, November 24, 1942, p. 103; MI, November 28, 1942, p. 3; *El Pampero,* November 27, 1942; *El Crisol,* November 28, 1942.

57. Lowrie, *Hunted Children,* pp. 222–25; DAIA Actas, session 80, November 12, 1942, p. 102, and November 29, 1942, p. 107. At this and later meetings, one of the topics of discussion was the punishment of Jews—among them activists—who did not close their businesses during the strike.

58. YHH, series 1, no. 13, letters of Mellibowsky dated January 21, February 2 and 10, and March 5, 1943; ibid., copy of memorandum to president on March 4, 1943, and summary of meeting; MI, March 6, 1943, p. 2.

59. YHH, series 1, no. 13, letter of Mellibowsky dated May 26, 1942; DAIA Actas, session 4, April 22, 1943, p. 116, and session 7, May 27, 1943, p. 121. Also see MI, May 22, 1943, p. 5; and Senkman, "Problemática de los refugiados," pp. 414–15.

60. Yad Vashem, MFA Germany, JM/2216, documents 210711–210732, memoranda of Wagner on July 21, 1943, October 28, 1943, and appendices.

61. Yad Vashem, 039/153, testimony of Doctor Rudolph Levy; 03/943, testimony of Betsy Andriess; 03/938, testimony of Maurice Jacob Levy. Also see Clara Ascher-Pinkhof, *Rakdanit beli raglaim,* pp. 25–40, on her experiences in the transit camp. On the exchange of citizens of Palestine, see Ruth Zariz, *Mi-Bergen Belsen la khofesh;* Senkman, "Problemática de los refugiados," pp. 417–18, who quotes cable of Foreign Minister Gilbert; and FORUS, 1943, vol. 1, pp. 204, 398–99, reports of the US ambassador in London on August 12, 1943, and December 27, 1943.

62. Yad Vashem, MFA, Germany, K1509 (Inland II A/B 83–26 Argentina), cables from Schleier, Paris, January 28, 1943, and June 6, 1943, response by Luther, January 30, 1943.

63. Ibid., K211078, note Referat DIII of March 1943, and Argentine embassy, note of November 17, 1943.

64. Ibid., note from Thadden, July 29, 1943.

65. Ibid., E411975-7, messages of February 4 and 5, 1944.

66. Yad Vashem, 039/153, testimony of Rudolph Levy; YHH, series 1, no. 13, letters of Mellibowsky, October 11 and 25, 1943; Avni, *Spain, Jews and Franco,* pp. 138–47.

67. Senkman, "Problemática de los refugiados," pp. 306–308, quoting *Memoria de la Oficina de Estadística de la Dirección de Inmigración;* Sop. Actas, July 20, 1942, p. 96; MI, January 23, 1943, p. 6. Jewish immigration figures are according to Wischnitzer, *To Dwell in Safety,* p. 291, and AJYB, vol. 47, 1946, p. 656.

68. Archives of the War Refugee Board, Box 112 IV E20, summary based on note 14547, dated April 21, 1944, from the US embassy in Buenos Aires. I am thankful to Yehuda Bauer for bringing this document to my attention.

69. CNCD, December 15, 1938, pp. 447–52; Giuvicich et al., *Fenómeno inmigratorio,* pp. 95–99.

70. Eduardo Labougle, *Misión en Berlin,* pp. 42–44, 46–49, and passim. This book is based on Labougle's reports from Berlin, and he quotes from them extensively. Cf., e.g., pp. 47–49, 81–82, 94, 104, 110, etc., with MFA, Argentina, Alemania 1935, Exp. 9.

71. JCA(Lon), file 539, Weill to JCA Paris and to Le Breton, February 15, 1940.

72. BPRO, FO 371/29210, Winterton's memorandum of his talk with Le Breton on August 5, 1941. Winterton's views are worth mentioning: Although he tried to intervene on behalf of the refugees, he accepted most of Le Breton's anti-Jewish arguments. His conclusion was that the great friend of the Allies, Ambassador Le Breton, should not be pursued any further on the subject of Jewish immigration. Also see ICJ, testimony of Eduardo J. Siri, secretary of the Argentine embassy in London, on the character of Le Breton.

73. Yad Vashem, MFA Germany, E411958, note dated Friday, September 11, 1942; Leonardo Senkman, "La problemática de los refugiados europeos a través de la inmigración limítrofe, 1938–1944," pp. 24–30.

74. DAIA Actas, session 60, April 2, 1945, p. 39, and other sessions leading up to session 92 on April 18, 1946, p. 139, when the letter of the Ministry of Foreign Affairs, dated April 11, 1946, was discussed.

75. Official figures for 1933–1937 are quoted by Wischnitzer, *To Dwell in Safety,* p. 291, and in AJYB, vol. 46, 1945, p. 517. Official data for 1938–1942 are given according to research material in Rissech "Final Report" and "Inmigración judía," and for 1943–1945, according to Senkman, "Problemática de los refugiados," p. 306; see also lists of names quoted by Rissech, "Final Report."

76. Weill, *Población israelita.* In his personal copy, Weill also noted data for the Jews for 1936–1945, which give a total of 30,336 immigrants in 1933–1939, and an-

other 7,824 in 1940–1945; also see JCA(Lon), file 539, report on 1939 (appended to Weill's letter no. 317, dated May 10, 1940), which lists 31,617 immigrants for 1933–1939 and states that 14,362 German Jews (or 45.4 percent of the total) entered the country during these years. As the author of the report attributed all illegal immigration to German Jews, this figure should be regarded as a maximum. According to the Immigration Department, two thousand tourists entered and remained in Argentina in 1940. Most of them were Jews from Germany. See Collins, "Desarrollo y distribución," p. 842. Bloch, "Hitpatkhut ha-okhlusiah ha-yehudit," who calculated the development of the Jewish population in Argentina retrospectively on the basis of the Argentine national census of 1960, found 17,300 immigrants in 1930–1934 (see his Table 26). When reckoned proportionately for each year, this gives 6,920 for 1933–1934. Together with the 23,300 that Bloch cites for 1935–1939, this brings us to a total of 30,220 for 1933–1939, which corroborates Weill's figures. While Bloch's calculation for 1940–1944—forty-four hundred immigrants—may be low, the figures quoted by Carlota Jackisch, "Los refugiados alemanes en la Argentina, 1933–1945," pp. 61–68, seem too high. M. Katz, "Los judíos alemanes en la Argentina," p. 163, mentions hundreds of Germans who re-emigrated.

77. Senkman, "Problemática de los refugiados," p. 271, table based on data from Immigration Department publications.

78. Weil, "Industrialización argentina," pp. 365–67; Blanco, "Industria," pp. 230–31.

79. Haim Avni, "Argentine Jewry," no. 13–14, pp. 178–84; Bejarano, "Ha-kehilla ha-sefaradit," pp. 52–74; Haim Avni, "Patterns of Jewish Leadership in Latin America during the Holocaust," pp. 94–98; Banco Israelita del Río de la Plata, *Yiddishe Folks Bank*, p. 72; Banco Comercial, *Banco Comercial de Buenos Aires, S.A.*, pp. 70, 129. Pesos rendered into US dollars according to Norman, *Outstretched Arm*, pp. 306–307, who provides data for 1932 and 1948; hence, the dollar amounts are only an approximation.

80. On German Jews in the capital and colonies, see Carlos Fogel, "Di daitshe yiden in Buenos Aires" and "Di kolonies fun di daytshe yiden bey Moisesville"; Katz, "Judíos alemanes"; *Filantropía* 10, no. 117 (December 1943):1–3, concluding article and social critique; Manfred Rehfeld, "Sinagogue in der Galuth"; and Bankier, "Jüdischen Flüchtlinge."

Chapter 6. The Survivors, 1945–1950

1. Yehuda Bauer, *Flight and Rescue*, pp. 113–16, 206–11; and Leonard Dinnerstein, *America and the Survivors of the Holocaust*, pp. 73, 278, Table A2.

2. Id. Ts., January 31, 1946, p. 3. Among fifty-eight arrested students, sixteen

had Jewish names. On relations with the Arabs, see *La Calle,* December 21, 1945; and CZA, S25/7502, memorandum of Moshe Tov to Moshe Shertok (1946?), p. 6.

3. See *La Prensa* and *La Nación,* both August 11, 1945; and *Noticias Gráficas,* December 7, 1945, the Communist party platform.

4. See *La Tribuna,* April 25 and May 4, 1946; and *El Laborista,* April 25, 1946, another paper that supported Perón. Of course, the immigration issue was dealt with in many other newspapers. See, e.g., *El Pueblo,* May 30 and June 4, 1946; *Hoy,* March 29, 1946; *Democracia,* March 12, 1946; *El Diario,* March 12, 1946; and especially the newspapers of various national groups, such as *El Diaro Español,* April 16 and 23, and May 6, 1946, *Buenos Aires Herald,* March 11, 1946, and *Italia Libre,* May 4, 1946.

5. Santiago M. Peralta, *La acción del pueblo judío en la Argentina,* pp. 67, 69, 110–11, 116–17; see MI, June 29, 1946, p. 3, for a sarcastic critique of this book.

6. YHH, series 1, no. 13, Arg/15, Mellibowsky to Shoshkes, December 27, 1945, and Arg/30, report by Shoshkes, p. 13.

7. See BO, March 30, 1946, order 435/46; and criticism in *La Prensa,* April 20, 1946, leading article. Also see *Diario Arabe,* January 30, 1946; responses in *Sábado,* July 20, 1946; *El Pampero* 10 (May 1946).

8. See *La Nación,* June 6, 1946; *La Hora,* June 3, 1946; *Democracia,* June 6, 1946; *Gobernantes,* June 9 and 29, 1946; and leading article in *The New York Times* on June 16, 1946, quoted in *La Razón,* June 17, 1946.

9. DAIA Arch., memorandum dated October 22, 1945, to the president, General Edelmino Farrell, with regard to the attacks on October 17, 1945. Also see Perón's statements in *El Laborista,* January 12, 1946; and see *Democracia,* January 14, 1946. See *La Época,* March 10, 1946, on the results of the elections in Entre Ríos and the journalist's assumption of broad Jewish support of Perón. According to Id. Ts., March 17, 1946, p. 1, Perón won 4,227, or 37 percent, of the votes in the Once quarter, the heart of Jewish Buenos Aires.

10. Sop. Actas, August 5, 1946, pp. 65–70, and November 13, 1946, pp. 89–96; and YHH, series 1, no. 13, Arg/13, 00140, report on the meeting. The delegation also asked Perón for permission to bring over one thousand children in place of those who had been approved as immigrants in 1942; Perón promised to consider the matter.

11. Id. Ts., February 16, 1947, pp. 2, 6, February 20, 1947, p. 5, February 21, 1947, p. 6; and MI, February 22, 1947, p. 7. *Naie Leben* 35–36 (January–February 1947):1; DAIA Actas, session 114, February 20, 1947, p. 14; and ICJ, testimony of Moshe Goldman.

12. DAIA Arch., appeals to President Perón on March 27 and April 1, 1947. Also see YHH, series 1, no. 12, Arg/18, report of Shoshkes and Harris on July 3, 1947. Ignacio Klich, "A Background to Perón's Discovery of Jewish National Aspiration," p. 209, assumes on the basis of circumstantial evidence that US ambassador

George Messersmith played a part in the dismissal of Peralta. This seems far-fetched.

13. See Enrique Siewers, "Obstáculos mentales a una política activa de inmigración," pp. 437–38. He claims that the Argentine economy required an annual manpower supplement of eighty thousand workers, whereas natural increase could supply only forty thousand. See Sociedad Rural Argentina, "Inmigración y reforma agraria," p. 319, memorandum to Perón on November 20, 1946, in which migration to the city was seen as a very serious problem. Also see Martínez de Hoz, "Agricultura," p. 197, for an economist's view of the activities of the Instituto Argentino de Promoción del Intercambio; and Juan Domingo Perón, *Doctrina peronista,* pp. 95–102, 110–67.

14. Perón's statements were quoted in the leading articles of *Hoy,* August 9, 1946, MI, June 8, 1946, *El Pueblo,* August 6, 1946, and *El Laborista,* August 6, 1946. See article titled "Peronism and Immigration" in *Democracia,* September 23, 1946. Also see "Ley de bases acerca de inmigración y colonización" in *La Nación,* October 25, 1946; and Sociedad Rural Argentina, "Inmigración," p. 300.

15. Leonardo Senkman, "Las relaciones EE.UU.–Argentina y la cuestión de los refugiados de la post-guerra, 1945–1948," pp. 91–94; Mario C. G. Nascimbene, "Los inmigrantes italianos a la Argentina," p. 4, Table 1. Figures based on Natale, *Aspectos jurídicos,* p. 220, Table 35.

16. Senkman, "Relaciones EE.UU.–Argentina," pp. 98–104, 107–109. This work records the entry into Argentina of ten thousand Yugoslavians, sixteen hundred of Anders' soldiers, who set sail with their families in October 1947, and another group of the same size that left in November.

17. Ibid., pp. 100–102; Louise W. Holborn, *The International Refugee Organization, a Specialized Agency of the United Nations,* pp. 401–402.

18. Tomás Eloy Martínez, "Perón and the Nazi War Criminals," deals with the problem of the Germans but tends to diminish their importance. So does Klich, "Perón's Discovery," pp. 203–204.

19. See BO, July 2, 1947, order 14.882/47 dated May 29, 1947; YHH, series 1, no. 13, Arg/18, letters of Turkow to Dijour on May 19 and June 11, 1947; MI, June 14, 1947, p. 2; Sop. Actas, September 16, 1947, pp. 157, 162, September 4, 1947, pp. 174–79, and October 16, 1947, pp. 182–86; and DAIA Arch., letter dated September 26, 1947, to the Comisión de Recepción.

20. Sop. Actas, November 6, 1947, p. 187, and April 6, 1948, report on 1947. The quotation is from the reply of the Comisión de Recepción on October 22, 1947. DAIA Actas, November 19, 1947, p. 36, December 18, 1947, p. 40, July 17, 1947, p. 29, and January 14, 1948, p. 48; YHH, series 1, no. 13, Arg/24, "Hias Activities," 1947, and memorandum dated February 18, 1949, and annual report of 1948.

21. Immigration by way of Paraguay and other countries is attested to in dozens of personal files in the Soprotimis Archives, now kept at the Central Archives of

the History of the Jewish People in Jerusalem. Also see YHH, series 1, no. 13, Arg/18, 00114, Turkow to Shoshkes, October 29, 1946. Soprotimis paid its agent in Asunción 100 pesos per visa; see Sop. Actas, April 9, 1947, pp. 132–37, May 22, 1947, pp. 150–52, and June 19, 1947, pp. 157–62.

22. DAIA Arch., cable on February 6, 1948 to Perón; DAIA Actas, June 24, 1948, p. 24; and Sop. Actas, July 6, 1948, p. 52, and July 27, 1948, pp. 55–58. Also see CZA, Z6/22, detailed report on the history of the OIA; and MI, August 21, 1948.

23. Sop. Actas, September 1, 1948, pp. 63–66; and BO, October 20, 1948, law no. 13.482 dated October 14, 1948.

24. Sop. Actas, June 14, 1949, p. 90, annual report on 1948; ibid., December 14, 1948, pp. 72, 76, March 8, 1949, pp. 78–79, and April 25, 1950, annual report on 1949, p. 140; BO, July 15, 1949, order no. 15.972 dated July 8, 1949. Also see BO, order no. 24.666 dated October 4, 1949.

25. Sop. Actas, June 14, 1949, annual report on 1948, pp. 91–92.

26. See Natale, *Aspectos jurídicos,* pp. 209–14, Tables 30, 33. These figures include all entries and departures from Argentina—not only immigration from overseas. The number of arrivals in 1947–1951 totaled 2,182,185, and the number of departures, 1,583,249. In 1933–1946, the number of arrivals totaled 2,138,509, and departures, 2,011,586. Compare with figures of Zulma Recchini de and Alfredo E. Lattes, *Año mundial de la población,* p. 200; and see Sop. Actas, March 7, 1946, p. 48, April 6, 1948, p. 14, June 14, 1949, p. 92, and May 9, 1950, pp. 136–47; Id. Ts., January 23, 1947, p. 7. Cf. Wischnitzer, *To Dwell in Safety,* p. 291, whose table for 1945–1947 gives a total of 1,149 persons.

27. See Weill, *Población israelita,* handwritten addendum.

28. DAIA Actas, March 7, 1946, p. 123, and November 3, 1946, p. 190. Soprotimis, which now enjoyed much greater support from the Jewish community, dedicated its funds to locating surviving relatives, sending food parcels, and so forth; see Sop. Actas, annual reports for 1949 and 1950.

29. See Dinnerstein, *America and the Survivors,* pp. 39–71, 117–82, 291–305; Wischnitzer, *To Dwell in Safety,* pp. 260–72.

30. In 1933–1945, Canada admitted only five thousand refugees. After the war, the Canadian Jewish Congress managed to arrange the immigration of one thousand children from France whose entry had been authorized in 1942 (as was the case for Argentina). Another one thousand permits were received for tailors and their families as part of the Canadian labor immigration program. See Harold Troper, "Canada and the Jewish Displaced Persons," pp. 188, 194–97, based on Abella and Troper, *None Is Too Many: Canada and the Jews of Europe, 1933–1948* (Toronto, 1982).

31. Klich, "Perón's Discovery," p. 213, quoting National Archives 835.00/1-2745, memo of Messersmith.

32. Ibid., pp. 216–18; Cristián Buchrucker, *Nacionalismo y peronismo,* pp. 354–55.

Also, see Avni, *Emantsipatsia*, pp. 71–91, and Haim Avni, "Religion at Government Schools," regarding the popular nationalism in the Peronist regime as reflected in the issue of Catholic education.

Chapter 7. Conclusion

1. EJ, vol. 16, "Migration," p. 1519. Our estimates for Jewish immigration to Argentina in maximal round figures are: until 1891, 1,500; 1896, 10,000; 1914, 85,000; 1932, 75,500; 1945, 40,000; 1950, 5,500. The total equals 217,500.

2. For a more detailed discussion, see Avni, *Argentina y inmigración*, pp. 187–202.

3. Avni, "Religion," pp. 164–66.

4. Avni, *Emantsipatsia*, pp. 22–25, 36.

5. Argentina, Directive Commission of the Census, *2° Censo*, pp. xlii–xliii.

Epilogue

1. Alfredo E. Lattes et al., *Dinámica migratoria argentina (1955–1984)*, vol. 1, pp. 39–49, esp. Tables 2, 3; Susana M. Sassone, "Migraciones ilegales y amnistías en la Argentina," esp. p. 267, Table 1. Amnesty for illegals was decreed in 1958, 1964, 1974, and 1984.

2. Bejarano, "Ha-kehilla ha-sefaradit," p. 160.

3. Lattes et al., *Dinámica migratoria*, vol. 1, p. 45; Bloch, "Hitpatkhut ha-okhlusiah ha-yehudit," p. 23, Table 5b.

4. Sergio della Pergola, "Demographic Trends of Latin American Jewry," pp. 88–100, esp. p. 99, Table C6.

5. Bloch, "Hitpatkhut ha-okhlusiah ha-yehudit," p. 9, Table 1.

6. Haim Avni, "La agricultura judía en la Argentina," p. 538.

7. For a detailed description of the organizational panorama of Argentine Jewry during the 1960s, see Avni, "Argentine Jewry," no. 13–14.

8. Bloch, "Hitpatkhut ha-okhlusiah ha-yehudit," p. 26.

9. Lattes et al., *Dinámica migratoria*, vol. 2, articles by César Moyano (pp. 185–87), Adela Pellegrini (pp. 156, 166), Marios Margulies (pp. 145–46), and Susana Schkolnik (pp. 98–99, Tables 10 and 11).

10. Pergola, "Demographic Trends," pp. 120–24.

References

Archives

Governmental

Argentina, Ministry of Foreign Relations, División Política, Alemania, 1935–1939.
Argentina, Archivo de la Dirección Nacional de Migraciones, *Partes Consulares* and *Libro de Pasageros*. This material was reviewed and listed by Elvira Rissech and presented in her "Final Report" of 1985, partially published.
France, Ministry of Foreign Affairs, Correspondance Politique, Argentine, and Correspondance Consulaire et Commerciale.
Germany, Ministry of Foreign Affairs, files photocopied at Yad Vashem Archives, Jerusalem.
Great Britain, Foreign Office, files kept at the Public Record Office, units on Argentina.
Spain, Ministry of Foreign Affairs, Correspondencia Embajadas, Argentina, 1889–1896.
United States of America, State Department, Papers kept at the National Archives, Washington: 840.48 Refugees.

General

Central Zionist Archives, Jerusalem.

Institute of Contemporary Jewry, The Hebrew University, Oral History Division.
Yad Vashem Archives, Jerusalem.
Yivo Archives, Buenos Aires.
Yivo Archives, Institute for Jewish Research, New York.

Institutional

Central Archives for the History of the Jewish People, Jerusalem.
Congregación Israelita de la República Argentina, Buenos Aires.
Delegación de Asociaciones Israelitas Argentinas.
HIAS-HICEM papers at the Yivo Archives, New York.
Jewish Colonization Association, Buenos Aires.
Jewish Colonization Association, London.
Soprotimis, Minutes of the Board on microfilm, kept at the Central Archives for
the History of the Jewish People, Jerusalem.

Periodicals and Newspapers

Argentine Jewish Periodicals

Argentiner Yivo Schriften
Filantropía
Di Idishe Tseitung
Der Imigrant
La Luz

Mundo Israelita
Naye Leben
Di Presse
Vida Nuestra
Der Yudischer Kolonist

Other Jewish Periodicals

Allgemeine Zeitung des Judentums
   (Leipzig)
American Jewish Yearbook (New York)
Les Archives Israélites (Paris)
Jewish Chronicle (London)

Jewish Journal of Sociology (London)
Jewish Social Studies (New York)
Di Jüdische Press (Berlin)
Ha-Melitz (Saint Petersburg
   [Leningrad])
Ha-Tsfirah (Warsaw)

Argentine Periodicals and Newspapers

El Argentino
Boletín del Museo Social Argentino
Boletín Oficial de la República
  Argentino
Buenos Aires Herald
La Calle
El Crisol
Criterio
Crítica
Democracia
El Diario
Diario Arabe
El Diario Español
La Época

Gobernantes
Hoy
Italia Libre
El Laborista
La Nación
El Nacional
Noticias Gráficas
El Pampero
La Prensa
El Pueblo
La Razón
Sábado
La Tribuna
L'Union Française

Books, Articles, Printed Records, and Manuscripts

Alberdi, Juan Bautista. *Bases y puntos de partida para la organización política de la República Argentina.* Santiago de Chile, 1852; Buenos Aires, 1974.

Alperson, Marcos. *Kolonie Mauricio: Dreysig Yehrigue JCA Kolonizatsie in Argentina* (The Colony Mauricio: Thirty years of JCA colonization in Argentina). 3 vols. Buenos Aires, 1922.

Alsina, Juan A. *La colectividad israelita al ex director de inmigración Don Juan Alsina, Dec. 12, 1910.* Buenos Aires, 1910.

———. *La inmigración en el primer siglo de la independencia.* Buenos Aires, 1910.

———. *La inmigración europea en la República Argentina.* Buenos Aires, 1898.

Amadeo, Tomás. *Museo Social de Buenos Aires: Fundamentos y anteproyectos.* Buenos Aires, 1910.

Anglo-Jewish Association. *The Thirteenth* [to *twenty-fifth*] *Annual Report of the Anglo-Jewish Association.* London, 1883–1896.

Ansel, Bernard David. "The Beginnings of the Modern Jewish Community of Argentina, 1852–1891." Ph.D. diss., University of Kansas, Lawrence, 1969.

———. "Discord among Western and Eastern European Jews in Argentina." *American Jewish Historical Quarterly* 60, no. 2 (December 1970):151–58.

———. "European Adventurer in Tierra del Fuego: Julio Popper." *Hispanic American Historical Review* 50, no. 1 (February 1970):89–110.

Argentina. *Registro Nacional de la República Argentina.* Buenos Aires, 1878–1881.

Argentina, Congreso Nacional. *Congreso Nacional: Cámara de Diputados, Diario de Sesiones.* Buenos Aires, 1938–1939.

———. *Congreso Nacional: Cámara de Senadores, Diario de Sesiones.* Buenos Aires, 1875–1876.

Argentina, Directive Commission of the Census. *2° censo de la República Argentina, May 1, 1895.* 3 vols. Buenos Aires, 1898.

———. *Tercer censo nacional levantado el 1°. de junio de 1914.* Buenos Aires, 1916–1917.

Argentina, Ministry of Agriculture. *Boletín del Departamento de Agricultura: Organo de la dirección de tierras, inmigración y agricultura,* vol. 16. Buenos Aires, 1892.

———. *Industrias, agrícolas y ganaderas en la República Argentina (datos para los inmigrantes agricultores),* by Hugo Miatello. Buenos Aires, 1901.

———. *Informes y estudios de la División de Estadística y Economía Rural,* by Emilio Lahitte. Buenos Aires, 1908.

———. *Ley de inmigración y reglamento de desembarco de inmigrantes.* Publicación Oficial. Buenos Aires, 1911.

———. *Memoria correspondiente al período* [1932, 1934, 1938, 1940] *presentada al Congreso de la Nación.* Buenos Aires, 1933, 1937, 1939, 1941.

———. *Memoria de las direcciones, 1898.* Buenos Aires, 1899.

———. *Memoria del Ministerio de Agricultura 1902/3, 6 presentada al honorable Congreso por el Ministro de Agricultura Wenceslao Escalante.* Buenos Aires, 1903.

———. *Resumen estadístico del movimiento migratorio en la República Argentina 1875 a 1924.* Buenos Aires, 1925.

———. División de Estadística y Economía Rural. *La Argentina—¿Qué es la Argentina? como País Agrícola, como país de inmigración.* Buenos Aires, 1911.

Argentina, Ministry of Foreign Relations. *Memoria del Ministero de Relaciones Exteriores y Culto.* Buenos Aires, 1942–1943, 1943–1945.

Asher-Pinkhof, Clara. *Rakdanit beli raglaim* (A footless dancer). Tel Aviv, 1971.

Asociación Filantrópica Israelita. *Diez años de obra constructiva en América del Sud, 1933–1943.* Buenos Aires, 1943.

———. *Libro aniversario: Bodas de oro.* Buenos Aires, 1983.

Avni, Haim. "La agricultura judía en la Argentina: ¿Éxito o fracaso?" *Desarrollo Económico* 22, no. 88 (January–March 1983):535–48.

———. "Argentina: A Case Study in Dimensions of Government Antisemitism." In *Antisemitism Through the Ages,* ed. Shmuel Almog. Oxford, 1988, pp. 321–38.

———. *Argentina ha-aretz ha-yeuda: Mifal ha-hityashvut shel ha-baron Hirsch be-Argentina* (Argentina, "The Promised Land": Baron de Hirsch's colonization project in the Argentine Republic). Jerusalem, 1973.

———. *Argentina y la historia de la inmigración judía.* Jerusalem and Buenos Aires, 1983.

———. "Argentine Jewry: Socio-political Status and Organizational Patterns." *Dispersion and Unity* 12 (1971):128–62; 13–14 (1971):161–208; 15 (1971):158–215.

———. *Emantsipatsia ve-khinuch yehudi: Mea shnot nisyona shel yahadut Argentina 1884–1984* (Emancipation and Jewish education: A century of Argentine Jewish experience, 1884–1984). Jerusalem, 1985.

———. "Latin America and the Jewish Refugees: Two Encounters, 1935–1938." In *The Jewish presence in Latin America,* ed. Judith Laikin Elkin and Gilbert W. Merkx. Boston, 1987.

———. "Patterns of Jewish Leadership in Latin America during the Holocaust." In *Jewish Leadership during the Nazi Era,* ed. Randolph L. Braham. New York, 1985, pp. 85–130.

———. "Religion at Government Schools: A Century of Argentinian Jewish Experience." In *Encyclopedia Judaica Yearbook, 1988.* Jerusalem, 1988, pp. 164–72.

———. *Spain, the Jews and Franco.* Philadelphia, 1982.

Bachi, Roberto. *The Population of Israel.* Jerusalem, 1978.

Banco Comercial. *Banco Comercial de Buenos Aires, S.A.: 1917–1950.* Buenos Aires, 1950.

Banco Israelita del Río de la Plata. *Yiddishe Folks Bank: Yovel Bukh, 1921–1951* (The jubilee book of the Jewish Popular Bank). Buenos Aires, 1951.

Bankier, David. "Die Verhältnisse zwischen jüdischen Flüchtlinge und deutschen Exilierten in Lateinamerika." In *Europäische Juden in Lateinamerika,* ed. Achim Schräder and Karl Heinrich Rengstors. Münster, 1987.

Baron, Salo W. *Steeled by Adversity.* New York, 1955.

Bauer, Yehuda. *American Jewry and the Holocaust: The American Jewish Joint Distribution Committee, 1939–1945.* Detroit, 1981.

———. *Flight and Rescue: Brichah, the Organized Escape of the Jewish Survivors of Eastern Europe 1944–1948.* New York, 1970.

Bejarano, Margalit. "Ha-kehilla ha-sefaradit shel Buenos Aires" (The Sephardic community of Buenos Aires). M.A. thesis, The Institute of Contemporary Jewry, The Hebrew University of Jerusalem, Jerusalem, 1974.

———. "Los sefardíes en la Argentina: Particularismo étnico frente a tendencias de unificación." *Rumbos* 17–18 (September–December 1986):143–60.

Benchimol, L. "La langue espagnole au Maroc." *La Revue des Écoles de l'Alliance* (1901):126–33.

Bennett, Marion T. *American Immigration Policies: A History.* Washington, DC, 1963.

Berikht funm yudishen kongres in Argentina, 1916–obgehalten in Buenos Aires, fun dem 26ten biz dem 29 februar 1916 (Report of the Jewish Congress in Argentina, convened in Buenos Aires, February 26–29, 1916). Buenos Aires, 1916.

Bernard, William S., ed., C. Zeleny and H. Miller, assist. eds. *American Immigra-*

tion Policy: A Reappraisal, published under the sponsorship of the National Committee on Immigration Policy. New York, 1950.

Binanyan, Narciso. *La colectividad armenia en la Argentina.* Buenos Aires, 1974.

Blanco, José A. "Industria." In *Argentina, 1930–1960,* comp. Jorge A. Paita. Buenos Aires, 1961.

Bloch, Bronislav. "Hitpatkhut ha-okhlusiah ha-yehudit be-argentina, 1900–1960" (The development of the Jewish population in Argentina, 1900–1960). Unpublished manuscript, Division of Demography, The Institute of Contemporary Jewry, The Hebrew University of Jerusalem, Jerusalem, 1977.

Bristow, Edward J. *Prostitution and Prejudice: The Jewish Fight Against White Slavery, 1870–1939.* Oxford, 1982.

Bronstein, Marcos and Manuel. "La inmigración israelita." *Boletín Mensual Museo Social Argentino* 56–60 (November–December 1916):1–19.

Brusilovsky, Hertz. "Der onteyl fun idishe arbeyter in di argentinishe arbeyter organizatsies" (Jews in the Argentine Workers' Organizations). In *Yovel bukh far di idishe tseitung tsu ihr 25 yohrigen yuviley* (Jubilee volume: 25 years of the *Idishe Tseitung*). Buenos Aires, 1940, pp. 563–80.

Buchrucker, Cristián. *Nacionalismo y peronismo: La Argentina en la crisis ideológica mundial, 1927–1955.* Buenos Aires, 1987.

Buenos Aires, General Directory of Municipal Statistics. *Censo general de población: Edificación, comercio e industrias de la Ciudad de Buenos Aires levantado en los días 11 y 18 de septiembre de 1904.* Buenos Aires, 1906.

———. *Censo general de la población: Edificación, comercio e industrias de la Ciudad de Buenos Aires levantado en los días 16 al 24 de octubre de 1909.* 3 vols. Buenos Aires, 1910.

Bunge, Alejandro E. "La cosmopólita argentina sera pronto un país sin extranjeros." *Revista de Economía Argentina* 39, no. 264 (June 1940):177–80.

———. "Ochenta y cinco años de inmigración: Análisis de su desarrollo." *Revista de Economía Argentina* 43, no. 307 (January 1944):31–65.

Canals Frau, Salvador. "La inmigración europa en la Argentina." *Anales del Instituto Étnico Nacional* 1 (1948):87–113.

Cárcano, Miguel Ángel. "La Conferencia Internacional de Roma y la política inmigratoria argentina." In *Anales del Instituto Popular de Conferencias,* vol. 10. Buenos Aires, 1924, pp. 47–68.

Castro, Donald Steven. "The Development of Argentine Immigration Policy, 1852–1914." Ph.D. diss., University of California, Los Angeles, 1970.

Cociovitch, Noe. *Génesis de Moisesville.* Buenos Aires, 1987 (Spanish translation of Noah Katsowitch. *Mosesviler Bereshis.* Buenos Aires, 1947).

Collins, Edgar W. "Desarrollo y distribución de la inmigración." *Revista de Ciencias Económicas, Comerciales y Políticas* 1, no. 3 (September–December 1942):818–57.

Comité Contra el Racismo y el Antisemitismo. *Actas del primer congreso contra el racismo y el antisemitismo.* Buenos Aires, 1938.

————. *2* [Segundo] *congreso del Comité Contra el Racismo y el Antisemitismo de la Argentina.* Buenos Aires, 1939.

————. *Tierra sin hombres: El problema inmigratorio argentino a través de la interpelación de la Cámara de Diputados al Poder Ejecutivo.* Buenos Aires, 1940.

Dickman, Enrique. *Población e inmigración.* Buenos Aires, 1946.

————. *Recuerdos de un militante socialista.* Buenos Aires, 1949.

Dinnerstein, Leonard. *America and the Survivors of the Holocaust.* New York, 1982.

Dorfman, Adolfo. *Historia de la industria argentina.* Buenos Aires, 1970.

Dotación Carnegie para la Paz Internacional. *Conferencias internacionales americanas: Primer suplemento 1938–1942.* Washington, DC, 1943.

Ebel, Arnold. *Das Dritte Reich und Argentinien.* Cologne, 1971.

Efron, Jedidia. "Informe presentado a la dirección general de la JCA en Buenos Aires, 1943." Manuscript in JCA(Lon) files, no. 514, (census presented separately for each province).

Elkin, Judith Laikin. *Jews of the Latin American Republics.* Chapel Hill, NC, 1980.

Eloy Martínez, Tomás. "Perón and the Nazi War Criminals." Paper presented at the Woodrow Wilson International Center for Scholars, Washington, DC, 1984.

Emigdirekt. *Der tsveyter idisher emigratsie tsuzamenfor in Berlin dem 9–12 August 1925: Kurtser berikht* (The Second Jewish Immigration Conference in Berlin, August 9–12, 1925: Concise report). Reprinted from *Idishe Emigratzie* 9 (1925).

Esh, Shaul. "Beyn haflayah le-hashmadah" (Between discrimination and extermination). In his *Iyunim be-kheker ha-shoah ve-yahadut zmanenu* (Studies in the Holocaust and contemporary Jewry). Jerusalem, 1973.

Ezrah (Hospital Israelita). *Libro del cincuentenario.* Buenos Aires, 1980.

Feinberg, Nathan. *Ha-agudot ha-yehudiot lema'an hever ha'leumim* (The Jewish League of Nation societies). Jerusalem, 1967.

Fingerman, Yisroel David. "Di geshikhte fun der idishe kolonizatsie in Argentine" (The history of Jewish colonization in Argentina). *Di Idishe Tseitung* (Buenos Aires), 1927.

Fliess, Alois E. *La producción agrícola y ganadera de la República Argentina en el año 1891.* Buenos Aires, 1892.

Fogel, Carlos. "Di daitshe yiden in Buenos Aires" (The German Jews in Buenos Aires). *Argentiner Iwo Shriftn* 4 (1947):174–80.

————. "Di kolonies fun di daitshe yiden bey Moisesville" (The colonies of the German Jews near Moisesville). *Argentiner Iwo Shriftn* 5 (1952):67–72.

Gallo, Ezequiel. *La pampa gringa: La colonización agrícola en Sante Fe, 1870–1895.* Buenos Aires, 1983.

Gartner, Lloyd P. *The Jewish Immigrant in England, 1870–1914.* London, 1960.

———. "Notes on the Statistics of Jewish Immigration to England, 1870–1914." *Jewish Social Studies* 22, no. 2 (April 1960):97–102.

Gerassi Navarro, Marysa. *Los nacionalistas*. Buenos Aires, 1969.

Giuvicich, Nelida et al. *El fenómeno inmigratorio*. Publication of the Instituto de Derecho Internacional de Buenos Aires, Ministry of Agriculture, vol. 3; Miscellaneous publication, no. 125. Buenos Aires, 1942.

Glauert, Earl T. "Ricardo Rojas and the Emergence of Argentinian Cultural Nationalism." *Hispanic American Historical Review* 43 (February 1963):1–13.

Great Britain, Foreign Office. *Accounts and Papers*. Miscellaneous Series, vol. 73, no. 172. London, 1890.

Grunwald, Kurt. *Türkenhirsch: A Study of Baron Maurice de Hirsch, Entrepreneur and Philanthropist*. Jerusalem, 1966.

Gurvitz, David, Aharon Gretz, and Roberto Bachi. *Ha-aliyah, ha-yishuv ve-ha-tnuah ha-tiv'it shel ha-okhlusiah be-eretz yisrael* (Immigration, settlement, and natural population trends in Palestine). Jerusalem, 1944.

Halperin Donghi, Tulio. "Crónica del período." In *Argentina 1930–1960*, comp. Jorge A. Paita. Buenos Aires, 1961, pp. 23–88.

Heras, Carlos. "Presidencia de Avellaneda." In Academia Nacional de la Historia, *Historia argentina contemporánea 1862–1930*. Vol. 1, *Historia de las presidencias: 1862–1898*. Buenos Aires, 1963, pp. 149–268.

HICEM (HIAS-JCA-Emigdirekt). *Bericht der HIAS-JCA-EMIGDIREKT über Südamerika*. Berlin, 1928.

———. *Four Years of Jewish Migration, 1927–1930*. Paris, 1931.

———. *Informatsie Bleter fun der Emigratsie Farainigung HIAS-JCA-EMIG-DIREKT* (Bulletin of information). Berlin and Paris, 1928–1932, 1936–1939.

Hilfsverein der Deutschen Juden. *Dritter [to zwölfter] Geschäftsbericht des Hilfsvereins der Deutschen Juden*. Berlin, 1905–1914.

———. *Festschrift Anlässlich der Feier des 25 Jahrigen Bestehens des Hilfsverein der Deutschen Juden: Gegründet am 28 ten. Mai 1901*. Berlin, 1926.

———. *Korrespondenzblatt des Central Büros für jüdische auswanderungs-angelegenheiten des Hilfsvereins der Deutschen Juden*. Berlin, 1904–1909, 1922–1929.

Hilfsverein der Juden in Deutschland. *Jüdische Auswanderung Korrespondenzblatt über Auswanderunges und Siedlungswesen*. Berlin, 1936.

Holborn, Louise W. *The International Refugee Organization. A Specialized Agency of the United Nations: Its History and Work, 1946–1952*. London, New York, and Toronto, 1956.

Ibáñez, José C. *Historia argentina*. Buenos Aires, 1968.

Intergovernmental Committee. *Proceedings of the Intergovernmental Committee, Évian, July 6–15, 1938: Verbatim Record of the Plenary Meetings of the Committee, Resolutions and Reports*. Geneva, 1938.

International Labour Office. *Emigration and Immigration: Legislation and Treaties.* Geneva, 1922.

Israelitische Allianz zu Wien. *Bericht über Ihre Bisherige Hilfsaction für die Rumänischen Juden.* Vienna, November 15, 1900.

Jackisch, Carlota. "Los refugiados alemanes en la Argentina, 1933–1945." *Cologuio* 17 (1988):53–71.

Jewish Colonization Association. *Le Baron Maurice de Hirsch et la Jewish Colonization Association.* Paris, 1931.

———. *Conditions d'installation des agriculteurs dans les colonies de la JCA: Argentine, Brésil, Canada.* Paris, 1929.

———. *Rapport de l'administration centrale au Conseil d'Administration.* Paris, 1892–1935.

———. *Recueil de materiaux sur la situation des Israélites de Russie d'après l'enquête de la JCA.* 2 vols. Paris, 1906.

Joseph, Samuel. *Jewish Immigration to the United States, 1881–1910.* New York, 1914.

Katz, M. "Los judíos alemanes en la Argentina." *Argentiner Iwo Shriftn* (1942):163–73, 202–203.

Klich, Ignacio. "A Background to Perón's Discovery of Jewish National Aspiration." In Amilat, *Judaica latinoamericana: Estudios historico-sociales.* Jerusalem, 1988, pp. 192–223.

Korn, Francis et al. *Buenos Aires: Los huéspedes del 20.* Buenos Aires, 1974.

Kreinin, Miron. *Di eynvanderungs meglikhkeyten keyn drom amerike un di dortige idishe yishuvim* (The possibilities of immigration to South America and the Jewish communities there). Berlin, 1928.

Labougle, Eduardo. *Misión en Berlin.* Buenos Aires, 1948.

Lappas, Alcibíades. *La Masonería argentina a través de sus hombres.* Buenos Aires, 1966.

Lattes, Alfredo E., et al. *Dinámica migratoria argentina (1955–1984): Democratización y retomo de expatriados.* 2 vols. Buenos Aires, 1986.

Lattes, Zulma L. Recchini de. "Demographic Consequences of International Migratory Movements in the Argentine Republic 1870–1960." In *United Nations World Population Conference (Belgrade).* New York, 1965, pp. 211–15.

Lattes, Zulma Recchini de, and Alfredo E. Lattes. *1974, Año mundial de la población: La población argentina.* Buenos Aires, 1975.

Latzky-Bertholdi, Jacob. *Di drom-amerikaner lender un di idishe eynvanderung* (The South American countries and Jewish immigration). Berlin, 1926.

Leibovitz, Adolfo. *Apuntes intimos, 1870–1946.* Buenos Aires, 1946.

Lestschinsky, Jakob. "Jewish Migration, 1840–1946." In *The Jews, Their History, Culture and Religion,* ed. Louis Finkelstein. New York, 1949.

———. "Jüdische Wanderungen im letzten Jahrhundert." *Weltwirtschaftliches Archiv* 25, no. 1 (January 1927):69–86.

————. "National Groups in Polish Emigration." *Jewish Social Studies*, 5, no. 2 (April 1943):99–114.

Levene, Ricardo. *Historia de las ideas sociales argentinas.* Buenos Aires, 1947.

Lewin, Boleslao. *La colectividad judía en la Argentina.* Buenos Aires, 1974.

————. *¿Cómo fue la inmigración judía a la Argentina?* Buenos Aires, 1971.

————. *La Inquisición en Hispanoamérica: Judíos, protestantes y patriotas.* Buenos Aires, 1962.

————. *Los judíos bajo la Inquisición en Hispanoamérica.* Buenos Aires, 1960.

————. *Popper: Un conquistador patagónico: Sus hazañas y escritos.* Buenos Aires, 1967.

————. *¿Quién fue el conquistador patagónico Julio Popper?* Buenos Aires, 1974.

López Alonso, Gerardo. *1930–1980: Cincuenta años de historia argentina.* Buenos Aires, 1983.

Lowrie, Donald A. *The Hunted Children.* New York, 1963.

McDonald, James G. *Draft of an Interim Report on the Mission to South and Central America of Dr. Samuel Guy Inman and the High Commissioner, March–June 1935.* Geneva, 1935.

Marco, Graciela M. de. "Extranjeros en la Argentina: Cuantía y continuidad de los flujos inmigratorios limítrofes, 1970–1985." *Estudios Migratorios Latinoamericanos* (August 1986):323–50.

Margaliot, Avraham. "The Problem of the Rescue of German Jewry during the Years 1933–1939: The Reason for the Delay in their Emigration from the Third Reich." In *Rescue Attempts during the Holocaust: Proceedings of the Second Yad Vashem International Historical Conference, April 1974.* Jerusalem, 1977, pp. 247–65.

Martínez de Hoz, José Alfredo. "Agricultura y ganadería." In *Argentina 1930–1960,* comp. Jorge A. Paita. Buenos Aires, 1960, pp. 189–210.

Martínez de Hoz, José Alfredo, and Jorge Pereda. "Inmigración y reforma agraria." *Anales de la Sociedad Rural Argentina* 71 (June 1947):299–320.

Matsushita, Hiroshi. "A Historical View of Argentine Neutrality during World War II." *The Developing Economies* (Tokyo) 11, no. 1–4 (1973):272–96.

Mellibowsky, Benjamin. "Meyne 51 yor tsu dinst bey der JCA, HICEM-HIAS un Sopromitis" (My fifty-one years of service with the JCA, HICEM-HIAS, and Soprotimis). *Argentiner Iwo Shriftn* 7 (1957):91–167.

Meltzer, Emanuel. "Ha-diplomatiah ha-polanit u-b'ayot ha-hagira ha-yehudit be-shanim 1935–1939" (Polish diplomacy and the problems of Jewish migration, 1935–1939). *Gil'ad* (Tel-Aviv) 1 (1973):211–49.

Mendelson, José. "A yovel idish lebn in Argentine" (Fifty years of Jewish life in Argentina). In *Yovel bukh far di idishe tseitung tsu ihr 25 yohriyen yuviley* (Jubilee volume: 25 years of *Di Idishe Tseitung*). Buenos Aires, 1940.

———. "Génesis de la colonia judía de la Argentina—1884–1892." In *DAIA: 50 años de colonización judía en la Argentina*. Buenos Aires, 1939, pp. 83–143, 317–23.

Miatello, Hugo. *La chacra santafecina en 1905*. Buenos Aires, 1905.

Mirelman, Víctor A. *En búsqueda de una identidad: Los inmigrantes judíos en Buenos Aires, 1890–1930*. Buenos Aires, 1988.

———. "The Jewish Community Versus Crime: The Case of White Slavery in Buenos Aires." *Jewish Social Studies* 46, no. 2 (Spring 1984):145–68.

———. "Jewish Life in Buenos Aires before the East European Immigration (1860–1890)." *American Jewish Historical Quarterly* 67, no. 3 (March 1978):195–207.

———. "The Jews in Argentina (1890–1930): Assimilation and Particularism." Ph.D. diss., Columbia University, New York, 1973.

———. "A Note on Jewish Settlement in Argentina, 1881–1892. *Jewish Social Studies* 33, no. 1 (January 1971):3–12.

Morgenstern, Manuel G. *De la Legión Judía a Medinat Israel*. Buenos Aires, 1972.

Museo Social Argentino. *La inmigración después de la guerra: Boletín mensual del Museo Social Argentino* (special issue) 85–90 (January–June 1919).

Nascimbene, Mario C. G. "Los inmigrantes italianos a la Argentina: Sus lugares de origen, sus lugares de destino, 1835–1960." Unpublished manuscript, Centro de Investigaciones Sociológicas, Universidad Católica, Buenos Aires, 1980.

Natale, Oscar A., ed. *Aspectos jurídicos, económicos y sociales de la colonización con inmigrantes*. Buenos Aires, 1967.

Navarro Viola, Miguel. "La primera boda judía en la Argentina." *Revista de Buenos Aires* 6, no. 67 (November 1868); reprinted in *Judaica (Buenos Aires)* 5, no. 51–53 (September–November 1937):185–89.

Newton, Ronald C. *German Buenos Aires, 1900–1933*. Austin, 1977.

Norman, Theodore. *An Outstretched Arm: A History of the Jewish Colonization Association*. London, 1985.

Oddone, Jacinto. *La burguesía terrateniente argentina*. Buenos Aires, 1967.

Officina Internacional del Trabajo. *La inmigración y la colonización en el Brasil, en la Argentina y en el Uruguay, Ginebra 1937* (extracted from the *Revista Internacional del Trabajo* 15, no. 4–5 [March–April 1937]).

Onega, Gladys S. *La inmigración en la literatura argentina*. Buenos Aires, 1969.

Opiniones de la prensa nacional sobre el proyecto-de-ley de inmigración: Documentos oficiales de la actual administración sobre la materia. Buenos Aires, 1875.

Ortiz, Ricardo M. *Historia económica de la Argentina*. 2 vols. Buenos Aires, 1964.

Panettieri, José. *Inmigración en la Argentina*. Buenos Aires, 1970.

———. *Los trabajadores*. Buenos Aires, 1968.

Pavlovsky, Aarón. *Problemas de Inmigración* (Conferencia dada en los salones de la Sociedad Rural Argentina el 5 de Diciembre de 1910). Buenos Aires, 1910.

Peralta, Santiago M. *La acción del pueblo judío en la Argentina*. Buenos Aires, 1943.

Pergola, Sergio della. "Demographic Trends of Latin American Jewry." In *The Jewish Presence in Latin America,* ed. Judith Laikin Elkin and Gilbert Merkx. Boston, 1987, pp. 85–133.

Perón, Juan Domingo. *Doctrina peronista: Filosófica, política, social.* Buenos Aires, 1947.

Protokoll der interterritorialen Wanderfürsorge-Konferenz: Kultusgemeinde Wien am 15 November 1937. Manuscript in the Jerusalem National Library, Jerusalem.

Rapoport, Mario. *Gran Bretaña, Estados Unidos y las clases dirigentes argentinas, 1940–1950.* Buenos Aires, 1980.

———. "El modelo agroexportador argentino, 1880–1914." In *Economía e historia: Contribuciones a la historia económica argentina,* ed. Mario Rapoport. Buenos Aires, 1988, pp. 168–217.

Ravignani, Emilio. "El Congreso Nacional de 1824–1827." In Academia Nacional de la Historia, *Historia de la nación argentina (desde los orígenes hasta la organización definitiva en 1862),* vol. 7. Buenos Aires, 1950, pp. 47–178.

———. "El tratado con la Gran Bretaña de 1825 y la libertad de cultos." *Boletín del Instituto de Investigaciones Historicas* (Buenos Aires) 1, no. 7–8 (March–April 1923):225–37.

———, ed. *Asambleas Constituyentes Argentinas: Seguidos de los textos constitucionales, legislativos y pactos interprovinciales que organizaron politicamente la Nación,* vols. 1–6. Buenos Aires, 1937–1939.

Rehfeld, Manfred (Michael). "Sinagogue in der Galuth." *Udim* (Frankfurt/M) 9/10 (1979–1980):57–69.

Rissech, Elvira. "Final report" and archival material in the Archivo de la Dirección Nacional de Migraciones, Buenos Aires. Unpublished manuscript, 1985.

———. "Inmigración judía a la Argentina 1938–1942: Entre la aceptación y el rechazo." *Rumbos* (Jerusalem) 15 (March 1986):91–113.

Rojas, Ricardo. *La restauración nacionalista.* Buenos Aires, 1909 (Third ed., ed. A. Peña Lillo. Buenos Aires, 1971).

Rondanina, Esteban F. *Liberalismo, Masonería y socialismo en la evolución nacional.* Buenos Aires, 1965.

Rosenstock, Werner. "Exodus 1933–1939: A Survey of Jewish Emigration from Germany." *Leo Baeck Institute Year Book,* vol. 1. London, 1956, pp. 373–90.

Rosenswaike, Ira. "The Jewish Population of Argentina: Census and Estimate 1887–1947." *Jewish Social Studies* 22, no. 4 (October 1960):159–214.

Rubel, Yaacov. "Argentina, ¿sí o no?" In Oficina Sudamericana del Comité Judío Americano, *Comunidades judías de Latinoamérica 1971–1972.* Buenos Aires, 1974, pp. 273–91.

Rülf, Isaac. *Die russische Juden: Ihre Leidensgeschichte und unsere Rettungsversuche.* Memel, 1892.

Sagarna, Antonio. "La organización nacional, la constitución de 1853." In Academia Nacional de la Historia, *Historia de la nación argentina*, vol. 7. Buenos Aires, 1947, ch. 4, pp. 163–204.

Sánchez Viamonte, Carlos. *Biografía de una ley antiargentina—La Ley 4144.* Buenos Aires, 1956.

Santander, Silvano. *Técnica de una traición—Juan D. Perón y Eva Duarte, agentes de nazismo en la Argentina.* Buenos Aires, 1955.

Sarmiento, Domingo Faustino. *Facundo: Civilización y barbarie.* Santiago de Chile, 1845; Madrid, 1970.

Sarna, Jonathan. "The Myth of No Return: Jewish Return Migration to Eastern Europe, 1881–1914." *American Jewish History* 71, no. 2 (December 1981):256–68.

Sassone, Susana M. "Migraciones ilegales y amnistías en la Argentina." *Estudios Migratorios Latino Americanos* (Buenos Aires) (August–September 1987): 249–90.

Sautu, Ruth. "Poder económico y burguesía industrial en la Argentina, 1930–1954." *Revista Latinoamericana de Sociología* (Buenos Aires) 4, no. 68-3 (November 1968):310–40.

Schallman, Lázaro. "Dramática historia de los pampistas o Stambuler." In Oficina Sudamericana del Comité Judío Americano, *Comunidades Judías de Latinoamerica 1966.* Buenos Aires, 1966, pp. 151–72.

———. "Historia del periodismo judío en la Argentina." In Oficina Sudamericana del Comité Judío Americana, *Comunidades Judías de Latinoamerica 1970.* Buenos Aires, 1970, pp. 149–73.

———. "Orígenes de la colonización judía en la Argentina." *Comentario* (Buenos Aires) 40 (1964):23–34.

———. "Proceso Histórico de la colonización agrícola en la Argentina." In Dardo Cuneo et al., *Inmigración y nacionalidad.* Buenos Aires, 1967, pp. 147–209.

Schöpflocher, Roberto. *Historia de la colonización agrícola en Argentina.* Buenos Aires, 1955.

Schusheim, A. L. "Der ershte idisher imigratsie kongres in drom amerike" (The first Jewish immigration congress in South America). In Miron Kreinin, *Die eynvanderungs meglijkeyten keyn drom amerike un di dortige idishe yishuvim.* Berlin, 1928, pp. 49–59.

Scobie, James R. "Buenos Aires as a Commercial Bureaucratic City, 1880–1910: Characteristics of a City's Orientation." *The American Historical Review* 77, no. 4 (October 1972):1035–73.

———. *Revolution on the Pampas: A Social History of Argentine Wheat, 1860–1910,* Austin 1964 (translated into Spanish as *Revolución en las pampas.* Buenos Aires, 1968).

Senkman, Leonardo. "Política internacional e inmigración europea en la Argentina de post-guerra (1945–1948), el caso de los refugiados." *Estudios Migratorios Latinoamericanos* (Buenos Aires) 1, no. 1 (December 1985):107–125.

———. "La problemática de los refugiados europeos a través de la inmigración limítrofe, 1938–1944." Paper presented at the Second International Days on the Study of Immigration, OEA, Buenos Aires, October 13–15, 1983.

———. "Lá problemática de los refugiados centro-europeos y su emigración a la Argentina, 1933–1945: Aspectos políticos, etnicos y culturales. Ph.D. diss., Universidad de Buenos Aires, Buenos Aires, 1985.

———. "Las relaciones EE.UU.–argentina y la cuestión de los refugiados de la post-guerra, 1945–1948." In Amilat, *Judaica latinoamericana estudios histórico-sociales.* Jerusalem, 1988, pp. 90–114.

Siewers, Enrique. "Obstáculos mentales a una política activa de inmigración." *Revista de Ciencias Económicas* (Buenos Aires), ser. 2, 34, no. 299 (June 1946):437–41.

Sociedad Rural Argentina. "Inmigración y reforma agraria" (A study by the Sociedad Rural Argentina, José A. Martínez de Hoz, president). *Anales de la Sociedad Rural Argentina* 71 (June 1947):299–320.

Sofer, Eugene. *From Pale to Pampa: A Social History of the Jews of Buenos Aires.* New York, 1982.

Solberg, Carl. *Immigration and Nationalism: Argentina and Chile, 1890–1914.* Austin and London, 1970.

Soprotimis. *Di arbeyt fun di yohren 1922–1927 mit statistishe tabelen* (Work in the years 1922–1927 with statistical tables). Buenos Aires, 1928.

Szajkowski, Zosa. "Di onhoyben fun der yidisher kolonizatisie in Argentine" (The beginnings of Jewish colonization in Argentina). *Argentiner Iwo Shriftn* 7 (1957):5–56.

———. "How the Mass Migration to America Began." *Jewish Social Studies* 4 (October 1942):295–306.

Szenkolewski, Silvia. "Di tsionistishe bavegung in argentine fun 1897–1917" (The Zionist movement in Argentina from 1897 to 1917). In *Anales de la comunidad israelita de Buenos Aires, 1963–1969.* Buenos Aires, 1969, pp. 101–30.

Tomezzoli, V. "L'Argentina e l'emigrazione italiana." *Bolletin dell'Emigrazione* (1907):pt. 1, pp. 1734–1846; pt. 2, pp. 1849–1946; and (1908):271–328.

Toribio Medina, José. *La Inquisición en el Río de la Plata.* Edition of Editorial Harpes, Buenos Aires, 1945 (published originally as *El Tribunal del Santo Oficio de la Inquisición en las Provincias del Río de la Plata.* Santiago de Chile, 1899).

Troper, Harold. "Canada and the Jewish Displaced Persons." *Michael* 10 (1986):181–225.

United States, Department of State. *Foreign Relations of the United States.* Washington, DC, 1943–1944.

Vago, Bela. *The Shadow of the Swastika: The Rise of Fascism and Antisemitism in the Danube Basin, 1936–1939.* London, 1975.

Verbitzky, Gregorio. *Afán de medio siglo.* Buenos Aires, 1955.

Wald, Pinie. *In gang fun tseiten: Geshikhte fun sotsializm in argentine* (In the course of time: History of socialism in Argentina). Buenos Aires, 1955.

——. "Yiden in der tragisher vokh" (Jews during the Tragic Week). *Argentiner Iwo Shriftn* 4 (1947):5–55.

——. *Yidisher arbeter klas un sotsiale bavegung in argentine—geshikhte in 7 tsen-diker yohren* (The Jewish working class and social movement in Argentina—a history of seventy years). Buenos Aires, 1963.

Weil, Felix J. "La industrialización argentina en los años '40." In *Economía e histo-ria: Contribuciones a la historia económica argentina*, ed. Mario Rapoport. Buenos Aires, 1988, pp. 330–79.

Weill, Simón. *Población israelita en la República Argentina*. Buenos Aires, 1936.

Wilde, José Antonio. *Buenos Aires desde 70 años atrás (1810–1880)*. Buenos Aires, 1964.

Willcox, Walter F., and Imre Ferenczi. *International Migrations*, vol. 1. Statistics compiled on behalf of the International Labour Office, Geneva. Demographic Monographs, vol. 7. New York, London, and Paris, 1969.

Winsberg, Morton D. *Colonia Baron Hirsch: A Jewish Agricultural Colony in Argen-tina*. Gainesville, FL, 1963.

Wischnitzer, Mark. "Jewish Emigration from Germany, 1933–1938." *Jewish Social Studies* 2, no. 1 (January 1940):23–44.

——. *To Dwell in Safety: The Story of Jewish Migration since 1800*. Philadelphia, 1948.

——. *Visas to Freedom—The History of HIAS*. Cleveland and New York, 1956.

Yahil, Leny. "Madagascar—Phantom of a Solution for the Jewish Question." In *Jews and Non-Jews in Eastern Europe, 1918–1945*, ed. Bela Vago and George L. Mosse. New York, Toronto, and Jerusalem, 1974, pp. 315–34.

Zariz, Ruth. *Mi-Bergen Belsen la khofesh* (From Bergen-Belzen to freedom), Sym-posium in memory of Chaim Pazner, published by Yad Vashem, Jerusalem, 1986.

Zionist Organization. *Stenographisches Protokoll der Verhandlungen des VII. Zionisten-Kongresses* (in Basel). Berlin, 1905.

——. *Stenographisches Protokoll der Verhandlungen des VIII. Zionisten-Kongresses* (in The Hague). Cologne, 1907.

Zuloaga, Manual Antonio. *Alberdi y la política inmigratoria argentina*. Buenos Aires, 1948.

Index

Acculturation of Argentine Jews. *See*
Assimilation, Jewish
Action Juive, 163
Agriculture, 38, 46; effect on
immigration and colonization,
60–62, 93; infrastructure not
developed for, 88–89; minister of,
102, 129, 143, 160
Agriculture, Ministry of, 143, 166;
immigration report demanded by,
146; and JCA, 151; Jewish colonies
praised by, 89; officials in, 157
Alberdi, Juan Bautista: beliefs of, 16, 17;
effect of writings, 15–16; exile and
return, 7–10; "Father of the
Constitution," 20; influence on
Constitution, 7–10; motto of, 9, 104
Alfonsín, Raul, 208
Alianza Anticomunista Argentina
(Triple A), 207
Alliance Israélite Universelle, 23, 26, 32,
67; attitude to Argentine
immigration, 24; immigrants
sponsored by, 66; relations with
Hirsch and JCA, 35–36; and *Weser*
immigrants, 27, 28

Allied powers: competition between,
158; and German prisoners, 163; and
Jews, 94, 160; victory of, 175
Allies. *See* Allied powers
Alsina, Juan, 39, 62, 88, 201; advocate of
assimilation, 85; attitude to Jewish
immigrants, 48–51; retired, 99
Alvear, Marcelo T., 106, 127, 168
Amadeo y Videla, Daniel, 160
American Jewish Committee, 45, 206
American Joint Distribution
Committee (the Joint), 125, 139, 189
AMIA. *See* Ashkenazic burial society
Amnesty for illegal immigrants, 189–93,
204
Anarchist party, 49, 71, 90
Anastasi, Leonidas, 146, 149
Anders, Wladyslaw, 185
Anglo-American Committee of Inquiry,
177
Anglo-Jewish Association of London,
32, 36
Anglo-Saxons, 84
Anti-Communism, 185–86
Anti-Jewish attitudes, 194–95, 199–200.
See also Anti-Semitism

Anti-Semitism, 35, 139, 203, 207; outside Argentina, 21–22, 129, 145–46, 163, 176, 185; of Catholics, 88, 134–35; and DAIA, 172, 193; in government, 15, 23, 101, 122, 140–41, 179–83; increase of, 149, 150, 168–70, 201–202; in Museo Social Argentino survey, 98–99; in publications, 22–23, 43, 86, 97, 147, 160. *See also* Anti-Jewish attitudes
Anti-Nazi Germans, 174
Anti-United States stance adopted by Argentina, 158
Arabs, 133, 177, 180
Argentine Confederation, 10
Argentine Delegation for Immigration in Europe, 184
Argentine immigration: opposition to, 6, 32, 71, 128, 129, 133–35, 198; versus emigration, 42, 43. *See also* Immigration; Immigration policy; Jewish immigration
Argentine independence, 1, 14–20
Argentine Jewry, 91–92, 139, 206–208; apathy of, 146–47, 150, 156; response to European events, 147, 149–50; solidarity of, 147
Argentine League for Human Rights, 146
Argentinidad, 195
Argentino Roca, Julio. *See* Roca, Julio Argentino
Aronstein, Georges, 135–36
Ashkenazic burial society, 75–76, 77, 126; Hevra Kadisha, 44, 72; renamed AMIA (Asociación Mutual Israelita Argentina), 173, 189
Ashkenazic community, 72, 80, 85; attitude to immigrants, 69–70, 126; established Communities' Committee, 206; Shomer Israel founded by, 69–70
Ashkenazim. *See* Ashkenazic burial society; Ashkenazic community
Asociación Filantrópica Israelita, 149,

173, 174, 199; aid to Holocaust survivors, 189. *See also* Hilfsverein Deutschsprechender Juden
Asociación Mutual Israelita Argentina (AMIA). *See* Ashkenazic burial society
Assimilation, Jewish, 98, 194–95; importance of, to Argentines, 201–203
Association for Protection of Girls and Women, 77
Association for the Protection of Jewish Immigrants, 69–70
Association of Polish Jewry, 114
Auerbach, Wolfgang, 58
Australia, 46, 94, 102
Austria, 99, 136, 141
Auxiliary farms, 64, 117, 119
Avelaneda, Nicolás, 12, 13, 18, 21

Balfour Declaration, 96, 99
Baltic States, 99–100, 156
Baron de Hirsch Fund in New York, 33
Baron Hirsch colony, 60, 61, 64
Bautista Alberdi, Juan. *See* Alberdi, Juan Bautista
Beiro, Francisco, 97
Bergen-Belsen, 163, 166
Bikur Holim. *See* Unions, labor: Union of Jewish Workers
Bolivia, 148, 166; visas to, 181, 204
Bolshevik conspiracy, 101
Boycotts, 118, 122, 129, 172
Braden, Spruille, 177–78
Bramuglio, Atilio, 183
Brazil, 123, 204; attitude to refugees, 113, 148, 155, 157
Brebbia, Domingo, 134
Bribery, 130–31, 149, 157
Britain. *See* Great Britain
British Isles. *See* Great Britain
Buenos Aires, 115, 125, 206; and JCA, 38, 60, 154; Jewish community in, 15, 31–32, 39, 43–44, 82, 126; closed to Jews, 107, 125; "German Colony" in,

131, 201; housing conditions in, 123; and illegal immigrants, 188, 191; population growth of, 6, 81, 123; unrest in, 49–51, 90, 100–101, 129, 161, 177; and *Weser* immigrants, 29–30
Bund, the, 45, 71, 101, 200
Burial society. *See* Ashkenazic burial society
Bustos, José María, 22–29

Calvos, Carlos, 22–24
Campaña, 182, 189
Canada, 102, 192; and DPs, 194; immigration to, 46, 67, 123; Jews in, 94, 194
Cárcano, Miguel Ángel, 160, 164
Castellanos, Aaron, 10–11
Castillo, Ramón, 154, 160, 161, 162, 172
Castro, Andres Maspero. *See* Maspero Castro, Andres
Catholic church, 185; anti-Semitism in, 88, 134–35; opposition of, 19, 134–35, 145, 167
Catholicism, 2, 4, 87; influence of, 16, 201, 207
Catholic loyalists, 177, 200–202
Cazés, Davíd, 55, 58, 59, 64
Celman, Miguel Juárez, 25, 33
Census, 82, 85, 89, 112, 126, 201, 205
Central Committee for the Relief of the War Victims (Central Committee): external relations, 108–110, 111–12, 198; fundraising by, 95–96
Chasanowitch, Leon, 53–54, 71
Children, Jewish, 154, 159–64, 168–69, 171, 172, 193
Chile, 148, 158–59, 204
Church and State, 4, 19–20
Clara Colony, 64, 65
Colonies, Jewish identity in, 86, 202, 205
Colonists: achievements of, 98; conflict with JCA, 39, 54–55, 125, 198; poverty among, 64–66
Colonization program, JCA:

development of, 36, 40, 91, 116–19, 135–36, 197–99; difficulties of, 54–66, 144, 151
Colonization proposal, government, 13
Comisión de Recepción y Encauzamiento de Inmigrantes (Commission for the Reception and Direction of Immigrants), 184, 185, 187
Comité Contra el Racismo y el Antisemitismo en la Argentina (Committee Against Racism and Anti-Semitism), 131, 139, 145–46, 180
Commission for the Protection of Jewish Immigrants, 108, 109
Commission for the Reception and Direction of Immigrants (Comisión de Recepción y Encauzamiento de Inmigrantes), 184, 185, 187
Committee Against Racism and Anti-Semitism (Comité Contra el Racismo y el Antisemitismo en la Argentina), 131, 139, 145–46, 180
Communists: exclusion of, 134, 139; Jewish, 131; policies of, 145, 178; reaction to, 139, 140
Communities' Committee, 206
Concentration camps, 155, 160, 175–76
Congregación Israelita de la República Argentina, 41, 97, 174; and attempts to rescue Jewish children, 160; development of, 18, 126; role of, in Jewish immigration, 31, 32, 42, 75–76, 105, 108
Congregación Israelita Latina, 44, 72–73
Congregation of Buenos Aires. *See* Congregación Israelita de la República Argentina
Congress, 162, 167; immigration policies of, 129, 146, 177
Constituent Assembly, 3, 4, 15–16, 20
Constitution, 42, 120, 146; adoption of, 4, 10, 16–17; Catholicism and, 16; legal status of Jews in, 15, 17; principles of immigration in, 9–10, 98

Consuls: and attempt to rescue Jewish children, 160; as deterrents to Jewish immigration, 107, 121, 144, 154, 159, 182; improper actions of, 105, 110; responsibilities of, 101, 103, 133, 146
Conventillos, 81, 123
Cooperatives, 65, 96, 118, 173, 205–206
Córdoba, 4, 31, 48, 85, 126
Craftsmen, 48, 67, 69
Culaciati, Miguel J., 169

DAIA (Delegación de Asociaciones Israelitas Argentinas), 147, 156; and attempt to rescue Jewish children, 160, 161, 162; established, 139; as immigration agency, 149, 172, 187; and OIA, 182; relations with Perón, 170, 182, 187–88, 189, 191; support for Jewish independence, 193, 203
de Hirsch, Maurice. See Hirsch, Maurice de
Delegación de Asociaciones Israelitas Argentinas. See DAIA
Demographics, Jewish, 1–2, 205–206, 208
de Rosas, Juan Manuel. See Rosas, Juan Manuel de
Desirable immigrants, 14, 16, 40, 84, 98, 140, 180, 185
Diana, Pablo, 187
"Dirty war," the (La Guerra Sucia), 207
Displaced Persons. See DPs
Displaced Persons Law, US, 194
DPs (Displaced Persons), 175–77; and Argentina, 192–95; and Canada, 194; and Great Britain, 193; and United States, 193–94
Dubrowsky, Ricardo, 191
Duhau, Luís, 134

Eastern Europe: Jewish emigration from, 22, 125, 158; plight of Jews in, 97, 99; repatriation to, impossible, 176; views on emigration from, 26, 32

Economy: affected by World War I, 94–97; affected by World War II, 151; decline in, 30, 32–33, 41–42, 88–91, 94, 125, 208; effect on immigration, 120–22, 127, 128, 196; effect on Jews, 55, 100, 141; global, 119–22, 192; improvements in, 46, 47, 69, 70–71, 95, 142, 171
Efron, Jedido, 181
Eichmann, Adolf, 141, 158, 164–65, 206
Emerson, Herbert, 168, 173
Emigdirekt, 112, 115
Emigration: Argentine, 55, 61, 121, 204, 208–210; Argentine, versus immigration, 42, 43; considered by Jews, 26, 125, 128; forced, 158; German, 132–33, 156, 157–58; JCA, policy, 59–60; Russian, 24, 36, 62. See *also* Mass emigration
Employment: conditions, 80, 204; infrastructure, 111, 115, 116; opportunities, 62–63, 78–80, 117
England. See Great Britain
Entre Ríos: colonial development in, 38, 65, 104, 136, 186; conditions in, 54, 55, 63; visitors to, 63, 79, 121
Erlanger, Michael, 28
Évian Conference, 142–43, 145, 147, 164, 168, 173
Exodus. See Mass emigration
Ezrah: activities of, 70, 72, 75–76, 77; established, 69, 70, 126, 173

Falcón, Ramón, 49
Family reunification program, 181, 187–88, 192
Farms, suburban, 130, 135–36, 199
Fascists, 139, 145, 176, 186
Faustino Sarmiento, Domingo. See Sarmiento, Domingo Faustino
Feinberg, David, 41, 56, 58
"Final Solution," the, 158
Foreign Relations, Ministry of, 143, 144, 146, 159; anti-Semitism in, 169; and attempt to rescue Jewish

children, 161–63
France, 94, 153, 154, 155, 166, 197
Franceschi, Gustavo, 134–35
Frank, J. B., 28–29, 31
Freemasons, 15, 19–20
Frondizi, Arturo, 146, 207
Fund-raising, 95–96, 108, 116, 147, 149, 172

Gauchos, 8, 16, 62, 84
German Foreign Ministry, 162–63, 164, 169
Germany, 132, 141, 145; Argentine economic interests in, 128; desirable immigrants from, 84; persecution of Jews in, 99, 129, 157–58. *See also* Nazi Germany
Glucksman, Max, 108, 110, 112, 114, 130, 189
Goldman, Moshe, 170, 182, 187–88
Goldschmidt, S. H., 35
Goldsmid, E. W., 36, 210
Goldsmid, Julian, 36
Grandi, Amadeo, 108
Great Britain, 96, 160, 162; Argentine embassy in, 96, 140; commercial ties with Argentina, 3, 94, 128; desirable immigrants from, 140; and DPs, 193; Foreign Office, 140; and JCA, 151–53; and Jewish immigrants, 67, 145, 163, 173, 197; and Palestine, 99, 133, 177; wartime economy of, 192
Gunzburg, Horace, 36

Halfon, Samuel, 72, 73–76; dispute with Central Committee, 109, 110, 198; in Jewish colonies, 79, 81; and Jewish organizations, 78, 108, 109; relations with authorities, 86, 105–106, 109–10
Harrison, Earl G., 193
Hart, Henry Naphtali, 15
Hassan, Davíd, 31
Hebrew Immigrant Aid Society. *See* HIAS

Hernández, Rafael, 28, 31
Herzl, Theodor, 52, 174
Hevra Kadisha. *See* Ashkenazic burial society
Heydrich, Reinhard, 158
HIAS (Hebrew Immigrant Aid Society), 115; established, 45; relations with authorities, 180, 181, 182–83, 187; relations with other organizations, 188, 189
HIAS-JCA-Emigdirekt. *See* HICEM
Hibbat Zion, 36, 40
HICEM (HIAS-JCA-Emigdirekt), 123, 129, 154; and attempt to rescue Jewish children, 159, 161; dismantled, 188; emigration efforts of, 125, 132, 199; established, 114; relations with other organizations, 115, 116, 121, 199; and spontaneous immigration, 119; views on immigration, 121, 139
High commissioner for refugees, 133–35
High Holidays, 18, 31, 87
Hildesheimer, Azriel, 28
Hilfsverein der Deutschen Juden, 45, 52, 53, 123, 132, 139
Hilfsverein Deutschsprechender Juden, 132, 137, 141, 149; established, 131, 199
Hirsch, Adolfo, 131, 137
Hirsch, Clara de, 54
Hirsch, Maurice de, 33, 52; died, 39; and JCA colonization project, 35–41, 42, 43, 197, 206; "new Moses," 36
Hirsch, Samuel, 55
Hitler, Adolf, 127, 175, 199
Holocaust survivors, 170, 174, 175–95; Argentine policy to, 199–200; immigration difficulties of, 192–95
Holy Land, 92, 176–77
Horne, Bernardino, 146, 149
Hostel, immigrants, 47, 121, 182, 189. *See also* Hotel de Inmigrantes
Hotel de Inmigrantes, 30, 148, 149. *See also* Hostel, immigrants
Housing conditions, 63–64, 81, 123

Illegal immigrants, 137, 155, 170; amnesty for, 189–93, 204; assistance for, 149, 188–92

Illegal immigration, 104, 112; increased, 150, 199; methods of, 137; versus legal, 188–92

Immigrant protection committee, 75–76

Immigrants: assistance for, 11, 108–14, 148–50; relatives of, 153–56

Immigrants hostel. *See* Hostel, immigrants; Hotel de Inmigrantes

Immigration: Argentine Jewry response to, 126–27, 146–47; affected by economy, 120–22; as central goal of Republic, 10; encouraged, 6, 9, 13, 23, 25–26, 67–69, 118–19, 197; halted, 8, 196; needed, 4, 9, 97–99, 183–84, 196; ratio to reemigration, 122–23; rate of, 48–49, 122–23, 150, 156–57, 168–69; restrictions on, 102, 103, 105, 120, 121. *See also* Argentine immigration; Immigration policy; Jewish immigration

Immigration and Colonization Law of 1876, 12, 21, 87; circumvented, 107; passed, 14; provisions of, 18, 20, 47, 196; violation of, 48. *See also* Immigration laws

Immigration Congress, 115–16, 118, 119, 125, 198

Immigration Department: established, 12; policy toward Jewish immigrants, 106, 107, 144, 180, 181, 182; and family reunification program, 155–56, 187; relations with Jewish community, 69, 111, 121, 122, 173

Immigration laws, 129, 139–41, 143–44, 183–84. *See also* Immigration and Colonization Law of 1876

Immigration pacts, 140

Immigration policy, 145–46, 166–67, 180, 184–86; changes in, 25–26, 119–22, 133–35, 183; debated, 11, 20, 149, 178–81; effect on Jews, 143–50,

167–70, 171–73, 187–88; JCA, changes in, 59–60; 1918–1925, 99–104; to Jews, 106–108, 180–81, 182–83, 192, 194, 199–200; US, 100. *See also* Argentine immigration; Immigration; Jewish immigration

Immigration statistics, 38–39, 78, 85, 110–13, 156–57, 166, 170–71, 185, 192–94, 196–97, 204–205

Independence, Argentine, 1, 14–20

Indeseables (undesirables), 186, 195

Industrial development, 142, 151, 166, 192, 205; effect on immigration, 183–85, 186–87

Inquisition, the, 2, 3, 6, 15, 23

Intergovernmental Committee, 145, 164, 168, 173

Interior, Ministry of the, 143, 166

International Labour Office, 101, 142

Irigoyen, Luís H., 164–65

Israel, 189, 191, 192, 193, 197; immigration to, 46, 208, 210; ties to Argentine Jewry, 206, 208, 210

Italy, 158, 184–85

JCA (Jewish Colonization Association): aid to immigrants, 38, 51–54, 66–67, 168; and attempt to rescue Jewish children, 160; conflict with colonists, 39, 54–55, 125, 198; criticism of, 39, 53, 73; difficulties encountered by, 151–54; established, 35–36; financial status of, 52, 117; and immigrant protection committee, 75–76; relations with authorities, 48–54, 106–108, 112, 116, 151; relations with other Jewish organizations, 41, 53, 69, 70, 72, 129, 199; scope of immigration activities, 197–99; staff as refugees, 154, 172; supported assimilation of Jews, 106–107. *See also* Colonization program, JCA

Jewish Argentine community. *See* Argentine Jewry

Jewish children, attempt to rescue. *See*

Children, Jewish
Jewish Colonization Association. *See*
JCA
Jewish Commercial Society (Sociedad
Comercial Israelita), 96
Jewish Congress: Canadian, 194;
general, 96
"Jewish conspiracy," the, 179
Jewish immigration: attitudes to,
23–24, 37, 53, 104–108; decline in, to
Argentina, 204–205; versus
emigration, 20, restriction of, 18–19.
See also Argentine immigration;
Immigration; Immigration policy
Jewish Immigration Association. *See*
JCA
Jewish National Fund, 52
Jewish organizations, 108–14, 132
"Jewish Question," the, 167–74
Jewish schools, 44, 72, 86
Joint, the (American Joint Distribution
Committee), 125, 139, 189
Joseph, Henry, 77
Judeo-Spanish (Ladino), 66, 126
Justo, Augustín P., 122, 142, 172
Juventud Israelita Argentina, 72, 97

Kahan, Zadok, 28, 35
Kaltenbruner, Ernst, 165
Kaplan, Isaac, 65
Katsovitch, Noah, 41, 56
Kelly, Sir David Victor, 157
Keren Hayesod, 113
Kherson, 22, 60
Klett, Carlos Lix. *See* Lix Klett, Carlos
Kramer, Simón, 32
Kreinin, Miron, 115
Kristallnacht, 141, 147, 172

Labougle, Eduardo, 167
Ladino (Judeo-Spanish), 66, 126
La Guerra Sucia (the "dirty war"), 207
Lamas, Carlos Saaverda. *See* Saaverda
Lamas, Carlos
Lamas, Pedro S., 27, 29

Landsmanschaften, 72, 96, 114, 115, 126,
189
La Semana Trágica (tragic week),
100–101, 122, 203
Latin America: immigration to, not
promoted, 139, 150, 158; and refugees,
133–35, 143
Latzky-Bertholdi, Jacob, 112, 125, 200
League of Nations, 99, 102, 133, 142
Le Breton, Tomás A., 102, 103, 106, 127,
14, 168–69
Levy, Elizabeth, 17–18, 19
Levy, Rudolph, 163
Levy, Solomon, 17–18, 19
Ley de Residencia (Residence Law), 47,
51
Lithuania, 26, 55
Lix Klett, Carlos, 29–30
Llamadas, 105, 135
Loeb, Isidore, 35
Löwenthal, Wilhelm, 28, 33–35, 38, 42
Lucienville, 63, 64
Lupo, Remigio, 105, 109

McDonald, James G., 133–35, 173
Martín Gracía, 177
Maspero Castro, Andrés, 155, 161
Mass emigration, 22, 45–46, 131, 198,
202; from Argentina, 66, 81;
encouraged by Perón, 186, 187, 188;
need for, 5, 98, 104; of Russian Jews,
33, 35–37; of Russian Jews
discouraged, 32
Mauricio, 54, 62
"Maximalist" uprising, proletarian,
100–101
Mellibowsky, Benjamin, 180, 189
Melting pot theory, 201, 202
Messersmith, George, 194
Mexico, 208–210
Mihajlović, Dragoljub, 185
Military junta, 164, 167, 172, 200–201;
Castillo overthrown by, 162; conflicts
within, 177; Peralta appointed by, 180
Military rule, 120, 175, 207, 208

"Ministry of the Diaspora," 53
"Mister Jacob," 14
Mitre, Bartolomé, 11, 23
Mohilewer, Schmuel, 36, 210
Moisesville, 55–56, 58, 61, 62, 64
Montevideo, 104, 148, 155
Mora, Cipriano Taboada. *See* Taboada Mora, Cipriano
Morocco, 66, 72, 78
Moss, Walter, 73
Mundo Israelita, 103, 121, 160
Museo Social Argentino: survey by, 97, 100, 101

Narcisse Leven Colony, 61–62
National Education Council, 86, 94, 106
Nationalism: cultural, 86; effect on immigration, 128, 133–35; growth of, 84, 87, 198, 201–202
Nationalists: persecution of Jews by, 90, 100–101; opposition to immigration, 93, 133–35, 172; support for Perón, 177
Natural disasters, 38, 54, 60, 61–62
Navarro, Samuel, 23, 26
Navarro Viola, Miguel, 18, 19
Nazi collaborators, 176, 185, 193
Nazi Germany: and Allied attempt to rescue Jewish children, 160–61, 162–64; relations with Argentina, 139, 149, 155, 158–67, 169; relations with Chile, 158, 159; repatriation to, 153–55. *See also* Germany
Nazis: actions to Jews by, 141, 142, 146, 203; in Argentina, 186, 193; Argentine Jewry response to, 131; opposition to, 145
Near East, 72, 125
Netherlands, 140, 155, 163, 165, 169
Neutrality, Argentine: during World War I, 94, 128, 158; during World War II, 150, 158–65
Non-Catholics, 140, 201; desirability of, debated, 20; rights of, 3, 4, 5, 10, 18

Non-Christians, 17, 88, 201
North Africa, 80, 160, 205
Nuremburg Laws, 132, 136

OIA (Organización Israelita Argentina): aid to illegal immigrants, 188–92; competed with DAIA, 182; relations with Perón, 189–91, 193, 194
Olivera, Ricardo, 162, 164
Organización Israelita Argentina. *See* OIA
Organized immigration. *See* Sponsored immigration
Oriondo, Simón de, 19
Oroño, Nicasio, 13, 19
Orphans. *See* Children, Jewish
Ortiz, Roberto, 142, 150, 154, 172
Oungre, Edouard, 115, 125
Oungre, Louis, 125, 127, 130, 198; criticized Central Committee, 110; criticized JCA, 73; and JCA colonization project, 64–65, 118–19, 135–36; at 1928 immigration congress, 115, 118; supported immigration agreement, 107–108

Palacios, Pedro, 31–32
Pale of Settlement, 56
Palestine, 123, 132, 189; compared to Argentina, 40–41, 59, 64, 91–92; Frankfurt orphanage transferred to, 149–50; and Great Britain, 99; immigration to, banned, 36, 37, 163, 176–77, 193; prospects for immigration to, 27, 133, 139, 149, 164; resettlement in, 147, 172; and Zionist movement, 72, 126, 131, 200
Paraguay, 12, 166, 188, 204; policy to Jewish immigrants, 137, 148, 155, 169, 181
Paris, 27, 28, 139, 154
Pavlovsky, Aarón, 24
Peddlers, 79, 80, 90, 95, 96
Peralta, Santiago M., 178–83, 187, 188, 194

Perón, Evita, 191

Perón, Isabel, 207

Perón, Juan Domingo: and anti-Semitism, 181, 193; election of, 177–78; and illegal immigrants, 189–92, 204; immigration policies of, 184–88, 202; inaugurated, 180; political actions of, 181–83, 205; and populism, 202, 207; relations with Jewish community, 187–95; relations with US, 185–86; and State of Israel, 189, 192; supported Zionist movement, 195

Perónists, 177–83

Philanthropic societies, 11, 45, 114, 200

Pluralism, cultural, 195, 197, 201

Poalei Zion party, 53, 71. *See also* Zionist movement

Podolia, 27, 32

Pogroms: aid for victims of, 108; in Buenos Aires, 101, 203; effect on Argentine immigration, 59, 67–69; in Poland, 176; in Russia, 22, 58, 99, 197

Poland, 114, 122; Jews refused admittance to, 99–100; plight of Jews in, 99, 141–42, 158, 165, 176

Politics, Argentine: Jewish involvement in, 206–207, 208

Popper, Julio and Max, 24–25

Population: decline in, 65, 97, 140; Argentine Jewish, 55, 91–92, 108; growth of, 46, 61, 81. *See also* Census

Proletarian: "maximalist" uprising, 100–101; movement, 90, 96, 126; opposition to, 66, 90, 93, 197

Proletarians, Jewish, 63, 71, 99

Propaganda: anti-Semitic, 134–35; Nazi, 131

Protestants, 4, 87, 140, 170

Quintana, Manuel, 53

Quotas, 100, 133, 194

Radical party, 119, 168; boycott by, 122; established, 30; leaders of, 94, 97,

146; views of, 90, 145, 146, 172

Radical synagogue, the, 208

Radovizky, Simón, 90

Ramírez, Pedro Pablo, 162

Ramos, Juan P., 102, 110; immigration policy of, 103, 108; and JCA, 106, 107, 112, 116, 127, 198

Red scare, 100–101; effect on Argentine immigration, 197–98; in United States, 197–98

Reemigration, 170, 196; effect of economic crisis on, 120–22; effect on population, 82; of preferential immigrants, 84; versus immigration, 122–23

Refugees: Argentine Jewish, 199–200, 208; Argentine policy to, 130, 143–50, 180–82, 198; between World War I and World War II, 112; HICEM directors as, 154; high commissioner for, 133–35; JCA staff as, 154, 172; Romanian, 58, 67; World War I, 99–100, 112; World War II, 135–36, 139, 142–43, 148–49, 155, 171–74; and Zionist movement, 131

Rega, José López, 207

Reich, 139, 141, 163. *See also* Third Reich

Religious freedom versus religious tolerance, 16–17, 88

Religious tolerance, 201; opposition to, 4; versus religious freedom, 16–17, 88

Repatriation: of Argentine Jews, 165–66; of DPs, 176; JCA's role in, 55, 145, 151; to Nazi Germany, 153–55

Residence Law (Ley de Residencia), 47, 51

Revolutionaries, 53–54, 100, 101, 120

Río de la Plata, 2, 102

Río Uruguay, 137, 177

Rivadavía, Bernadino, 5, 6

Roca, Julio Argentino, 21, 25, 43

Rojas, Ricardo, 84, 86, 88, 201, 202

Romania: emigration of Jews from, 24, 67; policy of, to Jews, 99–100, 105, 122, 142

Roosevelt, Franklin, 142, 167, 173
Rosario, 79, 85, 121, 126
Rosas, Juan Manuel de, 1, 4, 6, 15, 202
Rothschild, Edmond de, 27, 40
Rovizky, Simón, 49
Russia: compared to Argentine colonies, 64; emigration of Jews from, 24–25, 33, 35–36, 67, 105; equality for Jews in, 99; Pale of Settlement, 56. See also Soviet Union
Russian Jews, 27, 33, 37, 48, 51, 112; aid to, 33, 35–37, 69; immigration of encouraged, 22, 24; negative attitudes to, 24

Saaverda Lamas, Carlos, 140, 171
Sajarof, Miguel, 65
Salazar Altamira, Guillermo, 129, 134
Salzberg, Alexander, 24
Santa Fe, 4, 54, 55, 56, 61, 89
Sarmiento, Domingo Faustino, 6–7, 201; attitude to Jews, 15–16, 23, 159; opposition to, in Congress, 11–12; melting pot theory, 201, 202
Sarmiento, Ernesto, 159
Schiff, Jacob, 52
Schools, Jewish, 44, 72, 86, 150
Schusheim, A. L., 147
Sephardic community, 44, 126, 127, 174
Settlers' cooperatives. See Cooperatives
Shazar, Zalman, 53
Shomer Israel, 69–70
Shoskes, Haim, 180, 181
Sidi, Abraham, 65
Simmel, Siegmund, 28, 33
Socialist party, 90; aid to immigrants, 148, 172; growth of, 30, 49; views of, 71, 145, 146, 178
Socialist-Territorialist party, 71
Socialist-Zionist party, 200
Sociedad Commercial Israelita (Jewish Commercial Society), 96
Sociedad de Protección a los Inmigrantes Israelitas. See Soprotimis

Sociedad Hebraica Argentina, 126
Sociedad Rural Argentina, 184
Solari, Juan, 146, 148
Sonnenfeld, Nandor, 63–65, 73
Sonnenfeld, Sigismond, 55, 63
Soprotimis: achievements of, 110, 111, 113; and attempt to rescue Jewish children, 160, 161, 162; difficulties of, 110, 113–114, 120–121, 127, 166–167; and illegal immigrants, 137, 150, 188–192; relations with authorities, 109–111, 119, 122, 129, 161, 187; relations with Central Committee, 109–110, 111–112; relations with Peralta, 180, 181, 182–183; relations with Perón, 189, 193
South Africa, 46, 94, 102
Soviet "shadow government," 101
Soviet Union, 119, 121. See also Russia
Spain, 1–3, 166; Argentine immigration to, 208–210; desirable immigrants from, 185
Sponsored immigration: the first, 26; versus spontaneous, 10–14, 66, 67–69, 172
Spontaneous immigration, 37, 119; increase in, 66, 67–69, 120, 122; to Palestine, 40; versus sponsored, 10–14, 66, 67–69, 172
Spy network, German, 6, 155, 159, 165
Starkmeth, Isaac, 112, 121, 130
Strikes, 147, 161; labor, 30, 49, 100–101; rent, 81
Survey by Museo Social Argentino, 97–99
Synagogues, 85, 86

Taboada Mora, Cipriano, 148, 155
Thadden, Eberhardt von, 165
Third Reich, 157, 169, 175, 186. See also Reich
"To govern means to populate," 9, 104
Trade unions. See Unions, labor
Tragic week (La Semana Trágica), 100–101, 122, 203
Treaty of Friendship, 3–4, 9

Triple A, 207
Truman, Harry, 193, 194
Tucumán, 31, 48, 85
Turkey, 37, 67, 78, 99–100
Turkish immigrants, 66, 72, 80, 85, 126
Turkow, Mark, 187

Ukrainians, 99, 156, 185
Undesirable immigrants, 25, 98, 184, 186
Unemployment, 64–65, 95, 120, 123, 124, 129, 151
Unions, labor, 80, 114, 177, 183; Union of Jewish Workers (Unión Obera Israelita), 71–72, 77
United Evacuation Committee, 113, 114
United Kingdom. *See* Great Britain
United Nations, 182, 186, 189
United States, 123, 162, 177; and attempt to rescue Jewish children, 159, 160, 164; compared to Argentina, 78, 81, 102; and DPs, 193–94; German spy network uncovered by, 159; immigration policy of, 100, 108, 112, 197–98; immigration quotas in, 133, 194; Industrial Removal Office in, 53; Jews in, 15, 67, 96; preferred by emigrants, 112, 197, 198; Red scare in, 197–98; relations with Perón, 185–86
Urban immigrants, 88–89, 198
Urban immigration versus rural colonization, 171
Urquiza, José, 4
Uruguay, 104, 140, 155, 204

Veneziani, Davíd, 63, 73
Venezuela, 208–10
Vichy, 159, 161–62, 164
Vida Neustra, 101, 203
Vienna, 99, 139, 145
Viola, Miguel Navarro. *See* Navarro Viola, Miguel
Visas, 120, 144, 145, 146, 155, 188

Wald, Pinie, 101

Warsaw, 26, 110
Weill, Simon, 130, 154, 193
Welfare organizations, 69, 126, 131, 199; delegates to immigration congress, 115; membership expanded, 173; and unemployed immigrants, 95, 121
Welfare Society for German-speaking Jews. *See* Hilfsverein Deutschsprechender Juden
Weser immigrants, 27–30, 197; achievements of, 35; plight of, 30–32, 33–35
Western Europe, 15, 157
White, Arnold, 35
White slave trade, 25, 73, 75, 77, 198
White slave traders, 111, 114, 116, 125
Winterton, Lord, 168–69, 173
World War I, 96, 108, 126; Argentine neutrality during, 94; effect of, on Argentine Jews, 91, 93–97, 117; effect of, on immigration, 196
World War II, 151, 157, 173, 175
World Zionist Organization. *See* Zionist movement
WZO. *See* Zionist movement: World Zionist Organization

Yrigoyen, Hipólito, 94, 101, 105, 106, 119, 120

"Zion, Argentina will lead to," 36, 210
Zionist movement, 96, 174, 197, 200; in Buenos Aires, 85; and DAIA, 203; difficulties with, 72; efforts of, to establish national home, 126, 131, 176, 200; Hibbat Zion, 36; and Jewish National Fund, 52; Keren Hayesod, 113; new dominance of, in Argentine Jewish life, 206, 208; Poalei Zion party, 53, 71; support for, 99, 195; World Zionist Organization (WZO), 45

About the Author

Haim Avni is Professor of Contemporary Jewish History at the Institute of Contemporary Jewry, Hebrew University of Jerusalem. Avni is the author of many studies about Jews in Hispanic societies, including a book on modern Spain and the Jews and three other volumes on Argentine Jewry.